THE
20TH CENTURY'S
GREATEST
HITS

THE
20TH CENTURY'S
GREATEST
HITS

A "TOP 40" LIST

Paul Williams

A TOM DOHERTY ASSOCIATES BOOK

NEW YORK

This book is for
Frank J. Smith
and my other high school English teachers
and for Jane Manthorne and Fiona Kelleghan
and all librarians everywhere

Writing this book would not have been possible without the love and support of Cindy Lee Berryhill and the generous support of 150 readers and patrons, notably Andy Hertzfeld of Differnet.com. Thank you all.

THE 20th CENTURY'S GREATEST HITS:
A "TOP 40" LIST

Lyrics from "Smokestack Lightning" composed by Chester Burnett which appear on pages 203–207 are reprinted with permission of Arc Music Group and Copyright © 1956 (renewed) Arc Music Corp. All rights reserved.

This book is printed on acid-free paper.

Edited by David G. Hartwell

A Forge Book
Published by Tom Doherty Associates, LLC
175 Fifth Avenue
New York, NY 10010

www.tor.com

Forge® is a registered trademark of Tom Doherty Associates, LLC.

ISBN 0-312-87391-3 (trade paperback)
ISBN 0-312-87390-5 (hardcover)

First Edition: October 2000

Printed in the United States of America

0 9 8 7 6 5 4 3 2 1

Contents

Introduction

In the half of this century that I've lived in, it's quite common to encounter "best-of-the-year" lists of movies or records in newspapers and magazines, starting in late December. Indeed, the "idea" for this book came to me tonight when I noticed a "First Annual International Music Writers Poll Ballot" lying on the floor of my workspace, waiting to be filled in, and the notion entered my head that, um, this is January 25, 1998, must be time to start thinking about my "best-of-the-century" list. . . .

Hence the title and structure of the book. It's a tease. Intended to tease out of me (I have to entice the Muse, or the Writer within) comments on a buncha seemingly unrelated works of art of various sorts that have gotten my attention and greatly enriched or enlightened me in the last fifty years (I was born May 19, 1948, in Boston, Massachusetts—conceived nine months earlier in northern California). Including works from earlier in the century that I eventually discovered thanks to their reputations or serendipity or good luck. Okay, Picasso was always there, indeed there was one odd print of a card game with strangely shaped people and hunks of cheese, on the wall of the hallway in my childhood home. . . . But I hadn't actually made a connection with this well-known gentleman's oeuvre until a lucky day in 1980. I happened to be back in New York City with some free time, and a friend gave me his Museum of Modern Art membership card and pointed me toward MOMA's then-current exhibition, *Pablo Picasso: A Retrospective*. I wandered through the chronological presentation for a long afternoon—hey, the show was only there for four months, and all that stuff hardly ever has been together in one place before, nor, probably, will it ever be again. . . . I really did get lucky; ignorance would have kept me from the show, but for a gentle shove from my guardian or guiding angels—and on that day I got religion. Wow. What's the difference between that experience and seeing/hearing the Grateful Dead and Jefferson Airplane at the Fillmore Auditorium on December 31, 1966? Uh, you could say that in the MOMA case the artist wasn't present at the same time as the observer, but to say that, you'd have to deny the extraordinary degree to which the painter, especially that painter, is present in his work.

And I digress, or get ahead of myself. What I really want to be sure to say is that I'm teasing if I give the impression I'm going to try to rank the "top" artistic creations of this just-ending century in the Western world, or any world. That kind of hierarchical approach is contrary to certain philosophies of life that I hold dear. True, I did once write a book about "the 100 best rock and roll singles." I didn't rank 'em, but I did enjoy selecting 'em, even knowing that the best I could hope for was a 50 percent overlap between my list and the list any reader might construct for her- or himself. This book, though, is something different. It's a miniscule cross-section, a few of the 20th century's greatest aesthetic hits, necessarily limited to the rather small sampling that could reasonably come to one person's attention. I'm not even trying, actually, to make a carefully thought-out representation (or list) of my own preferences. These are all creations I believe are worthy to be on a list of, or in a collection of, great artistic works (achievements) of the 20th century. Okay, a catalog for some kinda future (multimedia) museum show.

They have been blindly selected by my Muse, or her Seeing Eye dog, with the intention of demonstrating (and therefore arguing; an essay is a kind of argument) that "art" is what we, the receivers, observers, listeners, readers, experience when we encounter it. "Great art," then, is not some objective phenomenon; it is an essentially subjective, and often profoundly spiritual, personal experience on the part of a person or many persons reading a book, listening to a recording, looking at a painting, watching a play or a film. The greatest hits of the 20th century happened mostly in private places. Um, even at a boxing match (speaking of hits in private places) there is a private catharsis of feelings experienced within each spectator. It's a public place, a public show, but the feelings generated are mostly internal, and personal.

And so let us move on, ladies and gentlemen, to the first entry, here not because it is my favorite Beatles song, nor because it is a recording that almost anyone would rank among the century's best. More because it isn't, and thus can be enjoyed simply for itself, not for any pretentious critical reasons. And because it did in fact hit me hard at one moment in my life (and still can), and because it speaks quite directly of the odd temporal nature of such experiences. Art exists not so much in the moment when it is created as in the moment when it is received. "Then we will remember . . ." True indeed.

T hings We Said Today" has always for me been a visionary song. Although it is a marvelously direct and unaffected love song, somehow for me the chorus has always sounded as though the singers (and I, the listener) are conscious at this moment of how precious these moments, these years (of the Beatles' creative flowering and of the listeners' youth and collective great awakening) will seem to us whenever we think of them in our future lives. What a wonderful message, and how perfect the melody and rhythm that accompany and carry it: "Someday when we're dreaming/Deep in love, not a lot to say/Then we will remember/Things we said today." This is what this book is about: things once said, moments shared, and how they endure. All great art is an expression of, and an opportunity to experience, this moment. What it puts us in touch with is this love for life, or this pain, that we are experiencing, and perhaps talking about, right now, today.

I get chills when Paul sings that word, "today," and the music changes, opens into another realm, moves forward and circles back to itself. This is a "hook," a quintessential device in rock and roll and most 20th-century popular music. The song (the performance, the recording) begins with a dramatic guitar flourish, fingers quickly down and up, repeated twice before the first word of the song, "You." This flourish returns

HIT

1

"Things We Said Today"

by The Beatles

(recorded June 2, 1964)

(very satisfyingly) after the end of the first verse-and-chorus, the word "today." By the time another verse-and-chorus have gone by, we are waiting for, anticipating, that guitar flourish, but this time it's a little different, bass and drums and percussion echoing but not reproducing the expected guitar riff—and then the third verse starts so suddenly, it feels more like a bridge, some kind of intriguing leap forward rather than a return to familiar territory.

Elegant simplicity. Four verses, each ending in a four-line chorus that ends with the title phrase. Great simple words that allow/encourage the reader to project profundity onto them. The guitar flourish/hook opens the song, closes the first verse, is echoed but teasingly held back at the end of verses two and three, and finally returns at the end of the fourth verse and of the songs—a fulfilling reprise, still somewhat restrained so you're left hoping to hear the whole song, and the sound of that full flourish, again.

Simple but not dumb. Remarkably artful. The gentleness of the vocal is moving after the energetic guitar opening, and this gentleness and the simple beauty of the melody notes that count out the first six syllables of the song (immediately repeated in the next six, the next line) all serve to communicate the singer's wish to be as lovingly "kind" as he praises "you" (the object of the song, the "girl") for being.

The subtleties of the verse structure, when you look closely, are surprising. The first verse is four lines, rhyming ABAB (nice two-syllable B rhyme: "love me"/"of me"). Then the four-line chorus, ABCB. Verse 2 rhymes AAAA, but with the marvelous twist that the first and third A rhymes are followed by an extra word, "girl" ("mine, girl"/"kind girl," similar to the "love me"/"of me" in the previous verse, except this time it's AAAA: "mine"/ "time"/"kind"/"find." Whew. The second chorus transforms itself with a lot of new language and shifting pronouns: "Someday when I'm lonely" becomes "Someday when we're dreaming." This rewritten chorus, which stays the same through the rest of the song, is a sharp change from first verse-and-chorus, which seem to be about someone (presumably the singer) facing a period of separation from a dearly loved one (like a world tour?) and being comforted by assurances of the power of love to transcend space ("You'll be thinking of me / Somehow I will know"). In the second verse and chorus the subject is not spatial separation but instead closeness enduring in time ("You say you will love me / Till the end of time"). Masters, or at least magicians, of space and time, singing in your ears right now, in 1964, and, presumably, till the end of time.

And the structural inventiveness continues. The third verse has eight lines instead of four, and as if to compensate for this break in symmetry, the fourth verse is the third verse repeated. And so the song ends. Those eight lines have this elegant rhyme scheme: ABABACAC. The third and fourth A's have "girl" appended: "kind"/"blind"/"mine, girl"/"time, girl." If that went by too fast to assimilate, don't worry, it's about to be repeated.

Just as those things we said today will be repeated, in our loving memories, for years (or perhaps centuries) to come. Listen, my man William Shakespeare, trying either to express love or to get living expenses from his Sponsor, said circa 1595, "So long as men can breathe or eyes can see / So long lives this and this gives life to thee." "This" is the poem, and man was he right!! In the same way, for many centuries, as long as humans can breathe and hear, we will indeed remember these "things" Paul and John and George and Ringo said that day. Many things, many days, many songs. But this special song acknowledges and describes the process.

That's enough on craft, perhaps, but it's hard to stop praising it. That powerfully gentle-and-assertive six-beat melody recurs in the first line of the chorus, part of that refrain's great power: "Someday when we're dreaming . . ." And how about those half-rhymes? The most brilliant is in the repeating verse 3 and 4: "be the only one"/"we'll go on and on." And they make it work. Milton would smile.

I realize, and hope, that some of you reading these comments are not from around here, temporally speaking. So it makes sense then that I should tell you (no way you would know, unless Beatles 101 is a required high school course in your century) that "Things We Said Today" was not a hit record in the Beatles' era, despite its prominent place in this book (#1 isn't higher than #2 or #40 in my system, but opening act is an honorable position anyway). "Things We Said Today" was the B-side (backside) of the hit single "A Hard Day's Night" in the U.K. In the U.S. it was on a little-remembered album called *Something New*. (Both were released in July 1964, close to the Gulf of Tonkin turning point in the Vietnam War.) Not a song that got a lot of attention in its day, as Beatles songs go. Nor since then, thus far. But listen: People don't just love the Beatles for their best-known or most-praised records. Talk to real listeners, real fans, and you'll find that there are "lesser" records and songs that are as precious to them as any of the famous ones. They have very strong feelings for and allegiance to certain songs, not just for sentimental reasons but because something about that song speaks to and for them. No matter when they first heard it. What I'm trying to say is that a common, and legitimate, relationship with great art is you find something, even in the repertoire of the century's most popular recording artists, that somehow becomes your secret treasure. This is one of mine. So as a "greatest hit" I'd like it to stand in for many hundred thousand other great moments in the art history of our era that won't necessarily make it into the curricula, you know, the official greatest-hits lists of academia and scholarship.

The Beatles themselves, like Picasso, are one of the obvious huge hits (artists like meteorites are measured by impact) of the 20th century. What isn't always said is that this was not simply a natural consequence of their enormous talent. Certainly they had talent, but also they came along at exactly the right moment. And to their credit, they made the best possible use of that moment. They let the world's attention inspire them. Again and again, starting over with each new record. For seven years.

There can't be another Beatles nor a reunion of the old Beatles, because the moment was part of the music, and that moment is not around anymore. But the music that did get made then is eternal, and its moment lives on within it. Like the fellows said, "Love is here to stay/And that's enough to make you mine." Like Shakespeare, they dare to boast that the love and attention of the "you" they're singing to will not fade in times to come. I like it that the song can be heard this way. And I like the rhymes and the guitar hook and the evident loving-kindness and sincerity of the writer and the singer. At least at the moment of writing and singing.

HIT 2

"Sister Ray"
by The Velvet Underground
(recorded September 1967)

And now for something completely different. That's what we want from art, isn't it? That's what we get from "Sister Ray." Henry Rollins once reminisced about this song (recording) being used at youth parties to clear rooms (because of its relentless discordant noisiness). It can also be used, and often is, by informed music lovers of all ages to clear minds (self-administered). A tonic. I absolutely guarantee its restorative powers. And it would be difficult for me to think of a single 20th-century work of art (perhaps to a lesser degree Fritz Lang's *Metropolis?*) that so powerfully and accurately evokes the human and other-than-human environment we find ourselves in at our historical moment. The noise of the machines. But most of all the inflamed racing of our own hearts as the awakening process rushes forward. These four artists (Moe, Lou, John, Sterling) captured the era in a performance so eloquent, it literally created a new musical and aesthetic language that has been of enormous use to many generations of avant-garde musical artists since. And that's not all. "Sister Ray" has been and continues to be a fantastic jumping-off place, and as such has had tremendous influence, but what's even better is that (I'm certain) it speaks to the ages—never going out of date because it provides its own context. This piece of artwork (using the relatively new "recorded music" medium) is another that "age cannot wither." It is a remarkably compact (although at seventeen and a half minutes it was and still is one of the longest works of its kind, i.e., rock-and-roll album tracks) articulation of a vision, a vision of an Order beyond what can be grasped by the cognitive mind. Structure and anarchy, coexisting in powerful (vibrant) interrelationship. A revelation. Not for the faint-hearted. "Just like Sister Ray said . . ."

Although contemporaries of a sort, the Beatles and the Velvet Underground have almost nothing in common, except that they're both sui generis. Rock and roll, that vaguely defined broad category of popular music that is so characteristic of the century, is I hope not overrepresented in this book (six entries out of forty) despite my long-standing interest in the genre. What I (and most of us) like about rock and roll is that it makes a lot of space for sui generis artists. Ones of a kind. That also applies to this song. Nothing else like it anywhere in God's creation (although I have heard a case made for "Sister Ray"'s similarity to John Coltrane's *Impressions*—see entry #30).

The triumph of "Sister Ray" is, indeed, its relentlessness. How do they *do* that? No one knows, not even them. It's one of the mysteries of the era (as great contemporary art so often is). Great expression is done in collaboration with the moment; what it expresses, what we respond to so enthusiastically, is among other things the mood (shared emotions, shared self-awareness, seemingly shared experience) of the historical moment in this place (Greenwich Village, USA, the postindustrial nations, the whole globe), this season of this year—that is, at exactly this point in the rising action of the drama we're playing out together. And how this expression is done so successfully (in, say, *Moby-Dick*, an acknowledged greatest hit of the 19th century) is ultimately a mystery to spectators and commentators. It isn't just that that novelist, that band, were objectively the best or most advanced craftsmen around in their art form and therefore "of course" producing the great works. Nah. That's now how I look at it, anyway. *Moby-Dick* and "Sister Ray" to me are extraordinary performances, similar to yet obviously miles above the novelist or the band's other acts of creation. Inspired works. How did he, how did they, do that? It's a mystery. Thank God. Such mysteries, like sunsets and other "natural" marvels, make life worth living.

Okay, as a commentator it is my job to comment, even if I'm struck dumb by the work in question. So I'll try to tell you what little I grasp of the mystery. *Moby-Dick* is an outburst of inspired language, a visionary performance (from first touching of pen to paper to the last) by a young man of much passion, knowledge, experience, and insight, who at the moment of writing, of story-telling and lecturing, was keenly aware of his whole species' rela-tionship with God and/or with its concept of God. He was astonishingly conscious of what it meant to be alive in 1851 and to have been born a human at this precise moment in "Man"'s relationship with nature, the wilderness, the biosphere, the universe of information, including information about whales, a whale of a lot of facts available to an interested cabin boy . . . Lou Reed and John Cale and cohorts? Similarly conscious, with simi-lar keenness and aesthetic success. For at least a few moments. Seventeen and a half minutes in a "second-rate" recording studio. Then Lou Reed returned to being the same irritating bumbler we students of his life know him to have been most of the time. But for eighteen minutes, and with the aid and support of his cowork-ers, he was a prophet absolutely equal to the performers we read about in the Bible (even Jonah as retold in *Moby-Dick's* great chapter 9, "The Sermon"). Speaking in tongues. Tongues that be-come prophecy and/or great art when we listeners can't help but feel we are enlightened by them, again and again. Revelation. "Too busy sucking on my ding-dong." *This* is one of the greatest hits of the twentieth century? You bet your ass.

Oh hell, let me just quote Melville quoting Father Mapple: "'Shipmates, this book, containing only four chapters—four yarns—is one of the smallest strands in the mighty cable of the Scriptures. Yet what depths of the soul does Jonah's deep sea-line sound! What a pregnant lesson to us is this prophet! What a noble thing is that canticle in the fish's belly! How billow-like and boisterously grand! We feel the floods surging over us; we sound with him to the kelpy bottom of the waters; sea-weed and all the slime of the sea is about us! But *what* is this lesson that the book of Jonah teaches? Shipmates, it is a two-stranded lesson; a lesson to us all as sinful men, and a lesson to me as a pilot of the living God. . . .'" This is very good; Melville demonstrates awareness that the content of the song or scriptural chapter varies significantly depending on who is listening to or reading it at a particular moment.

So I'm not Father Mapple and can't speak for you, shipmates, but I will endeavor to tell you what I believe "Sister Ray" teaches almost every one of us who has the fortune and fortitude to connect with it at all. Like I said, it gestures in the direction of knowledge of that awesome greater Order in which we find ourselves enmeshed. This is difficult to articulate, of course. Let me quote that other sixth-decade-of-the-20th-century prophet, Bob Dylan: "i accept chaos. i am not sure whether it accepts me." He spoke these words on the back cover of his fifth album, in 1965, and it is quite likely Messrs. Cale and Reed had read them before they recorded "Sister Ray" two years later, but they didn't need to. Like Dylan, they were alive and young in the urban Western world in mid-century, so they intuitively understood that this relationship between man and chaos was as central to any of our lives as, say, the relationship between man and God was for Captain Ahab whenever the white whale crossed his path. In "Sister Ray," I the narrator and I the musicians and I the listener *become* that chaos, joyfully, even as we remain the baffled and often terrified man at the same time. And we (even the musicians) watch in wonder as order is created using chaos as building blocks and foundation and even as aesthetically pleasing decoration. How is it done? I don't know. But watch me (us) do it again!

It's done, as every painter and musician and poet would like to accomplish, by changing the nature of our perception of and thus our participation in (relationship with) the universe, the other, God, the world, the five skandhas. (See entry #3, *Girl Before a Mirror.*) Put very simply (and for the third time): This uniquely chaotic recording is wondrous in the way it manages to be both fiercely disorienting and astonishingly and reassuringly orderly, that special kind of order that the best music and paintings offer, an order that goes beyond (or violates) patterns the mind can recognize easily, but speaks directly (and eloquently) to the heart, the soul.

Great art creates misunderstanding (*The Rite of Spring* and *Les Demoiselles d'Avignon* and Bob Dylan going electric are obvious 20th-century examples). "Sister Ray," whose great accomplishment is its precise sonic and rhythmic palette, has been criticized (along with the *White Light/White Heat* album as a whole) by both John Cale and Lou Reed for being an inadequate representation of the band's sound due to willfully sloppy recording. So perfect sound (recognized as such by untold thousands of listeners, particularly "serious" rock musicians, over the last three decades) is dismissed by its creators as not what they think they were capable of, while in fact it may be the finest document we have of what the medium itself was capable of—more than a document, a living piece of art.

Artists routinely misunderstand their own work. One primary source of this is the spiritual nature of the creative experience, and an intense love-hate relationship that the artist may thus have with his or her work, like, say, Ahab's relationship with the white whale. "Don't know if I saw you, if I would kiss you or kill you," Bob Dylan sings in a 1997 song. This seems to me a quite accurate description of Lou Reed's feelings about the band, the gestalt, with which he did his best work. Indeed, in the 1990s he both kissed (embraced, reunited with) and killed the Velvet Underground.

The most obvious misunderstanding likely to be experienced by the uninitiated reader who goes out to listen to this "Sister Ray" that I'm praising so effusively (in 1998 you can find it most easily in the Velvet Underground box set, *Peel Slowly and See*, which should be, but probably isn't, at your local library) has to do with the song's lyrics. The primary ones, the only ones you can hear clearly, are: "I'm searching for my mainline / I couldn't hit it sideways / Too busy sucking on my ding-dong / Ah, just like Sister Ray said." The rest of the lyrics are a narrative, a scene described by the same narrator-participant: "He aims it at the sailor / Shoots him down dead on the floor / 'Oh, you shouldn't do that / Don't you know you'll stain the carpet? / 'Oh no, man, I haven't got the time-time. / Too busy sucking on a . . .'" Reed's biographer Victor Bockris says the song's lyrics "echo scenes from *Last Exit to Brooklyn* by Hubert Selby, one of Lou's favorite writers." Bockris quotes Reed: "'Sister Ray' has eight characters in it and this guy gets killed and nobody does anything. The situation is a bunch of drag queens taking a bunch of sailors home with them, shooting up on smack and having this orgy when the police appear."

So an easy misunderstanding in 1998 would be that this song romanticizes heroin use, and therefore could be a dangerous influence on young listeners. Um, I won't argue with that, since there's always a possibility that a particular listener may be irony-deaf. Some people read Nietzsche and get very bad ideas. That doesn't mean *Thus Spake Zarathustra* wasn't one of the 19th century's greatest hits.

But if you don't understand rock and roll, or for that matter sung music in general, you might imagine that the supposed greatness of the musical work must depend largely on the "greatness" of the song's words. No, not necessarily. The ways that words in songs speak to and for listeners and singers can be quite mysterious. Bob Dylan is a great songwriter. But I argue that it is a mistake to assume his powerful voice can be heard just by reading his lyrics on a page. Dylan's best lyrics ("It's Alright Ma," "Blind Willie McTell") are enormously improved (given added power) by the sound of his voice and the rhythmic and melodic shape of his instrumental accompaniment. And so, to a certain extent, they do not exist meaningfully when separated from their performance(s).

But still, you ask, how can such a supposedly "great" song as "Sister Ray" have such dumb words? And I'm forced to admit: I love the words! Why? Because like every other element of the performance—Cale's organ crescendos, Reed's guitar solos and vocal phrasings, Tucker and Morrison's rhythmic infrastructure, and that one glorious chord change that is repeated fanatically all through the song—just like these, the words contain (and shine with the brightness of) the performance as a whole and all its other elements. I love the performance as a whole, every time I hear it (even twenty times in two days) at different stages of my life, and so I love the words. "Just back from Carolina"—the phrase, or something about the singer's voice, can hit me with the force of revelation. Ridiculous! But every moment of this recording awakens me.

And "speaking in tongues" means, precisely, speaking profound feelings or insights or messages that cannot be deciphered by examining the text of the speaker's utterances. These messages are *felt*, and are by their nature, transcendent. "Glossolalia" is defined as "an ecstatic or apparently ecstatic utterance of unintelligible speechlike sounds, viewed by some as a manifestation of deep religious experience." Lou Reed couldn't have gotten into that state without the simultaneous performances of Tucker and Morrison and Cale (who all actually wrote the song's "music" without him one afternoon), and without the circumstances of the moment, including the fact that this was a single take that would be on the band's album just as they played it now, which famously stimulated a competition between the musicians to play louder in order to be heard in the final mix. So I'm not saying Reed's lyrics were created spontaneously during this performance. The glossolalia in this case is not the words—they're a sort of script, and he's a method actor—it's the ecstatic truths communicated through his voice as he sings. This vocal performance is exactly equal to the individual instrumental performances and solos. Indeed, Reed's voice here is almost precisely the equivalent of a great jazz innovator's trumpet or saxophone playing in the midst of a top-quality improvisatory performance. True, Reed's guitar *sounds* like a jazzman's horn throughout "Sister Ray," but his voice explores the same musical realm, and the triumph of the song's lyrics is that their absurdity and the rebelliousness of singing this kind of a story and these bits of language in a song serve to liberate the singer and the song from any preconceptions either the band or its listeners might have about what's supposed to happen when you perform or hear a rock and roll song. Liberation is the goal, and, mysteriously, it seems to be achieved over and over again in this song about confused beings defiling themselves pathetically and banging on trash cans to celebrate the fact.

Is there anybody left in the room? The power of the song and its vocals can be heard at almost every moment of the track, but if someone wants a closeup of what I consider "speaking in tongues" and inspired vocal riffing, I can point out, for example, "c-c-c-c-couldn't" at 3:45 and "now just like . . . now just like . . . I said, oh . . . Just like!" at 16:29. And finally, I need to call attention to the closing minutes of the performance. Everything about them suggests conscious and brilliantly planned structure, as though these four madpersons knew exactly what they were doing all along. They didn't, of course. Yet their piece ends with a series of musical summations and false climaxes and magnificent rhythmic and melodic and lyrical resolutions that seem to this listener and many other listeners to be filled with conscious meaning, intelligence, very important information. Vital food for the soul. How'd they do that? I suspect only by being in touch, for a few moments, with a higher truth.

Which is why the chorus line of the song is in the form of religious testimony: "Just like Sister Ray said!" "I'm searching for my mainline . . ." (i.e., my purpose in life, at least for right now). And I repeat, Moe's tom-toms and Sterling's rhythm guitar are just as integral to the essence of this great creation as John's viola and organ and Lou's voice and guitar. Collective authorship. And don't forget the role of the moment. Came and went pretty quick, didn't it?

HIT 3

Girl Before a Mirror
by *Pablo Picasso*
(painted March 14, 1932)

Pablo Picasso was fifty years old when he painted *Girl Before a Mirror*. Backtracking for a moment, Lou Reed was twenty-five when "Sister Ray" was recorded, Paul McCartney was twenty-one when he sang "Things We Said Today," and Herman Melville was thirty-one when he wrote *Moby-Dick*. The model for the painting, Picasso's mistress Marie-Thérèse Walter, was twenty-two in the winter of 1932. As for the person looking at the painting, I'm forty-nine as I write these sentences and gaze at the reproduction of the girl (and her reflection) included in *Pablo Picasso: A Retrospective*, the book/catalog I bought at that 1980 Museum of Modern Art show. So I was thirty-two when *Girl* first inflamed my imagination and my soul and my sexual organs of perception (ears, fingers, tongue, mind, and, in this case, eyes).

"A poem should be palpable and mute/As a globed fruit," Archibald MacLeish told us in his poem "Ars Poetica" (in 1926; he was thirty-four). This comes to mind of course because *Girl Before a Mirror* is full of images of globed fruits—breasts, belly, even face and head—images the viewer's mind immediately, intuitively and/or consciously associates with other recent Picasso paintings, *Pitcher and Bowl of Fruit* and *Still Life on a Pedestal Table* (which the catalog helpfully tells us is a "secret portrait" of Marie-Thérèse). What a thrill for any unschooled museum-walker or book-thumber like myself to look from *Pedestal* (March 11, 1931) to *Girl* and be able to see one image as a recognizable transformation or rearrangement of the other! When is a desirable woman like a colorful bowl of fruit? In the eyes of her hungry lover. It also happens that Picasso's painting sublimely realizes the standard young Archibald defined (six years earlier) for a "poem." It is "motionless in time as the moon climbs." And it certainly embodies (no pun intended) the last lines of "Ars Poetica," the only part of the poem that shows up in my edition of Bartlett's *Familiar Quotations* (though that "globed fruit" line is the one that has most stuck with me): "A poem should not mean/But be." *Girl Before a Mirror* is. It does not need to be interpreted or understood. It speaks silently and directly and profoundly and oh-so-palpably.

I don't intend to call much on certified "experts" to justify my selections here (Hey! This one really is a "20th Century Greatest," the big boys all say so) since, after all, my premise is that you and I as individuals have as much right as any expert to form our own ideas of what is/was great art in our time or any time. The value of this book, if any, is that it's an honest reflection of the taste and "art experiences" of one person-in-the-street. I'm foolhardy enough to presume that what a Picasso painting means to little old me is as useful a morsel of information as the informed opinion of a scholar. (Picasso himself said on this subject, in 1935, "Academic training in beauty is a sham. Art is not the application of a canon of beauty but what the instinct and the brain can conceive beyond canon.") But anyway, rules need exceptions, and here's a quote from H. H. Arnason's 1977 *History of Modern Art* (found in many public libraries), just because I like what he says and the way he says it. He says *Girl* is a "moment of summation" between Picasso's "cycles of fertile and varied experiment." Arnason:

> *Girl Before a Mirror* brings together Picasso's total experience of curvilinear cubism and classical idealism. The painting is powerful in its color patterns and linear rhythms, but above all it is a work of poetry: the maiden,

rapt in contemplation of her mirror image, sees not merely a reversed reflection but a mystery and a prophecy. This lyrical work revives the poetry of the blue and rose periods and of his period of classical idealism; it adds a dimension of strangeness to the exotic Odalisques that Matisse painted, and anticipates Braque's haunting studio scenes.

Okay, it is fun for art scholars that every one of Picasso's works is another installment in an ongoing narrative that tells the story of this artist's aesthetic adventures and to a degree the story of *all* artists' and art-watchers' evolution as perceivers during Picasso's century (he lived and worked 1881–1973). But for the aspect of this painting that speaks most strongly to me, aside from its sheer beauty and eye-pleasure, I like this quote from John Berger (1965): "What makes these paintings [the portraits of Marie-Thérèse] different is the degree of their direct sexuality. They refer without any ambiguity at all to the experience of making love to this woman. They describe sensations and, above all, the sensation of sexual comfort."

Yes. These more than all the others on display at MOMA that day are the paintings that caused me to fall in love with Picasso. Because I could see we'd been to the same place. And it meant as much to him as it did and does to me. This reaffirms my humanity, in a world that is often hostile to and judgmental of sexual love. "Look!" I thought. "This painter understands. And worships the same God. At last, a friend I can talk to about this." (He talks to me and I talk to him when I'm looking at his paintings. Boy before a mirror.)

The really radical and experimental move for an artist to make in any era or art form is to find a way to tell the truth. *Girl Before a Mirror* is very simply Picasso telling the truth about his happiness at this moment in his life, while also employing a new visual language he has been developing in his work in order to more honestly represent what humans see when they look at each other's faces. Look, he famously tells us in so many paintings and drawings: You see the person's profile and their full face both at once—two eyes on one side of a nose!—and your mental picture of the friend you're looking at is actually a composite of the information conveyed by both perspectives. Just as we see with our hearts and our minds both at once, and try to form composite pictures of reality out of this sometimes contradictory input.

In the case of the girl before the mirror, her eyes are properly on opposite sides of her nose; but as we look at her face it changes like an animated cartoon, from a beautiful, evocative face seen full on, shining like a full moon, to a calm pensive profile, to subtle differences in whether she's seen as looking right at the camera (or painter) or half-looking toward the mirror. The whole effect is as if her head were seen in the process of turning from a deep gaze into the mirror to glance inquisitively (and affectionately) toward the observer.

And then there's the twin girl on the right side of the painting, the one in the mirror. This reflection is at once the same woman and a different one. And again, we are paradoxically treated to the sight of one girl from her side (beautiful pooching-out curve on that ready-to-be-pregnant belly) and the other turned toward us (her torso facing us, but her head and features turned away as though looking at the girl to her right). So much action in this still picture! The real girl almost has her arm protectively on the shoulder of the mirror girl. But the same lines suggest the mirror girl too is reaching toward her double (maybe fondling her breasts). And one more trompe l'oeil: Is the girl on the left (and therefore both of them) naked or wearing clothes? She's obviously naked because you can see so much of her body (including an X ray of her womb), but she's obviously clothed because we can see that those stripes belong to a sweater or blouse. And the backgrounds! Are those colorful checkerboard markings the walls of the boudoir, or are they a representation of how the observer's mind feels looking at this scene? We can *see* that he feels affection and deep admiration, and genuine wonder at the miracle of God's creation that this woman, his lover, is. Not just her lovely face and exquisite body—everything about her, including her relationship with herself, her mirror companion.

This painting is a passionate love poem. And full of humor. And very revealing of who the unseen member of this relationship (the painter, the lover) is. I love the way he expresses love and desire in this series of paintings of Marie-Thérèse (*The Dream*, *The Dream (Reading)*, *Nude on a Black Couch*, *The Mirror*, and others). With such immediacy. So for the first time I can actually show somebody how I feel when I feel this way. You think I'm mad? Or sex-crazed? Look at these paintings! You see, this is part of the human experience for many of us. Look at this man boasting about how voluptuous his young girlfriend is, and about how wild and tender she makes him feel.

It took a lot of courage for this fifty-year-old man who felt increasingly trapped by his wife's moods and their bourgeois lifestyle to speak so forthrightly and eloquently of his great sexual happiness (and self-discovery) with his twenty-two-year-old mistress. But we expect courage of Picasso. Courage and honesty. And an indomitable will to change the nature of our perception of the universe. "Gotcha!" he laughs as he throws up this mirror before us. And flatters us by suggesting we might possibly love women and life as much as he does.

For me, Marie-Thérèse comes across as a real person in these paintings, as tangible and knowable as any character in Shakespeare. Her every look and gesture seem genuine to me; I can feel her personality and presence. I adore her as one loves a favorite movie star of the opposite sex. I long for her, and I sense her comforting presence, her affectionate support. And I thank Pablo Picasso for saying some things that needed to be said about what it's like to be a male person. And for sending out such a positive message, for once, about a love relationship that works. At this moment. Most of all, I celebrate this painting for being such a fabulous portrait of two particular people, and their special moment in time, in which each has become so delicious to the other's eyes and hands and heart.

The *I Ching* or Book
of Changes

Translated by Richard Wilhelm

(completed in the summer of 1923)

I nquire of the oracle once again," this book says to its reader in chapter eight. *Hexagram* eight. The chapters are called hexagrams because each is defined by an ideogram made out of six lines. The *I Ching* is one of the few books I've ever read that's written in the second person imperative voice. The book speaks directly to and about its reader, confidently and compellingly. It is surely the book I've read the most number of times of all the books in my life. I've read each chapter, each hexagram, carefully, attentively, more than a hundred times, maybe many hundred.

And every time I read this book or read its chapters is different, because the book *is* an oracle and expects to be asked questions and reliably gives answers—each answer very personal, because it's about what's going on in my life and consciousness right now, it's about what I just asked. What a good friend! Book-oracles always keep their confidences. Are always ready to listen. Are always—in the case of this one, once you learn how to read it—ready to give very clear and practical and wise responses. Responses that articulate a deep and consistent philosophy. Which it teaches me as I ask it questions about my life situation and thus read and study bits of its text again, as I've done many thousands of times over the course of thirty years. And every time I learn something new. Or I see a little more deeply. This is not a process I expect or seek to complete. It's a lifetime course. If this book were a novel it would be the never ending story, the one that never loses interest or ceases to nourish.

It's a five-thousand-year-old book. And yet it belongs on a list of great cultural accomplishments of the 20th century, because between 1913 and 1923 a German man named Richard Wilhelm (with the energetic assistance of a Chinese man named Lao Nai-hsüan) gathered these texts and commentaries and read them as a supplicant (question-asker) himself and then translated them from Chinese into German (so his text could in turn be translated into other Western languages, including French and English—the version I've been reading and consulting since 1968 was translated from Wilhelm's 1924 edition by an American woman, Cary F. Baynes, and published in the United States in 1950).

What an accomplishment for a writer/editor/scholar! Wilhelm brought this most venerable of Eastern texts across the great water from Orient to Occident, brought it home alive, very much alive. I cannot imagine a more significant achievement by any word-artist anywhere in any century. He (they) brought the two worlds together, in the most useful domains, the domain of perception (of everyday human reality) and insight, and the domain of moral ("right") action. Practical philosophy. Collected in a book as old as civilization—a living, evolving being throughout its fifty centuries—and as broad as two hemispheres. When Rudyard Kipling wrote in 1889, "East is East, and West is West, and never the twain shall meet," he didn't see Richard Wilhelm on his horizon.

How to read the *I Ching*: Ask it a question. Carl Jung gives a good demonstration in his foreword to the American edition. He asks the Sage (that is to say, the old book, personified as a being, which it is) what its judgment is "about my intention to present it to the Western mind" (by writing a foreword to this new edition). He then uses the "coin method"—you throw down three coins six times, each time generating a line which is either broken or solid (unbroken), depending on how many coins are showing their "heads" sides or "tails" sides. This gets him a "hexagram," a set of six lines, each of which is either broken or solid (yin or yang, female or male, on or off). There are sixty-four possibilities in such a sequence. This is easy to perceive when you think of the six lines as two groups of three lines. There are eight possibilities for the three lines (all solid, all broken, solid at top and bottom and broken in the center, etc.). Since any of these eight could be the bottom three lines of the hexagram, and any of the eight could be the top set, there are eight times eight possible hexagrams.

Thus the book is divided into sixty-four chapters, one for each hexagram, with a sentence or two attached to each called "The Judgment," plus another sentence or two called "The Image." Wilhelm has organized the text with commentaries (gathered from the last three thousand years of Chinese commentaries on the *I Ching*, texts that have attached themselves to the original "system" over the centuries). Some of these commentaries are Wilhelm's own syntheses of various traditional interpretations, sometimes including his own related insights or clarifications, as a modern Westerner. Jung is his foreword then discusses the "answer" he got from the book, to let the reader see the process at work, and see how strikingly relevant the book's answer can seem to be in relation to the question asked or the situation inquired about.

The *I Ching*, which began to be widely available for interaction with Western minds in the 20th century, thanks to Wilhelm and Lao (and Baynes), is not only the world's oldest book but also the ancient forerunner of the modern computer. Computers, like the one I'm writing this essay on, operate by using a set of information-carrying languages all written by means of an underlying network of tiny stitches that are either on or off. That's what the *I Ching* is. In antiquity, more than three thousand years before the birth of Christ, someone in China invented this system for organizing all information relevant to daily human existence (i.e., the answers to the questions "What's going on?" and "What should I do about it?"), based on solid lines and broken lines, on- and off-switches, precisely equivalent to the 1 and 0 units of the mathematical binary system, organized in groups of six. An ancient digital computer. And—you gotta hand it to the Chinese—much friendlier than the one I'm using right now.

I suppose the question that remains is, didn't I say this was going to be a list of "works of art," and if so where does the *I Ching* fit in? Well, I for one consider the Bible and the Koran to be works of art as measured by my aforementioned yardstick: the impact they have on individuals at the moment that the individual is reading or listening to these Books. And if you argue that spiritual texts are by definition in a category separate from "art," I will concede the point regarding received texts; but this job of editing and translating that Wilhelm did with Lao's tremendous help is not a received text. It's a daring and inspired creative undertaking, and unquestionably "art" if the writing of nonfiction prose is ever considered art and if editing is recognized, as I believe it should be, as a legitimate art form.

And finally, like a play or a poem or a novel, Wilhelm's *I Ching* is a work of language. For example: "Revolution (Molting). The Chinese character for this hexagram means in its original sense an animal's pelt, which is changed in the course of the year by molting. From this the word is carried over to apply to the 'moltings' in political life, the great revolutions connected with changes of governments." This well-expressed and intriguing bit of etymology, and its implication that "revolution" is an ordinary and necessary process, speaks directly to the portion of the reader's consciousness that has ever questioned authority, in any era or any part of the world. It certainly had a great consciousness-raising impact on me when I first read it in 1968, when the word *revolution* had an extraordinary vibrance and relevance in the circles I traveled in, circles that were of course very excited and not too surprised when President Johnson lost the New Hampshire primary and then in effect resigned as president, over the Vietnam War issue. How could the definition of a single word have such an influence on my view of the world around me? I even came to see that not just my government but even I myself had some skin that was really due for shedding. "He who is not busy being born is busy dying," Bob Dylan has said in 1965, and now this *I Ching* book seemed to be saying the same thing. The Judgment: "Revolution. On your own day you are believed. Supreme success, furthering through perseverance. Remorse disappears." Encouraging words. Hey, enticing kids like me circa 1968 and '69 to feel optimistic about the outcome of our revolutionary efforts could be considered aiding and abetting seditious activities. But as far as I know, the Bollingen Foundation, publisher of the Wilhelm/Baynes *I Ching* that was becoming so popular amongst counterculturites in those years, was never investigated by any of Nixon's or Johnson's agencies. . . .

A little bit more language: "Someone does indeed increase him. Ten pairs of tortoises cannot oppose it. Supreme good fortune." This is a "line." With the coin method, if you get three heads or three tails facing up at once (a system later adopted by gambling machines worldwide) that particular line "changes," it's a "changing line." There's a part of the text Wilhelm assembles in each chapter, in addition to the Judgment and the Image and the commentaries on those and the opening comments on the name and form of the hexagram (the "Revolution" sentences quoted above are from the name-and-form comments)—a part of the text called "the lines." You read only the changing lines you got, if any. The tortoise line is from Hexagram 41, Decrease. Wilhelm's commentary (or Wilhelm and Lao's commentary, based on their knowledge of centuries of comments by Confucius and many others on the meanings of these lines) is: "If someone is marked out by fate for good fortune, it comes without fail. All oracles—as for instance those that are read from the shells of tortoises—are bound to concur in giving him favorable signs. He need fear nothing, because his luck is ordained from on high." A pleasant message to get from one's friend the book-oracle—even though the Judgment on Decrease includes the sentence "One may use two small bowls for the sacrifice." Because if you're the kind of person who's willing to ask the book a question (by phrasing a question, maybe on a piece of paper, then throwing the coins and using the little guide in the back of the book to figure out which hexagram-chapter you got) and then to endeavor to read and consider the answer with an open mind, words like *sacrifice* won't scare you too much. You'll have already learned from your experiences with the book that it's up to you to find out and decide what each of these words ("perseverance") means to you.

Okay, so how does it work? C. G. Jung, who says, "I was already fairly familiar with the *I Ching* when I first met Wilhelm in the early nineteen twenties," has a word for it: "synchronicity." (See that vitally important but insufficiently discussed 20th-century essay "Synchronicity: An Acausal Connecting Principle," in *The Structure and Dynamics of the Psyche*.) Jung does not presuppose an all-knowing Man behind the curtain who arranges that you, Julie, will get the exact right answer (out of the 4,096 available) from the *I Ching* to the specific question you just asked or to shed light on the situation you're in at this moment. In his Foreword, Jung writes:

> While the Western mind carefully sifts, weighs, selects, classifies, isolates, the Chinese picture of the moment encompasses everything down to the minutest nonsensical detail, because all of the ingredients make up the observed moment. Thus it happens that when one throws the three coins, these chance details enter into the picture of the moment of observation and form a part of it. . . . In other words, whoever invented the *I Ching* was convinced that the hexagram worked out in a certain moment coincided with that moment in quality no less than in time. To him the hexagram was the exponent of the moment in which it was cast—even more so than the hours of the clock or the divisions of the calendar could be . . . the hexagram was understood to be an indicator of the essential situation prevailing in the moment of its origin.

Jung goes on to say:

> This [ancient Chinese] assumption involves a certain curious principle that I have termed synchronicity, a concept

> that formulates a point of view diametrically opposed to that of causality. . . . Synchronicity takes the coincidence of events in space and time as meaning something more than mere chance, namely, a peculiar interdependence of objective events among themselves as well as with the subjective (or psychic) states of the observer or observers.

In short, the *I Ching* does not tell the future, it tells the moment. It does help the inquirer get insight into the possible future, and how to favorably or unfavorably influence the outcome of the current situation, because the seeds of the future lie in the present moment, and the more deeply you look into the moment, the more present and therefore the more ready you are. But most of all, the *I Ching* answers our questions by helping us look more deeply into our present situation and moment—even such questions as "Where did I drop the car keys?" or "What have I done with so-and-so's phone number?" Read the *I Ching's* answer openly and contemplatively, and you'll be surprised at how helpful this twenty-four-hour free confidential Help service ("Answers to all your questions!") can be.

So we really have to thank Wilhelm and Lao and Baynes and five millennia of Chinese wisepersons for making this service available to us in a language that can speak clearly and helpfully and poetically to anyone who encounters it and feels attracted to this text (this practice) and spends a little earnest and attentive time with it. Who were they? Richard Wilhelm was a Christian missionary only in the sense that he was brought to China at age twenty-six (1899) to teach at the German mission in Tsingtao. According to the anonymous author of the introduction to a 1956 collection of Wilhelm's essays, he was an intellectual with "a predilection toward fine arts, literature, music, sculpture, and especially the poetry of the great German writer Johann Wolfgang von Goethe (1749–1832)." He had served very briefly as a parish minister before going to China.

In 1913 in Tsingtao, Wilhelm began translating the *I Ching* with the aid of Lao Nai-hsüan, a seventy-year-old government

bureaucrat (Wilhelm was forty) and a scholar "of considerable re-
pute, steeped in traditional learning." These quotes are from the
introduction to a collection of Wilhelm's lectures, which tells us:

> Through Lao, Wilhelm came to understand the *Changes* not
> as a book to be critically and "scientifically" studied, and, as
> happened later, to be reevaluated, but as a work rooted
> within the fabric of Chineses thinking. The distinction is
> important. Chinese scholars and intellectuals continued to
> read and examine the *I Ching* in the twentieth century,
> much as they had done earlier. However, insofar as their ap-
> proaches to tradition were rapidly changing, their reading of
> traditional texts also changed. To read a text because it jus-
> tifies all there is, and to read a text in order to find *whether* it
> justifies all there is, are two different activities. That Wil-
> helm infused his translation and interpretation of the *I
> Ching* with a living reality, as such communicable to the
> West, may in part, at least, reflect Lao's position.

This gives your humble servant the romantic notion that the
old book chose Lao and Wilhelm as its agents, to help it escape
China at a dangerous historical moment and continue its life in a
different, global milieu.

And for any of you who may need to be reminded of the
importance of eternal vigilance when it comes to questioning
authority, I'd like to call your attention to the following quote
from the "Yi jing" entry in the seemingly authoritative Western
volume *Merriam-Webster's Encyclopedia of Literature* (Springfield,
Mass., 1995):

> Modern scholars have been troubled by the inclusion of
> the *Yi jing* among the Confucian classics, for Confucius
> (551–479 B.C.) seems to have deliberately avoided speak-
> ing of anything that suggested esoteric doctrines. The
> answer seems to be that Han dynasty Confucianists (*c.*
> 2nd century B.C.), influenced by the Daoist quest for im-
> mortality, justified their use of the *Yi jing* by attributing
> certain of its commentaries to Confucius.

I'm not a sinologist, but I can say fairly authoritatively that this is crap, reminiscent of the 20th-century Chinese government pronouncements that Tibet has always been part of China (see entry #38, *Kundun*) but the local people are confused and oppressed by a religious tyranny that claims otherwise. Confucius devoted much of his life to studying the *I Ching* and his excellent commentaries are quoted often in the Wilhelm/Baynes edition. But hey, don't believe me, believe the jerks who write the daily TV news, believe this anonymous corporate committee of experts in Springfield, Mass. (I'm from Cambridge—maybe some old regional rivalry is flaring up here).

About Cary Baynes, I know only that she is an American woman (she was living in Connecticut in 1949 when she finished translating Wilhelm's German edition into English) who had done some translations of C. G. Jung before getting this assignment. And I appreciate her choices of words whenever I read this work of hers and Wilhelm's and Lao's, sometimes every day of the year but recently more like once or twice a week.

In summation, Jung says, "In the *I Ching*, the only criterion of the validity of synchronicity is the observer's opinion that the text of the hexagram amounts to a true rendering of his psychic condition." Yeah, and if that happens to you, impressively and powerfully and very helpfully, more than twice, you just might find yourself going back for more. "Great art," as I said back in the introduction, "is an essentially subjective, and often profoundly spiritual, personal experience." So, talk to the *I Ching* and/or listen to "Sister Ray" if you find they work for you. You won't be alone.

HIT 5

Ulysses by **James Joyce**

(published February 2, 1922)

Ulysses is in this book because it seems to me a perfect example of what a "greatest hit of a century" can be, both publicly (collectively) and privately (to just one individual, you or me, at the time of reading or listening). Even though, or maybe especially because, I've never read it.

You can't read/hear/see/experience 'em all. I believe this is an important truth to remember about the greatest hits of any century. Even if their greatness were widely acknowledged and agreed upon, you shouldn't expect yourself or your friends to have seen/heard/read every one of them. It doesn't work that way. There's too much great art, and our individual attention spans are (relatively) small. If it's extraordinary for a man or woman to write two or three great books in a lifetime, then it should also be recognized as an extraordinary achievement to read and really savor seven or eight in a lifetime. Great writers need great readers. That's what this chapter's about. I can praise the reader of *Ulysses* unashamedly, because I'm not talking about myself. Except that I want to say, "what *Ulysses* has been to you, 'Sister Ray' and Philip K. Dick's meta-novel have been to me."

The Columbia Encyclopedia (3rd edition, 1963) says, "The effect of Joyce on writers of the 20th century is incalculable; he is probably the most-discussed author of his time. His techniques and forms have had enormous influence. . . ." Indeed. Also true of the Velvets and PKD, though classes on their work haven't sprung up quite as quickly as was the case with Joyce (who was thirty-eight when he finished this novel).

Enough of the public acclaim side of the story. Here's a nice tale of a private encounter with a great hit. The biographers of comparative mythology scholar Joseph Campbell report that Campbell bought a copy of *Ulysses* in Paris in 1927 (not surprising—he was twenty-three, and the novel had been banned in the United States and the United Kingdom and was prominently displayed in every bookstore in town). "To his dismay, when he tried reading it, it made no sense to him. 'Upon first opening *Ulysses*, I thought,' Campbell later said, 'Good God, what is this?' I thought, 'I had got my degree, but I don't know what he's talking about.'" The biographers, Stephen and Robin Larsen, go on to quote a still later Campbell reminiscence about his first weeks with the book: "No one in the world knew more than what James Joyce knew of what I was trying to find out! To translate knowledge and information into experience: that seems to me the function of literature and art." Interesting that the person who helped Campbell through the process of making sense of and learning how to read this book that was to change his life was the visionary and courageous woman (bookstore owner Sylvia Beach) who had published *Ulysses* in the first place. There really was something going on in Paris in the 1920s; it wasn't just (sorry, Joseph) a myth.

What does it take to be a great reader? Energy, intelligence, compassion (for the characters in the tale), commitment to the task, and an ability to suspend disbelief. Certainly, these qualities are to a significant degree dependent on the author, the storyteller; he or she must encourage and inspire and successfully engage the reader, sometimes causing him (as in the case of Campbell) to make an energetic commitment to a particular task of reading in a way that he or she has never considered before. Nor imagined possible. And thus the reader discovers how rewarding a truly attentive and even unconventional commitment to a novel (or any work of art) can be. New techniques and forms of reading. That's the legacy of Joyce's readers. Bless 'em.

Because *Ulysses* is such a recognized classic, my mind is going crazy as I write this with defensive thoughts about other already-acknowledged 20th-century "classics" that don't show up on my list. Even ones I've read and liked, such as Proust's *Du côté de chez Swann* (1913)—read it in French in high school and loved it, I've never forgotten that madeleine, and a few years later I eagerly acquired the two-volume Moncrieff translation of the whole *Remembrance*, imagining how happily I would read through it in my adulthood. Well, I never did. I could have, but it didn't happen that way; there is something fated about our relationships with works of art, I believe, like love stories. My list of "greatest hits," like yours, is a kind of autobiography. And the same is true of all critics and art historians and members of curriculum committees. But what do they talk about? Reputations. yeah, but the truth of art (I argue) lies in personal experiences, not reputations. Reputations are yardsticks as absurd as sales figures. *Ulysses* will survive as long as it can seduce individual readers into entering its world ("yes and how he kissed me under the Moorish wall and I thought well as well him as another"). Its reputation could get in the way, of course. That's the danger with greatest-hits lists.

I have this outrageous claim that I frequently make about Bob Dylan. I claim that the songs he so famously wrote in his heyday only found or achieved great power and beauty when he sang them. *Then* they meant something to their listeners, something they could not possibly have meant if they were just words on a piece of paper. He's not that kind of poet. He makes poetry with his musical voice, his performances.

So does Billie Holiday. Great, beautiful, profound, memorable poetry. These two songs, only one of which was kinda sorta written by her in the words-on-paper sense, are excellent examples. Her voice has the power to make written words (the actress's script) extraordinarily and very personally meaningful. To every listener. Few among us will ever forget what we have heard and felt when Lady Day sings:

> I cover the waterfront, I'm watching the sea . . .
> Will the one I love be coming back to me?
> I cover the waterfront, in search of my love
> And I'm covered by a starless sky above.

This (Billie Holiday's 1941 recording of this song) is beautiful. We love Billie's recordings like we love paintings and handicrafts that seem full of beauty to us, their observers, when we drink them in with our senses. "I cover the waterfront." You have to hear the ways she sings these four words (she sings them three times in the three minutes of this performance, and each time the phrase has different connotations, evokes different feelings and images) to even be able to imagine the extraordinary beauty they can contain and convey. It's all in the textures of her voice, and the very clear, strong images that arise in the listener's emotional imagination when he or she hears these four words—images evoked by those textures and by the keenly felt presence of the singer's persona, the narrator who's pacing back and forth before the ocean. We *feel* Billie. We know what these words mean to her right now as she's singing them. And that (what they mean to her, what she evidently hears and feels in them) is something deep and complex and moving. Something profound. Great fucking art.

Where did it come from? From Billie Holiday's heart, in combination with the hearts of the other musicians who co-created this performance. But if you're asking about the song itself, its origins are the soundtrack of a 1933 film for which this was the title song (not sung by Billie). In the film, Ben Lyon is an investigative waterfront reporter who pretends to love Claudette Colbert in order to entrap her father, who is smuggling Chinese immigrants. This is not the story Billie sings or that we hear. Wow, did she write a universal epic out of this song! With that voice and that presence of hers. And that incomparable gift she had for working with other jazz musicians as an equal. A sister. Soloing with her ax. Speaking that remarkable and always newly-invented-at-this-moment telepathic language called jazz. This is it. Not a pop singer accompanied by jazz musicians. A combo of nine jazz musicians, including Billie, blowing at and with each other: "Billie Holiday accompanied by Teddy Wilson and his Orchestra." At the same August 1941 session where she and they recorded two other masterpieces: "Love Me or Leave Me" and "Gloomy Sunday."

The lyrics and music of "I Cover the Waterfront" were written by Edward Heyman and Johnny Green. When Billie Holiday recorded the song, she was twenty-six years old, and had been recording for eight years, and performing in New York City and elsewhere for at least eleven years. She was young. And seasoned. And loved and admired by her peers, other musicians—and just starting to become known to the public. She had sung with two traveling big bands: Count Basies's and Artie Shaw's. She'd had a few "hit" records (a relative term at a time when the market for jazz or any recorded music was limited), notably "Fine and Mellow" in 1939 and the very famous B-side of that hit 78, the notorious "Strange Fruit," a poem about the common but seldom-spoken-of phenomenon of the lynching of black men by white mobs in the American South. The first "protest song" in modern American pop music, "Strange Fruit" had a considerable impact and was certainly one of the seeds of the civil rights movement of the 1950s and 1960s. At the time it brought Lady Day some notoriety, not because she wrote the song (she didn't), but because she dared to sing it in a club (Café Society in Greenwich Village), and then dared to record it. Raised her voice, so to speak. On behalf of her people.

But of course Billie Holiday didn't sing only for black people. Like Hank Williams a little later, she was (and is) universally recognized as an effective and articulate spokesperson for the emotionally downtrodden. Which bring us to the immortal lines that *were* partly written by Billie Holiday, from the other performance being honored in this entry:

Them that's got shall get.
Them that's not shall lose.
So the Bible said, and it still is news.
Mama may have, Papa may have,
But God bless the child that's got his own.

"God Bless the Child" is the best-known and most widely loved of all of Lady's songs:

She began to hum and then to sing. Both the song and the phrasing were tantalizingly familiar. "Billie!" he said suddenly. She turned and grinned at him. "God rest her soul. Played all them records till nothing left but a scratchy hiss, then boughten some more and played those out too. Withouten Lady Day, I'd have hardly no career at all, sugar. There are any one of hers you like special?"

"God Bless the Chile."

She clapped her hands with delight. "Damn *all*, Kirk, honey, that there is *my* song. Seven thousand times I sung that, all alone and for the people, and not one time it wasn't like my heart turning over slow. I can *cry* to that song, thinking of that poor lost broad and how the world broke her down. After this here food, I'll sing it to you good, and you shuten your eyes, you'll think she's come on back for sure."

—Bonnie Lee Beaumont and Kirk Winner in *The Girl, the Gold Watch & Everything* by John D. MacDonald (1962)

I'm including both "God Bless the Child" and "I Cover the Waterfront" in this "greatest hits" entry because I began to feel that focusing on just one Billie performance would not be an accurate representation of the nature of her greatness as an artist. As with most beloved singers, her greatness is in her *presence*. And much of that presence comes from getting to know her, which happens as you listen to her sing more than one song. An interface is created between her voice and your mind, enabling large quantities of awareness and beauty to be communicated and shared the instant the two come in contact. "Rich relations give crusts of bread and such/'You can help yourself, but don't take too much . . .'" Billie Holiday's voice singing these words in this musical setting (the May 1941 session with Eddie Heywood, Roy Eldridge, et al.) has enormous power. The very gentleness of her voice in this passage contributes to the electrifying nature of the listener's experience.

Billie Holiday was primarily a song-interpreter, not a writer, so there's a story behind her getting co-author credit for "God Bless the Child." Songwriter Arthur Herzog recalls:

One night I said to Billie, I want you to give me an old-fashioned Southern expression that we can turn into a song. She scratched her head and came up with nothing. . . . We turned to conversation about her mother, Sadie, and about how she was opening up an after-hours illicit joint, and wanted money from Billie, and how Billie didn't want to give it to her, didn't have it, and in a moment of exasperation she said, "God bless the child." And I said, "Billie, what does that mean?" She said, "You know. That's what we used to say—your mother's got money, your father's got money, your sister's got money, your cousin's got money, but if you haven't got it yourself, God bless the child that's got his own." And I said, "This is it, Billie." The song took twenty minutes to do as it stands today.

Herzog wrote the music and the rest of the words, and gave Holiday credit as co-songwriter of "God Bless the Child."

Every listener has a different set of favorite Billie Holiday songs. In the 1988 film *Rocket Gibraltar*, Burt Lancaster plays a dying man surrounded by family but most comforted by the recorded voice of his favorite singer, Billie. Like the scene from MacDonald's novel quoted above, it's a powerful portrait of the ongoing presence singers so often have in the lives of people who love them. The Billie performances we watch Lancaster listen to are "Don't Explain," "You Better Go Now," and "Foolin' Myself." Lancaster tells his daughter, "I gotta have someone sit down with me when I listen to Billie Holiday. Otherwise I cry. Sometimes I lose control. . . ."

What *does* "God bless the child that's got his own" mean? I don't know. But I think it's a good example of how this art form works. Some songs are like Zen riddles. We hear a phrase and we *feel* very clearly the resonance of it. We know it's true and that it speaks for us in a very personal way, but we can't rephrase it, explain it. His own *what*? His own money? Yeah, but the song is about not having money. So I guess "that's got his own" must be about self-sufficiency. "God helps them that help themselves." Is the chorus a prayer? Or a complaint? Or a declaration of independence? Depends on the listener. The art form goads us into finding our own truths. Songs are emotional mirrors.

Just to demonstrate how arrogant and wrong one listener's interpretation can be (in the eyes of another listener), check out

this comment from the liner notes of a 1991 Sony box set called
Billie Holiday—The Legacy (1937–1958). The entire entry, by
Michael Brooks ("digital producer" of the box set), says:

> GOD BLESS THE CHILD. Billie's most successful excursion into songwriting. The redoubtable Arthur Herzog does his usual fine job with the melody, and although I know this was written from the heart and the lyrics make perfect sense, the song doesn't work for me. It's a virtual updated version of Bessie Smith's "Nobody Knows You When You're Down and Out," but whereas Bessie's message was a defiant shout in the dark and God help those who did her down if she ever gets back on her feet, there is a whininess about "God Bless the Child" which makes me want to use the record as a frisbee.

At an Artie Shaw gig in St. Louis in 1938, when a redneck fan
in the crowd shouted, "Let the nigger wench sing again!" Lady
called him a motherfucker from the stage (a fight ensued). By all
accounts, she was a tough woman with a quick temper. I have no
doubt she would have decked Michael Brooks for his rude
remark. A *legacy* is "something handed down from the past, as
from an ancestor." Respect for one's ancestors is so central to
Asian culture that I have to wonder if the president of Sony
would have to consider committing suicide to atone for this horribly
public disrespect to an ancestor if he were aware that this
condescending criticism of the great singer was included in a
Sony box set called *The Legacy*. Hey, in the West we don't even
respect beloved and great artists. The ego of the critic or liner-
note writer takes precedence. Brooks goes on in his next note to
communicate his immense disdain for "Gloomy Sunday" (which
Billie once described as one of her favorites among her recordings).
This in a booklet that is the sole source of information
about Billie Holiday included in the most widely available and
most-likely-to-be-found-in-libraries anthology of her work as of
1998. And incidentally, if there is any "whininess" to be heard in
Billie's voice on this track, that is only the result of a failure on
the part of the digital producer to compensate for an unpleasant

distortion in the treble range caused by differences between the compact disc technology and the original analog recording. There is a slight shrillness at moments (the word "money") in the compact disc vocal that is not to be heard on a vinyl pressing of the same track (I've compared them recently). So let the buyer beware. The great artworks of the 20th century may be lost in some cases because their archivists are philistines (as if the cura- tors of the Picasso Museum in Paris painted over some of the mas- ter's "mistakes" in their disdain for the clumsy Spaniard).

Billie in heaven at least has the consolation of knowing that Michael Brooks, whoever he is, is not one of her peers, all of whom speak and spoke of her lovingly and respectfully. Frank Sinatra said, in 1958:

> With few exceptions, every major pop singer in the U.S. during her generation has been touched in some way by her genius. It is Billie Holiday who was, and still remains, the greatest single musical influence on me. Lady Day is unquestionably the most important influence on Ameri- can popular singing in the last twenty years.

Also in 1958, Miles Davis said, "I love the way she sings . . . like Lester Young and Louis Armstrong play . . . she doesn't need any horns. She sounds like one anyway." Max Jones read this comment to Lady Day on her last visit to England: "Billie smiled faintly and said: 'That's how I *try* to sound; I didn't know I suc- ceeded.'"

The beauty and poetry of Billie Holiday's great work is not hers alone. It is an expression and extension of a community of dedicated artists who lived and worked together. All of her work, from 1930 till her death in 1959, was created within and out of this world of loving friends and courageous coexplorers of the frontiers of music and life. For an example of this, listen to "All of Me" (1941) and her other legendary recordings with her dear friend the great saxophonist Lester Young, who gave her the nickname "Lady Day" (she in turn gave him his nickname, "Prez"). Other great jazz musicians she performed or recorded with at one moment or another include: Benny Goodman, Louis

Armstrong, Count Basie, Paul Whiteman, Duke Ellington, Teddy Wilson, Ben Webster, Dizzy Gillespie, Charles Mingus, Coleman Hawkins, Benny Carter, Artie Shaw, Johnny Hodges, Roy Eldridge, and Gene Krupa.

You don't have to recognize any of these names to enjoy and appreciate the two performances under discussion here. But, because disrespect for great artists is common in the American music business and throughout the "entertainment industry" at century's end, you have to be careful as you go looking for Billie Holiday CDs containing "God Bless the Child" and "I Cover the Waterfront." If you want to hear what I'm citing as examples of some of the greatest art created by humans in our era, you need to locate the May 9, 1941, performance of "God Bless the Child" with Eddie Heywood and his orchestra and the August 7, 1941, performance of "I Cover the Waterfront" with Teddy Wilson and his orchestra. This may not be easy. The *Legacy* box omits "I Cover the Waterfront," and the recording of "God Bless the Child" in that box set is actually an alternate take from the May 1941 session, not the version millions have grown up with, a fact Brooks doesn't bother to mention in his notes (it's in tiny print on the back of the package). Most of the Billie Holiday CDs you will find if you search the stores don't bother to identify their tracks by date of recording or even to give the names of the other musicians who participated in these collaborative creations. I have here a 1994 MCA CD called *God Bless the Child*; there are no liner notes, and no musicians are credited inside the package or on the back or anywhere. More disgraceful is a 1996 CD called *American Legends* with a reproduction of the U.S. Postal Service Billie Holiday "jazz singer" postage stamp on the cover. This one, "produced" (i.e., compiled) by Rod McKuen, names the band for three out of its twelve tracks, and never lists musicians nor gives any dates for the performances. A Polygram compilation called *The Billie Holiday Songbook* does offer dates and personnel on the inner sleeve. The version of "God Bless the Child" included, from a 1956 recording session, is a little weak, although there are live performances of this song from the 1950s that are certainly worth hearing; the version of "I Cover the Waterfront" here, from a 1956 Carnegie Hall concert, is powerful and quite worthwhile, but again not at all similar to the August 1941 recording which I consider such a prime example of the genius of this artist and her collaborators.

To further complicate matters, the exquisite August '41 recording of "I Cover the Waterfront" was not released by Columbia Records as a 78 until after the rather different 1944 Commodore recording was released as a 78 that year. (The 1941 "God Bless the Child" *was* released by Columbia in 1941, and was something of a "hit" at the time.) There are three alternate takes available of the 1944 "I Cover the Waterfront," of interest to dedicated fans, but to hear the particular magic I've been transported by you need to find a wonderful European CD called *The Complete Billie Holiday Mastertakes Collection, Vol. 7, 1940/42*, or an old Columbia Records vinyl anthology like *The Billie Holiday Story* or *Billie Holiday, the Golden Years*. Or if you're lucky you might find a Sony compilation other than *Legacy* that draws from the same source as those vinyl collections. *The Golden Years* includes liner notes by Ralph Gleason, with this fine quote from Billie: "I don't think I'm singing. I feel like I'm playing a horn. I try to improvise like Les Young, like Louis Armstrong, or someone else I admire. What comes out is what I feel. I hate straight singing. I have to change a tune to my own way of doing it. That's all I know."

The Universal Declaration of Human Rights

by the Drafting Committee of the United Nations Commission on Human Rights, Eleanor Roosevelt, Chairman

(adopted by the General Assembly December 10, 1948)

One great American woman after another. Throughout 1947 and 1948, Eleanor Roosevelt was the "chairman" of a committee that wrote the most important and wonderful piece of writing produced by any committee in this century or era. Dr. Peng-Chun Chang of China was vice-chairman, Dr. Charles Malik of Lebanon "rapporteur." The other five members of the committee were from Australia, Chile, France, the United Kingdom, and the Soviet Union.

The drafting committee worked in part from draft declarations and proposals submitted by the governments of Chile, Cuba, India, Panama, and the United States, but in the end the eight men and women wrote these 1,774 words themselves.

In this case the essence of the creative act was not the choosing of words but the process of agreeing to agree on them (before collectively publishing them, making them public, which in this case meant offering them as a text to be adopted by a yes or no vote on the floor of the fairly young United Nations General Assembly).

All observers and commentators agree that Mrs. Roosevelt deserves primary credit for making this act of agreement possible, through her own artful presence. Not the same as Billie Holiday's role in her performing and recording bands, but not all that differ-

ent. Billie led by inspiration, Eleanor by devotion to worthy principles and by loving kindness. And look at what was created,
back on the first Human Rights Day, December 10, 1948, as a result! "The Magna Carta of all mankind."

The thing that baffles me is why this isn't the first thing
people think of when the subject of the 20th century's "greatest
hits" comes up. Okay, the mass media have kind of ignored the
Universal Declaration so far, to their discredit—but what song or
novel in this century has spoken for or had an impact on or liber-
ated more people?

Article 19

*Everyone has the right to freedom of opinion and expres-
sion; this right includes freedom to hold opinions without interference and to seek, receive and impart information and ideas
through any media and regardless of frontiers.*

Article 23

*1. Everyone has the right to work, to free choice of employ-
ment, to just and favourable conditions of work and to protection against unemployment.*

*2. Everyone, without any discrimination, has the right to
equal pay for equal work.*

*3. Everyone who works has the right to just and favourable
remuneration ensuring for himself and his family an existence
worthy of human dignity, and supplemented, if necessary, by
other means of social protection.*

*4. Everyone has the right to form and to join trade unions
for the protection of his interests.*

Article 27

*1. Everyone has the right freely to participate in the cultural
life of the community, to enjoy the arts and to share in scientific
advancement and its benefits.*

*2. Everyone has the right to the protection of the moral and
material interests resulting from any scientific, literary or artistic production of which he is the author.*

Article 1

All human beings are born free and equal in dignity and rights. They are endowed with reason and conscience and should act towards one another in a spirit of brotherhood.

Article 2

Everyone is entitled to all the rights and freedoms set forth in this Declaration, without distinction of any kind, such as race, colour, sex, language, religion, political or other opinion, national or social origin, property, birth or other status.

Furthermore, no distinction shall be made on the basis of the political, jurisdictional or international status of the country or territory to which a person belongs, whether it be independent, trust, non-self-governing or under any other limitation of sovereignty.

Article 3

Everyone has the right to life, liberty and security of person.

Eleanor Roosevelt was sixty-two years old when she began the work of guiding and participating in the creation of a universal declaration of human rights. She had been a widow for a year and a half. Her biographer Joseph P. Lash speaks eloquently (in his preface to *Eleanor: The Years Alone*) of who she was at this moment in her life:

> The same qualities that had turned this protected daughter of old New York into an uncompromising champion of the poor and oppressed, that had enabled her to remake her marriage after the discovery of her husband's unfaithfulness into a journey of self-discovery and a partnership of immense usefulness to America . . . foretold that Eleanor Roosevelt, now standing alone and speaking for herself, would leave her mark on the times.
>
> She had overcome so much, turned so many difficulties into points of growth. She had emancipated herself from the insular and caste-minded society into which she had been born and, in a relentless battle of wills, had freed her-

self from the domination of a strong-minded mother-in-law who had embodied the values of that society. She had established a unique relationship of independence and partnership with her husband. A homely adolescent with a deep sense of inadequacy because of her physical plainness, she had grown into a woman of poise, dignity, and gracious beauty. She who had been anti-Semitic and prejudiced against "darkies" had become the epitome of a concern that excluded no one from the circle of its compassion and love. Although she had opposed the woman's suffrage movement, she was now a tough-minded and astute political figure in her own right. She for whom speaking had been an ordeal had become one of the most self-possessed and moving speakers in public life.

She had even learned to cope with the sense of alienation, of being an outsider, that she had acquired in childhood with the death of her parents. Work and loving people no matter what they did were her formulas for transcending loneliness and disappointment. She was only sixty-one [when the President died], full of vitality, at home in the corridors of power, and adept at using power to help others. She had a vast political constituency and felt an obligation to promote her husband's objectives, especially the achievement of peace through the United Nations.

Thus the background of the principal author and a few samples from the text. Be assured that the other twenty-four Articles include all the basics almost any of us would wish declared and embraced: freedom of movement within, and the right to leave or return to any country; freedom from arbitrary arrest; the right to education; freedom of religion; the right to a standard of living adequate to health and well-being. But why include the Universal Declaration in this book? Because it is a work of expression, a short piece of prose, and therefore in my view as much an example of human art from its era as any film or sculpture or poem. What greater or more memorable poem that this? It's a distillation into a few well-chosen words (in five languages simultaneously) of the standards virtually all nations and persons agree apply to the circumstances of every human being everywhere, a song of love and a grand essay on the many twists and turnings in the relationships between individuals and states, between personal power and consciousness and collective power and consciousness. And because I cannot bear to contemplate a world in which our understandable and appropriate appreciation for the Beatles and Picasso and James Joyce distracts us from or blinds us to awareness of the significance and reality of our having somehow agreed, in the middle of this difficult century, on the basic ground rules for human coexistence on this ball of dirt.

We did agree, that's the point. All of the work of human rights organizations like Amnesty International is completely based upon, made possible by, and carried out by reference to, this Declaration that was passed resoundingly by an assembly of the representatives of all nations and peoples of the world. Every nation that has ever joined the United Nations has by that act formally expressed its willing acceptance of the Charter of the UN and by extension of the text of the Universal Declaration. The progress toward the realization of Mrs. Roosevelt's and the UN's original intention, an International Bill of Human Rights accepted as law and given the support necessary to make it enforceable in the realpolitik of international affairs, is another story, one which the reader is urged to inform her- or himself about (www.globalrights.org, or ask your library for a copy of *The International Bill of Human Rights*—the 1981 book edition has a very readable "brief history" which can also be found at the aforementioned website).

And finally, dear reader, a bit of homework. The Preamble to the Declaration concludes:

Now, therefore, THE GENERAL ASSEMBLY proclaims this Universal Declaration of Human Rights as a common standard of achievement for all peoples and all nations to the end that every individual and every organ of society, keeping this Declaration constantly in mind, shall strive by teaching and education to promote respect for these rights and freedoms. . . .

That's where we come in. Have you told your kids? Your friends and neighbors? Yourself? How can we live by such a beautiful code if we don't educate ourselves as to its content and its existence?

HIT 8

Winnie-the-Pooh
by A. A. Milne
(published 1926)

In 1966 Philip K. Dick (see next entry) wrote a thought-sequence going through the mind of the protagonist of his novel *Ubik* in a fictional 1992 as he (Joe Chip) contemplates the death of a friend: "Didn't Plato think that something survived the decline, something inner not able to decay? The ancient dualism: body separated from soul. The body ending as Wendy did, and the soul—out of its nest the bird, flown elsewhere. Maybe so, he thought. To be reborn again, as the *Tibetan Book of the Dead* says. It really is true. Christ, I hope so. Because in that case we all can meet again. In, as in *Winnie-the-Pooh*, another part of the forest, where a boy and his bear will always be playing . . . a category, he thought, imperishable. Like all of us. We will all wind up with Pooh, in a clearer, more durable new place."

The year before, 1965, songwriter Richard Fariña (college chum of Thomas Pynchon; see entry #18) wrote or completed his first and only novel, *Been Down So Long It Looks Like up to Me*, which opens with its protagonist (prototypical 1960s campus rebel Gnossos Pappadopoulis) being identified as (this is understood to be how the character thinks of himself) a "furry Pooh Bear, keeper of the flame." And closes, after adventures with primary characters nicknamed Heffalump and Piglet, with the phrase "Bump bump bump, down the funny stairs." A fabulous novel, by the way, worth seeking out.

And in 1967, popular rock band Jefferson Airplane recorded and began performing live a signature song called "The Ballad of You and Me and Pooneil." You had to be an insider (like me, ahem) to know this, but the title referred to a projected subjective world evoked by the stories about Winnie-the-Pooh and the songs of Fred Neil. This reference (good song, by the way) was a little more evident when the group recorded a 1968 follow-up called "The House at Pooneil Corners."

Thus the presence of Pooh, a character in a 1926 children's book, in the Western world's literary or aesthetic collective consciousness four decades later. How "greatest hits" reverberate within and against each other. (Notice Plato still hanging around after two millennia. . . .)

Alan Alexander Milne was thirty-eight years old when his first and only child Christopher Robin Milne was born in London in 1920. One year later the boy was given a teddy bear, soon to be joined by other stuffed animals, including a tiger, a pig, and a donkey.

Speaking again of the impact, direct and indirect, of *Pooh* on all of us, it is difficult to imagine Walt Kelly's *Pogo* and its Okefenokee Swamp inhabited by talking animals who know each other, or Bill Watterson's *Calvin and Hobbes* and its a-boy-and-his-friend-the-stuffed-tiger, ever having been invented and drawn without *Pooh* (and the *Pooh* drawings by Ernest Shepard) first blazing the path.

Why is Pooh so important to us?—and he is, have no doubt about it. This is one inarguable greatest hit of the century, unless you're a literary snob who has trouble imagining a *children's book* (one that can be understood and responded to by four-year-olds) being considered the equal of a more obviously "literary" work like *The Sound and the Fury* or *Ulysses*. Which brings us back to the question: What is great art? My answer is, a creative work that provokes in many observers powerful feelings leading to or affirming great insights, resulting in significant degrees of self-understanding. An attractive messenger of profound and awakening truths. *Winnie-the-Pooh* is that. And how this memorable work of art achieves its profound impact, and why it's so important to so many who've read it or had it read to them, is this:

A. A. Milne, writer of humorous verse for *Punch* and already author of one quite successful (thanks particularly to Ernest Shepard) book of humorous verse for contemporary children (which did introduce his infant son's teddy bear as a peripheral character)—this new father, when he wrote his book of children's stories, took a very unusual and, as it turns out, universally meaningful perspective. His characters are not just animals, they are *stuffed* animals who have a community together because they belong to the same child. And we as readers are allowed to perceive them, particularly Pooh, from inside their own minds. This is charming, since Milne so skillfully sketches them as real, recognizable people with human fears and vanities and appetites and neuroses. It is a very safe way to be inside other people's minds. But best of all is the constant implied presence of Christopher Robin, the felt understanding that these animals have feelings consistent with what a child might project onto his or her imaginary creatures, animas, alter egos. Who has not looked at or held a teddy bear or other stuffed animal and felt strong feelings of mysterious sympathy and understanding, and, therefore, self-love? It is a universal experience. *Winnie-the-Pooh* captures it, and in so doing says a lot on behalf of each of us about our private experiences since infancy of getting to know other people—the social world, with its Rabbits and Eeyores, and the world of close friends, with its Poohs and Piglets. This intensity of feeling and this depth of felt understanding and insight is what we want from literature or any kind of art. Milne, with his love of language and his (gently expressed) love of people and of children, really comes through in *Winnie-the-Pooh* and its companion, published two years later, *The House at Pooh Corner*. Milne and Shepard successfully combine adult perspectives and child perspectives, and produce a very satisfying portrait of the human community as a result. Not a very "British" or even very "Western" book. A universally articulate and pleasing work of storytelling, picture-drawing, literature, great art.

HIT 9

Martian Time-Slip

by *Philip K. Dick*

(published 1964)

In the penultimate chapter of *Winnie-the-Pooh*, Christopher Robin and Pooh float to the rescue of Piglet in a boat (actually, an upside-down umbrella) called *The Brain of Pooh*. This is notable because, as I tried to convey in the previous entry, the special magic of the Pooh stories is the opportunity they give us to spend time in the mind of Pooh. Just as the almost-irresistible attraction of Philip K. Dick's science fiction novels is the opportunity they give us to float in (and sometimes be rescued by) the mind of Phil.

> What had tormented him ever since the psychotic episode with the personnel manager at Corona Corporation was this: suppose it was not a hallucination? Suppose the so-called personnel manager was as he had seen him, an artificial construct, a machine like these teaching machines? If that had been the case, *then there was no psychosis*.
>
> Instead of a psychosis, he had thought again and again, it was more on the order of a vision, a glimpse of absolute reality, with the façade stripped away. And it was so crushing, so radical an idea, that it could not be meshed with his ordinary views. And the mental disturbance had come out of that.

—*Martian Time-Slip*, chapter 5

Philip K. Dick was the Dostoyevsky, the great questioner, the doubting prophet, of the mid-20th century. He, perhaps more than any other novelist of his era anywhere in the world, explored and expressed the great ambiguities of the human situation, the dilemma of the individual human being trying to locate himself vis-à-vis perceived reality, at this rapidly changing historical moment.

"Things are seldom what they seem, skim milk masquerades as cream," said W. S. Gilbert in his musical drama *H.M.S. Pinafore* in 1878, and Philip K. Dick devoted his life to writing one huge novel (more than two million words) expanding on this single sentence. "You've heard the song, now read the metanovel!" Forty-five novels by one man, published as separate books over the course of his lifetime, but intuitively understood by his many readers around the world to be one continuous or discontinuous story, one big book. A book about fictional characters getting glimpses of absolute reality, constantly discovering that things are not as they seem. This is your life, *Homo sapiens*, 1964 C.E. Get used to it. And if you can't get used to it, reading Philip K. Dick novels will at least help you to laugh at it, and to feel less alone. The mind of Phil is an oddly reassuring place because we've all had his insane suspicions and visions. He makes our personal crazinesses seem smart . . . maybe even wise. Do you see what I see?? And if so, do you have any idea how we can get through the next few minutes or hours or years?

I mean, after all, you have to consider we're only made out of dust. That's admittedly not much to go on and we shouldn't forget that. But even considering, I mean it's a sort of bad beginning, we're not doing too bad. So I personally have faith that even in this lousy situation we're faced with we can make it. You get me?—From an inter-office audio-memo circulated to Pre-Fash level consultants at Perky Pat Layouts, Inc., dictated by Leo Bulero immediately on his return from Mars.

—*The Three Stigmata of Palmer Eldritch* (1965)

In Dick's 1969 novel *Ubik*, the protagonist Joe Chip is on his way out of his futuristic condominium-apartment:

> He strode to the apt door, turned the knob and pulled on the release bolt. The door refused to open. It said, "Five cents, please." He searched his pockets. No more coins; nothing. "I'll pay you tomorrow," he told the door. Again he tried the knob. Again it remained locked tight. "What I pay you," he informed it, "is in the nature of a gratuity. I don't *have* to pay you." "I think otherwise," the door said. "Look in the purchase contract you signed when you bought this conapt."

Joe Everyman, arguing futilely with the computer that operates the door to his crummy futuristic urban apartment, is perhaps the quintessential comic image in Philip K. Dick's oeuvre, just as the defeated protagonist of *Now Wait for Last Year* asking for and receiving sympathetic advice from a talking robot taxicab on whether to leave his wife is the quintessential tragicomic moment in the metanovel. But it is another apartment building, autistic child Manfred Steiner's chronologically displaced crayon drawing in *Martian Time-Slip* of AM-WEB, the slumlike public housing structure where he will someday be confined for 123 years as an aging, unwilling ward of the state, that manages to endure in many readers' imaginations as the quintessential postmodern nightmare object in a body of work thickly populated with nightmarish images of contemporary reality. Not comic. Too close to home for most readers, even though the public housing complex has not yet been built in the Martian badlands (the "Franklin D. Roosevelt Mountains") and is still the object of fiercely competitive land speculation at the time of the novel's action.

Manfred's dread vision is simultaneously the ineradicable horror of the (recent, remembered) human past, of his unavoidable future, and of his and our present moment. In Dick's hands, the horror of AM-WEB is palpable and the time-perception confusion that Manfred experiences and generates (entrapping the novel's protagonist and its readers in his disturbed perceptual field) is mysteriously familiar, believable, recognizable. Manfred is a paradoxically cynical, and dangerous, innocent, and we can't help identifying with his bizarre circumstances and caring about him and caring about the people whose lives he comes into: Jack, the bumbling ex-schizophrenic repairman; Doreen, Jack's beautiful and surprisingly compassionate mistress; Silvia, his confused barbiturate-addicted wife; and even Arnie Kott, the self-indulgent, self-doubting comic despot of the Martian plumbers' union. This is not an ordinary novel. It's a Philip K. Dick experience, and the danger is, as many have discovered, that after tasting it you may find yourself craving more. Even the author found himself dealing with withdrawal crises in relation to his novels or metanovel:

> What matters to me is the *writing*, the act of manufacturing the novel, because while I am doing it, at that particular moment, I am in the world I'm writing about. It is real to me, completely and utterly. Then, when I'm finished, and have to stop, withdraw from that world *forever*—that destroys me. The men and women have ceased talking. They no longer move. I'm alone, without much money, and, as I said before, nearly forty. . . . I promise myself: I will never write another novel. I will never again imagine people from whom I will eventually be cut off. I tell myself this . . . and, secretly and cautiously, I begin another book.

The world Dick is writing about is as real to his readers as it is to him, and that is the key to his achievements as a novelist. Patricia Warrick, in her book *Mind in Motion: The Fiction of Philip K. Dick*, offers valuable insight into how this is accomplished:

> In *Martian Time-Slip*, we see the world not only as it looks to the major characters like Jack Bohlen and Arnie Kott, but also as it appears to almost all the minor characters, too— Otto Zitte, Anne Esterhazy, Dr. Glaub, Silvia Bohlen. The result is a richness and depth of characterization that makes us feel sympathy and compassion for each individual. The economy in characterization is impressive—a rapid sketch-

ing with sure strokes, like an artist bringing a character to
life on a sketch pad while we watch. In a short chapter, Norbert Steiner, with his tormented, guilt-ridden inner life, becomes so real that we understand the inevitability of his
suicide.

Dick's quote about his experience of the act of writing, and
Warrick's quote about the experience of reading him, explain
each other. He can sketch his characters so easily and effectively
because he has no distance from them. He does not use them as
symbols (although they become full of symbolic meaning in the
reader's perception), does not manipulate them for purposes of
plot or message. They are real to him, he writes down what he
hears them saying and sees them doing. If, at times, the things
they do echo moments and events from his own life, that is
because they are projections of his unconscious, like characters
and situations in dreams. He makes us feel compassion for each of
them because he does too. This is not a matter of technique. It's
his actual experience in the act of writing, which we share as we
read.

Dr. Milton Glaub is a fascinating example. He's the only psychiatrist in the novel, and although Dick (and his primary alter
ego here, Jack Bohlen) has considerable resentment for psychiatrists and has seen them as oppressors imposing a false reality on
their patients, Glaub (his name is the German word for faith or
belief) is not a villain, not the kind of symbolic character you
might expect a novelist to invent for his major work on the topic
of the subjective world of schizophrenia. Dick doesn't use Glaub
as a symbol in the ordinary dramatic sense. He observes him,
honestly and with curiosity and empathy. This in spite of a powerful biographical parallel that perhaps Dick did not know he was
going to write until he observed it happening to his characters
and recorded it.

Um, he *seems* to have known, because he sets the stage so
carefully ahead of time, when he describes Jack Bohlen in chapter 5 thinking back to his schizophrenic hallucination regarding that personnel manager: "The man was dead . . . his organs,

which had withered away, were replaced by artificial components . . . everything was made of plastic and stainless steel." This sets up a less dramatic moment in chapter 7: "Jack saw the psychiatrist under the aspect of absolute reality, a thing composed of cold wires and switches, not a human at all, not made of flesh." Less dramatic because now Jack can "cope," he conceals his vision, the psychiatrist doesn't notice Jack's momentary terror, nor does his boss Arnie, but the girl Doreen, who had a brother who was schizophrenic, does notice what Jack is going through, and responds with concern and affection. "I'd love to fool everybody," he tells her when they're alone. "But I'd have to say to Dr. Glaub, 'Doc, I can see you under the aspect of eternity and you're dead.'"

The biographical parallel I'm referring to can be found in Dick's comments to an interviewer in 1977:

> I remember I was in my teens and I saw a psychiatrist—I was having trouble in school—and I told him that I had begun to wonder if our value systems—what was right and what was wrong—were absolutely true or whether they were not merely culturally relativistic. And he said, "That's a symptom of your neurosis, that you doubt the values of what is right and what is wrong." So I got hold of a copy of the British scientific journal *Nature* . . . and there was an article in it which said virtually all our values are derived essentially from the Bible and cannot be empirically verified, therefore must fall into the category of the untestable and the unprovable. I showed it to him, and he got very angry and said, "I consider this nothing but horseshit. *Horseshit*, I say!" Now I look back and see that this man was cemented into a simplistic mold. I mean his brain was *dead* as far as I could determine. Somewhere along his life-track, his brain had ossified. He thought certain things were absolutely right, empirically right. Psychiatrists are philosophically naive. Most of them, except people like Laing and so forth.

So how do we meet Dr. Glaub in *Martian Time-Slip*? He enters the novel (described as "tall, slender, in his white coat, carrying his clipboard") by approaching and addressing the viewpoint character for this brief section of the narrative, Norbert Steiner, unhappy father of autistic boy Manfred Steiner. Manfred lives in Camp Ben-Gurion, a home for "anomalous children" in the Israeli sector of colonized Mars. Dr. Glaub is a resident psychologist at Camp B-G. And as we meet him he impresses us (well, this reader) as compassionate and committed, talking enthusiastically of a recently published theory about autism as "a derangement in the sense of time," which he believes will enable him to help his patient, Manfred, to lead a more normal and happy life. Dr. Glaub's hope is contrasted with the dismissive pessimism of Manfred's father: "'Dreams,' Steiner interrupted, 'You will never make contact with my boy.' Turning, he walked away from Dr. Glaub."

So Glaub arrives in the novel as a portrait of a caring and intellectually engaged scientist/practitioner, a symbol, if you will, of hope. Then when he returns twelve pages later he gets his moment as viewpoint character (Philip K. Dick was a master of the "shifting viewpoint" narrative, in which succeeding sections of a novel show us the same world as perceived by the mind of another major or minor character), and we discover that in the privacy of his mind this symbol of hope is fretting and worrying all too humanly about his money problems. So this "best psychiatrist on Mars" is portrayed not so much as an authority figure (indeed he has his own problems dealing with Arnie Kott as an authority figure who has power to hire him and ease his money worries or not) but as sympathetic and human and, like Joe Chip, kind of comic.

And because he's a Philip K. Dick character, the author's (and, therefore, the reader's) view of Glaub does not stay fixed. In a climactic scene, not only does Jack see Glaub as an inhuman thing composed of cold wires and switches but Jack's lady friend Doreen notices (because she's tuned in to how people react to Arnie's power) how envious the Doc is of Jack's seeming sinecure with the Big Boss. From here forward, the best psychiatrist on Mars deteriorates into a more and more neurotic and unlikable, or anyway weak, human being. Characters in Dick novels shift roles as the author's perception of them is altered by the other characters' perceptions of them and as their own perceptions of themselves alter. Nothing is permanent. Except certain difficult-to-define human values and a pervasive uncertainty about the real meaning of sanity and reality and right behavior. "What's going on???" becomes a subjective as well as an objective question, and we see the collective human view of reality creating itself and shifting even as the personal views of the individual characters resist that consensus and yet also shift from moment to moment.

In a marvelously PhilDickian bit of off-handed satire, we discover in chapter 6 that on Mars or in this future world you can hire a psychiatrist to be your stand-in for difficult social situations: "'I sure appreciate your going [to the party] in my place, Doc. You psychiatrists really take a load off a man's back; I'm not joking when I say I been losing sleep over this.' 'Don't worry any further about it,' Dr. Glaub said. For after all, he thought, what's a little schizophrenia? That is, you know, what you're suffering from. I'll take the social pressure from you, and you can continue on in your chronic maladaptive state, at least for another few months. Until the next overpowering social demand is made on your limited capabilities. . . ."

So not only do *Martian Time-Slip's* characters shift roles (good guy to bad guy, friend to foe, etc.), they can hire each other to assume roles for them. One realizes that if Arnie Kott suspected Philip K. Dick existed he'd have to find a way to bribe him to alter the plot of the novel to Arnie's benefit. And Phil suggests that if so, he'd be as buyable as any of his characters; he doesn't presume any moral superiority just because he's the author.

Anyway, by the time Glaub makes his last appearances in the novel (chapter 14) he's acting out his own neuroses quite helplessly, stalking Arnie Kott in cahoots with Kott's ex-wife, supposedly in a heroic act on behalf of Jack Bohlen but (we readers perceive) actually acting out his own irrational hostility at the man who declined to solve Glaub's money problems when Glaub imagined he could have. No longer a sympathetic character, depending of course on how much the individual reader happens to dislike Arnie Kott (who actually is pretty helpless himself by this point).

So we could, if we like, see Glaub as the psychiatrist redeemed, definitely flesh and blood and not a very effective machine after all. Not that Jack's perception wasn't absolute reality. . . .

So I include *Martian Time-Slip* as an inarguable (I believe) greatest hit of the 20th century as an act of synecdoche, that literary device wherein a part is mentioned to represent the whole (e.g., "hired hands" for workmen). The metanovel in a certain sense is indivisible, so you can't single out *Martian Time-Slip* or *The Man in the High Castle* or *Valis* or *Ubik* or *The Transmigration of Timothy Archer*, superb novels though they are, and ask them to stand up like *Moby-Dick* or *The Adventures of Huckleberry Finn* or *Bleak House* as single works for which the author may be remembered. *Martian Time-Slip* is indeed as perfect a representation of Dick's entire oeuvre and of his genius as can be found. But don't think, after you as reader have lived through the experience of reading the party scene, one of the more psychedelic moments in 20th-century literature, that you're going to be able to stop after just one brilliantly disordering novel: ". . . secretly and cautiously, I begin another book." The mind of Phil (or Jack, or Manfred) is not so easily escaped from.

HIT 10

by **Allen Ginsberg**

"**Howl**"

(written August–October 1955)

In the summer of 1955 (the first summer of rock and roll; "Rock Around the Clock" by Bill Haley and the Comets hit #1 July 9), twenty-nine-year-old aspiring poet Allen Ginsberg was visited by Spirit and found himself speaking in a language he had never used before (though he had been searching for it and yearning for it for years), a language which in hindsight we recognize as the voice of the historical moment, just as much as Bob Dylan's related invention would be a decade later. A new voice very much in the tradition of (but not imitative of) Walt Whitman's "Song of Myself" in *Leaves of Grass* exactly one hundred years earlier. So, rather unexpectedly, aspiring poet Ginsberg found himself with a "hit" on his hands, and in the writing and publishing (making public) of this poem he accomplished what every poet oughta aspire to: He reinvented the art form, thus allowing the voice of Spirit, of the collective human unconscious, to thunder forth.

So "Howl" is notable both for being that voice and conveying its message and for introducing a new poetic form and language that would be echoed in the work of many other artists around the world for decades (and perhaps centuries) to come. And like literary "greatest hits" oughta, it immediately made its way into Bartlett's *Familiar Quotations* (1968 edition):

"I saw the best minds of my generation destroyed by madness . . ."

This famous opening line not only evokes but very accurately summarizes the entire poem. "Howl" *is* about madness and minds and destruction and its author's (and readers') generation. And, like Bob Dylan's "A Hard Rain's A-Gonna Fall" (1963), it's about what one young man has seen. A catalogue. A litany. A proclamation of independence and fierce, uncompromising compassion. A song of ourselves.

The story of the title is illustrative. Ginsberg mailed to Jack Kerouac (who was in Mexico City writing his immortal "blues") the first-draft typescript (keeping a retyped copy for himself) and handwrote "Howl for Carl Solomon" on the top of the first page. And perhaps forgot that he'd done so, as Ginsberg biographer Michael Schumacher suggests, so when Jack wrote back commenting on "Howl for Carl Solomon" Allen thought he was inventing a title. Hence the line in the dedication to the book: "Several phrases and the title of *Howl* are taken from him [Kerouac]." More likely, I think, is that Allen hadn't thought of shortening the title to one word until his friend Jack referred to it that way later in the same letter, and so what in Ginsberg's mind was "taken from" Jack was the powerful one-word version of the title. I suppose it's even possible, though not documented, that at some point in San Francisco in response to an expression of uncertainty from Allen about which way to go with the title in the book, Jack pulled out a pencil and invented the bit of visual play whereby the title of the poem in the book could be both: "HOWL [and under that] For Carl Solomon" . . . so the reader could read it as full title or as title plus dedication. In any case, Allen's impulse to give Jack the credit for his poem's memorable (indeed, rather earth-shaking) title surely also reflects the well-established fact that Ginsberg would not have written so spontaneously and frankly (the day he wrote Part I of "Howl" and the later days when he resisted the urge to edit and obscure parts of that first outburst) without Kerouac's very specific encouragement to do exactly that in his writing. A footnote to Kerouac's August 19, 1955, letter in Ann Charter's book *Jack Ker-*

ouac: Selected Letters says, "Responding to this letter, Ginsberg wrote Kerouac on August 25, 1955, that the process of creating 'Howl for Carl Solomon' had made him realize 'how right you are, that was the first time I sat down to blow [jazz reference], it came out in your method, sounding like you, an imitation practically. How far advanced you are on this'" [see entry #21, *On the Road*].

Schumacher further informs us, in a superb footnote of his own, that "in his 1954 journal, Ginsberg had written a poem to which he had affixed the same title ["Howl for Carl Solomon"] . . . the journal poem was not about the same subject matter." This tells me that whatever it is that whispers in poets' ears had been readying Ginsberg for this particular outburst/ song/statement/howl for some time. And of course further points to what is made explicit in Part III: that the poem is something the poet feels driven to express in response to the news of his friend (whom Allen met when he was in an East Coast mental hospital himself) being locked up in the nuthouse again. "Carl Solomon! I'm with you in Rockland/where you're madder than I am." This is not an insult, it's a humorous compliment within a cry of anguished compassion.

What these tales of the title illustrate is how "Howl" functions as a song, not of myself, but of *our*selves. Kerouac and Ginsberg co-creating, looking for a prose and a poetry that would sound like Lester Young's horn just as Billie's voice did. Allen Ginsberg speaking for Carl Solomon (because he's "with" him, knows that they are one) and for every crazy holy fool he has known. We are us! We are suffering. We are holy. And we are not afraid to announce out loud that we use forbidden drugs and engage in unconventional sexual activities. And, finally, not afraid to name the Enemy that is the source of our madness, and not afraid to recognize and describe ourselves and our outrageous lifestyles as "holy." The "Sixties" obviously begin here, on a typewriter in a San Francisco apartment in the summer of '55. And in the Six Gallery in the same city that October when Allen Ginsberg, in the company of Kenneth Rexroth, Michael McClure, Gary Snyder, Philip Whalen, Jack Kerouac, Lawrence Ferlinghetti ("us"), read "Howl" in public for the first time. Astonishingly, that very famous performance was also the first time Allen Ginsberg had read his poetry in public. So a lifetime of great work as a powerful and influential performing poet also started with "Howl." Funny how these things happen.

Oh, and the Sixties or anyway the mid-century "counterculture" also begin on the day in August 1956 when *Howl and Other Poems* was published (in a unique format, little black-and-white pocket booklet) by Ferlinghetti's new City Lights Books. "Underground" newspapers and comix would not be far behind.

And certainly the Sixties also begin on the August 1955 night when Allen Ginsberg on peyote with his lover Peter Orlovsky had a vision remarkably similar to Manfred Steiner's vision of the AM-WEB building in *Martian Time-Slip*: "Saw Moloch smoking building in red glare downtown Sir Francis Drake Hotel, with robot upstairs eyes & skullface." That very night he wrote most of Part III of "Howl" in a cafeteria at the foot of the Sir Francis itself: "Moloch whose skyscrapers stand in the long streets like endless Jehovahs! Moloch whose factories dream and croak in the fog! Moloch whose smokestacks and antennae crown the cities!" In a letter the following June, Ginsberg summarized the first three-fourths of the poem:

> Part I deals sympathetically with individual cases [i.e. himself and his friends and acquaintances, "us"]. Part II describes and rejects the Moloch of society which confounds and suppresses individual experience and forces the individual to consider himself mad if he does not reject his own deepest senses. Part III is an expression of sympathy and identification with C.S. who is in the madhouse— saying that his madness basically is rebellion against Moloch and I am with him, and extending my hand in union.

(Part IV, of course—also known as "Footnote to Howl"—is apotheosis: "The poem is holy the voice is holy the hearers are holy the ecstasy is holy!")

So what is it about rebellion and 1955? Of course the great uprisings against the Soviet Union in Hungary and Georgia would come the following year. As would Elvis Presley's first hit records and television appearances. But in the months before the writing of "Howl" what was pushing "Rock Around the Clock" to #1 was its inclusion as theme song in *The Blackboard Jungle,* a movie about juvenile delinquency that was provoking the first teenage "riots" (vandalism of movie theaters, college students setting trash cans on fire and running into the streets) of the modern era. "Howl," of course, by 1957 was at the center of an obscenity trial, Moloch swatting at a pesky fly.

Generational brotherhood and rebellion against Moloch. Obviously the appeal of this sort of poetry is that it "tells it like it is," and communities can be formed or strengthened around such public articulations of private (but shared) truths. This fits nicely into the tradition of Thomas Paine's *Common Sense.* Poet as pamphleteer, or vice versa.

Not to overlook the beauty of the language and imagery, or the obvious musical power of the rhythms of the poem. My favorite lines: "I'm with you in Rockland/in my dreams you walk dripping from a sea-journey on the highway across America in tears/to the door of my cottage in the Western night." He's actually talking about Peter Orlovsky, who's just returned from such a journey. But the point is that in dreams "I" am with Carl and Carl becomes Peter, and all of us, friends and readers, are the antecedents of the pronoun "who" that provides the gorgeous African backbeat throughout Part I. And just when you think you're doomed to 123 years in AM-WEB, Allen, who at this moment counts himself as student of both the Buddha (Jack, see "Howl"'s dedication) and of the autobiography-writer who "enlightened Buddha" (Neal Cassady), offers these encouraging words: "Holy the solitudes of skyscrapers and pavements! Holy the cafeterias filled with the millions! Holy the mysterious rivers of tears under the streets! . . . Holy the crazy shepherds of rebellion!" Odd that no rock group of the next "generation" ever called themselves The Crazy Shepherds. . .

HIT 11

by **Pet Sounds** by **The Beach Boys**
(recorded January–April 1966)

Great works of art have no more affecting lesson for us than this: They teach us to abide by our spontaneous impression with good-humored inflexibility then most when the whole cry of voices is on the other side.
—Ralph Waldo Emerson, "Self-Reliance" (a greatest hit of the 19th century, 1841)

I know perfectly well I'm not where I should be. . . . I keep looking for a place to fit in where I can speak my mind. . . . I know there's an answer, I know now but I have to find it by myself.
—Brian Wilson and Tony Asher, *Pet Sounds*

As I write this (mid-1998), *Pet Sounds* is as firmly established (in the minds of critics and the public and "the academy") as a greatest hit (memorable work of art, recognized "classic") of the 20th century as *Ulysses* and *2001* and *Guernica*. So I don't need to make a case for its greatness here; suffice to say I've always loved it—I was one of relatively few Americans who fell in love with this album the summer it was released; it wasn't a hit at home that year, though the British were discerning enough to make *Pet Sounds* an immediate critical and commercial success in the United Kingdon of unprecedented proportions for an American rock album—and still do love it. Hell, the near-universal recognition of this album's great beauty, and its enduring ability year after year to provide pleasure and comfort and substantial nourishment whenever I (and others) turn to it, is a remarkable validation of the "century's greatest hit" concept. There really is such a thing. And as Emerson pointed out, we can learn a lot by contemplating such great achievements: "To thine own self be true." If you don't, whoever you are, you'll never come within a parsec of Allen Ginsberg's or Brian Wilson's accomplishments.

So let's look at the circumstances of this album's creation. Well first, just for historical context, what is an "album" and why is it called that? In 1966, an album was a recording pressed on both sides of a twelve-inch piece of black plastic and prepared for commercial distribution, usually in a cardboard jacket. Also called a "record," but there were other records then, seven-inch ones called "singles" (or 45s), one song to a side, like the 78s of an earlier era (Billie Holiday's 1941 records were 78s). Those 1966 twelve-inch records were played on turntables at 33⅓ revolutions per minute and provided fifteen to twenty-five minutes of music per side (thirty-six minutes altogether in the case of *Pet Sounds*). They were called "albums" because in the days when my mother was buying Billie Holiday 78s, single records were sold in paper sleeves and it was possible to get longer recordings (such as a classical symphony or a collection of more than two songs by a jazz or pop or folk artist) in the form of an "album," a gatefold within stiff covers of sleeves containing two or more 78s, kind of like a photograph album. When "long-playing" records were introduced in 1948, they were called albums by the marketers and the public, because the music contained on them was the equivalent of what had been available on a 78-rpm album. Now, most music recordings are sold on laser discs or audiotape cassettes, but a collection of songs like *Pet Sounds* or any audio recording longer than thirty minutes is still called an album, though it bears no physical resemblance to a photo album. So an album is a collection of songs, a kind of art container like the canvas of a painting, thought of by audiences/consumers as the "natural" form in which to receive and experience this kind of art. Art is a concept, okay? And we receive it in containers, which are also concepts. "Things We Said Today" and "Sister Ray" are songs, or "album tracks." *Pet Sounds* is a set of thirteen songs recorded and released together, an "album."

Circumstances: It's the beginning of 1966. Brian Wilson is a twenty-three-year-old self-made millionaire, the leader of a pop group called the Beach Boys which he and his younger brothers and cousin started when he was nineteen. Since then, the Beach Boys, self-taught, amateur musicians, have had fourteen top-ten hit songs in the United States, including two #1 records, all written and arranged by Brian Wilson (who also wrote a #1 song for another Southern California group, Jan and Dean). Now you might imagine that if you had this kind of success you could do anything you wanted. Not necessarily. Success brings power, and freedom, and self-confidence, but it also tends to create a lot of pressure (resulting in loss of freedom and powerlessness) for the simple reason that suddenly other people—the other members of your group or the executives of your record company—are very dependent on your continuing success. Which usually means they will use all their power to press you to keep doing exactly what they think you have been doing. "Don't change a winning formula." If you say you want to, they'll say they can't afford to give you that freedom. This is a difficult situation for a sensitive, creative twenty-three-year-old to find himself in. But Brian Wilson, who has always said of his *Pet Sounds* album that "there's a lot of love in it," found ways to make use of the positive aspects of his circumstances while dodging the negative aspects—found ways to fulfill his creative inspiration and vision of that moment, with good-humored inflexibility. The result, the whole world agrees, was his, and rock and roll's, masterpiece.

I could write a book about *Pet Sounds,* but I don't have to because it's been done, and excellently, by David Leaf, in two booklets included in a 1997 multimedia (print and audio) package called *The Pet Sounds Sessions.* The more than 150 pages in these booklets offer an extraordinary amount of information and history—including thoughtful interviews with the studio musicians and the members of the Beach Boys and the two songwriters and such notable "fans" of the album as Paul McCartney of the Beatles, who asserts that his group would not and could not have recorded their memorable album *Sgt. Pepper's Lonely Hearts Club Band* without the impact and influence of *Pet Sounds*, just as Brian Wilson asserts that he would not have been inspired to create *Pet Sounds* without first hearing the Beatles' album *Rubber Soul*. Most of all, the listener/reader who wants to do his or her own study of how such great work comes to be created can find in these booklets and in the audio part of the package—the album itself in original mono mix and a careful and respectful new stereo mix, and many recordings of producer Wilson verbally directing the musicians at the recording sessions for these songs, and various alternate vocals and mixes and so forth—ample raw material for arriving at one's own personal nondogmatic understanding of how this work of art came into being. Wonderful! As the reader of this book can tell, I believe such contemplation can be of great value, and I further believe that it is just as much a place for "self-reliance" as is the creating of the artwork in the first place. Listeners/readers/art-appreciators are also creators, working in the present moment as they read the novel or watch the film or listen to the recording.

So I refer you, dear reader, after you've fallen in love with the *Pet Sounds* album (if you do, and most will or already have), to *The Pet Sounds Sessions* package if you wish to pursue the eternally fascinating riddle of how such a miracle as this actually gets created by one or two or seven people at a particular moment in time. Don't expect to find the answer in a neat summarizing paragraph. You find the answer(s) in your heart and mind as you read and listen and enjoy, as you contemplate the Mystery. Contemplating the album alone would be enough (as listening over and over to recordings that Phil Spector produced was enough for Brian Wilson, according to him, to understand in a way that was very helpful to him what it could mean to make a record and how he could do it). The package and Leaf's book just make it possible to clear up false assumptions and to see ever more deeply into the wonder of the process, though admittedly nothing could be more wondrous than the finished product itself. "There are words we both could say . . . but don't talk, take my hand and listen to my heartbeat. Listen, listen, listen . . ."

What you hear when you listen to *Pet Sounds* is words and music, voices and orchestral instruments, "layered vocals and sound textures" (to quote David Leaf). Remarkably, like Monet's or Picasso's brushstrokes on canvas, these units of creative effort add up to a whole that touches us immediately, and often remarkably deeply. Moment after moment. How is this done? In the case of Monet and Picasso and Brian Wilson, sincerity is as important as craft and talent. The artist genuinely wants to express something, and cares deeply about doing the job "right" according to inner guidelines that seem to be dictated to him by an unseen force—Inspiration, the Muse, truly a power higher than the intellect or "professionalism" or any sort of ego-identity or separate self. Monet studied, and tried to express, light; Wilson studies and tries to express the human heart. Feelings. Objects of perception, just like Monet's water-lilies. On *Pet Sounds* the relationship between a man and a woman ("don't talk, put your head on my shoulder") and between a young person and the world ("I wanted to show how independent I've grown now, but that's not me") become as abstract or all-inclusive as the relationship between sun and cathedral or sun and haystacks in a Monet painting. The artworks are a study of these (and all) relationships. Experiencing the enormous compassion in the words and music and performances of *Pet Sounds*, the listener finds himself identifying with both "I" and "thou" at once. Your head, my shoulder. Your feelings, my feelings, a whole universe filled with enormous feelings. It is easy to believe, listening to this music, that Brian held prayer sessions with his collaborators (as reported in Leaf's booklets) during the recording of this album: "We prayed for guidance, to make the most healing sounds." Asking for guidance is the most modest, and perhaps the most powerful, declaration of intention.

Intention is something we observers easily get confused about when contemplating and discussing great works of art. For example, we all know that music and musical sounds can be healing ("hath charms to soothe a savage breast"), but it is not so obvious to most of us how one sets out to make sounds that will heal. For another example, a listener needs no background information when he or she hears Brian Wilson sing, "And after all I've done to you, how can it be you still believe in me?" to suppose that he must be speaking to his wife or life-partner. Or we can think of it as "current girlfriend" or boyfriend, if—as the opening song ("Wouldn't it be nice if we were older?") invites us to—we hear the album as the emotional diary of an adolescent. But what did Wilson (and his songwriting collaborator Tony Asher) intend? Was it just to write songs that would appeal to the "teenage market" when played on the radio? Was Brian Wilson really speaking autobiographically? In which case, we could ask (if we do have some background info to be confused by), why does he sing, "every time we break up you bring back your love to me" when in fact he and his young wife weren't yet known to have had any breakups?

Or we could ask, if Brian is speaking of his own life experience, how did the songwriting collaboration work? Did he tell the lyricist what he wanted the song's words to say? For still another example, suppose we read the surprising passage on page 135 of Brian Wilson's autobiography, *Wouldn't It Be Nice*, where Brian recalls telling Tony Asher, "'I was watching Diane [his wife's sister] and God, she's so beautiful.' 'Brian, you're married,' he said. 'I know,' I shrugged. 'But wouldn't it be nice if I could lie down beside her and nestle myself in her long hair?'" Brian reports that Asher then went home and "the next day he arrived with a completed set of lyrics to 'Wouldn't It Be Nice' and an apology. 'For what?' I asked. 'I thought maybe the words were too personal, too close to home,' he said. 'No, that's exactly what I want.'" Um, how can we fit this in with our ideas about the songwriters' intentions?

Only by letting go of our ideas that songs that intend to tell personal truths must be true to the details and circumstances of their writer's lives—and realizing that there really is something universal about true feelings, and they can be expressed by constructing story-songs in which situations are described that seem somewhat different from the situations in which the feelings actually arose. This is possible because, as noted above, songs communicate not only by words but by melodies and rhythms and musical sounds—and by performance, which means the feeling that the singers or instrumentalists put into their singing or playing. Even the arranger and "producer" can be a kind of performer, communicating what he's feeling by the spirit in which and with which he does his task. In the case of *Pet Sounds*, the result of all this focused creative intent is a thirty-six-minute work of recorded music in which the stories the songs tell and the words the singers speak and the rich textured music the instruments and the voices make and the mood created by the sounds of all of the foregoing, all work together with supernatural grace to create a work of art that can have a profound emotional impact on listeners of all ages and backgrounds, a work of such startling originality that musicians and composers and producers and even artists working in other media credit it with being a source of ideas and inspiration for much of the work they've done since hearing it. It's an astonishing accomplishment. And it did indeed require Brian Wilson (the primary author, although the album is properly catalogued as "*Pet Sounds* by the Beach Boys") to stay true to himself and abide by his own creative impulses in the face of considerable skepticism on the part of many people around him. Brian has been quoted as saying about track 11, "I Just Wasn't Made for These Times":

> It's about a guy who was crying because he thought he was too advanced, and that he'd eventually have to leave people behind. All my friends thought I was crazy to do *Pet Sounds*.

So what I wanna call your attention to, dear reader, is that it is not only the outspoken honest "howls" of young artists that require courage of their creators. A gentle, healing work of exceptional beauty may also come into existence primarily through the artist's willingness to withstand opposition and stay courageously true to his inner vision, however mysterious it may be at times, even to himself. Of course it also comes into existence via the artist's exceptional craft and talent and hard work. No matter how willful (and demanding of his coworkers) Brian Wilson was, he could not have created *Pet Sounds* without the gift he was apparently born with of an uncommon ability to hear the component parts of vocal and instrumental music and to hold them in his head. Along with this he also had (and still has, as I write this) a keen energy for experimentation, in musical dynamics and song structure and creating and combining musical sounds. A nice tale of how this gift and interest manifested themselves long before the first Beach Boys surf records is told by younger brother Carl Wilson: "As a twelve-year-old, Brian was heavy into the jazz vocals of the Four Freshmen. He could listen to their records and play the harmonies on the piano. What he would do is sit at the piano and figure out each individual part; then he would teach Mom and I a part. He would sing the third part, record the three of us singing together, and then he would sing to the playback to hear the fourth part."

Brian Wilson believed, as firmly as Allen Ginsberg's mentor Jack Kerouac, in subtle techniques for allowing inner truth and the poetry of the human heart to reveal themselves through spontaneity in the creative act, techniques that make it possible to be guided effectively by accidental and unconscious and invisible forces. Tony Asher has said, describing writing *Pet Sounds* with Brian: "He used to go in and record [instrumental] tracks. We didn't know what they were going to be. They didn't even have melodies. They would just be a series of chord changes that Brian liked, with some weird or not-so-weird instruments. . . . Then we would bring these back [to the house] and play them and kind of write a melody to them and then write some lyrics." Next, "Brian would just be banging out at the piano. He or I would sing dummy lyrics . . . whatever popped into your head. By the time you had spent two or three hours you had kind of written the song. . . . He'd have a pretty complete melody, partial lyrics, and a kind of bridge and some other stuff. But not a complete song. I'd go home at night and work on the lyrics a little bit . . . then go back, and he might say, 'Hey, that's terrific' or 'I don't like those lines.' He did a lot of editing on them."

One final quote from Brian Wilson, speaking for all of the artists in this volume: "I find it possible to spill melodies, beautiful melodies, in moments of great despair. This is one of the wonderful things about this art form—it can draw out so much emotion, and it can channel it into notes of music in cadence. Good, emotional music is genuine and healthy and the stimulation I get from it and from adding dynamics is like nothing else on Earth."

HIT 12

Old Path White Clouds

Walking in the footsteps of the Buddha

by Thich Nhat Hanh

(published 1991)

This is a biography of Siddhartha Gautama (Indian philosopher and teacher, circa 500 B.C.) written near the end of the 20th-century in Vietnamese in France by a Zen monk/poet/scholar/peace activist who had traveled to North America at the height of the Vietnam War "to try to help dissolve some of the wrong views that were at the root of the war." In the United States, Nhat Hanh spoke with students, teachers, government officials, and other peace workers; in 1967 he was nominated for the Nobel Peace Prize by American civil rights leader Martin Luther King, Jr.

This thorough biography is the major work of one of the great world literary figures of the second half of this century, a man not yet known in literary circles but author of a substantial (and, I predict, enduring) body of work consisting of more than thirty books, including a novel, collections of poetry, collections of short stories, translations of Buddhist sutras, and many books of practical philosophy directed to the general public, of which two of the most widely read are *Peace Is Every Step* and *Living Buddha, Living Christ*. In a very real sense, everything that Thich Nhat Hanh shares with us in all his other writings can be found in *Old Path White Clouds*. And although I am aware of such European retellings of the Buddha's story as *Siddhartha* (Hermann Hesse, 1922) and *The Light of*

Asia (Sir Edwin Arnold, 1879), I do not believe there has ever been another book like this, a straightforward narrative nonfiction account of the life and work of the man who inspired a million statues ("Buddha was not a God. He was a human being like you and me, and he suffered just as we do," TNH tells us in another book), carefully researched by comparing and contemplating the surviving documents that tell pieces of the story with keen attention to the contexts of those documents, who wrote them and when, and what elements of the story they had reason to emphasize or ignore or exaggerate. The resulting narrative is told with the confidence of a biographer who is certain he knows as much as any modern person could of what happened day to day and how it felt to the protagonist and other participants as it was happening. The reader can feel this in the narrator's voice, and can't help but be further reassured by the careful notes in the back of the book identifying the specific sources for the stories told in each chapter.

But for all of its loving faithfulness to the 2,500-year-old "Pali canon" that is the basis of all "Buddhism" since, the greatest value of *Old Path White Clouds*, exactly like every other work cited herein as a "greatest hit," is what it tells us about the consciousness and feelings and (by extension) experience of the 20th-century person who wrote it. Jorge Luis Borges (see entry #32) in his tale "Pierre Menard, Author of the *Quixote*," imagines a 20th-century man who undertakes to compose chapters of *Don Quixote* that may be word-for-word the same as the 17th-century original but will have enormously different implications because of the new author's consciousness and identity: "It is not in vain that three hundred years have gone by, filled with exceedingly complex events." So the Vietnam War is in this biography, and a fierce, infectious idealism that is startlingly recognizable to me as the idealism of my youth in the sixth decade of this century, the era of the Beatles and Martin Luther King and the Vietnam War. Nhat Hanh is so palpably proud (for example) of the fact (and he has painstakingly satisfied himself that it is a fact) that this son of the Indian nobility called "the Buddha" was adamant (in the face of opposition from friends, students, strangers, and other teachers) that he would let himself be touched by members of the "untouchable" caste and would accept them as his students and brothers because: "Our way is a way of equality. We do not recognize caste. Though we may encounter difficulties over Sunita's ordination now, we will have opened a door for the first time in history that future generations will thank us for. We must have courage."

Obviously, the purpose of Nhat Hanh's book is to transmit this sort of courage to its reader, as the Buddha's writings did for Henry David Thoreau and Thoreau's did for Mahatma Gandhi (see entry #34) and as the Buddha and his dharma-heirs did for the current Dalai Lama of Tibet (see entry #38). I can hardly imagine the reader who could turn page after page of *Old Path White Clouds* without feeling intense (and sometimes awkward, and implacable) tides of idealism surging in his or her own veins. Reader beware. This is a heady brew. Hero worship—sincere admiration for and emulation of another human being's life and deeds and motives—is exceedingly rare in modern literature, but very welcome and affecting in this case.

Reading this book, and finding the protagonist very interesting and likable, I find myself steadily aware that what so attracts me is the Buddha as seen through Thich Nhat Hanh's eyes. Like Yogananda's *Autobiography of a Yogi*, this book is actually a passionate love story (Yogananda calls himself "a blissful devotee in a cosmic romance"). Thay (TNH's nickname; it means "teacher," like the Japanese *sensei*) loves the Buddha. Loves him from the perspective of a mid-20th-century man who saw the best minds (and hearts and bodies) of his generation destroyed by a senseless war and who found refuge—and the opportunity to be genuinely helpful to his countrymen—in the example of the Buddha.

I have never in my life been what anyone would call "religious," but I can relate to this. Largely because Buddhism (which is to say Thich Nhat Hanh's Buddhism, the version I'm most familiar with) is almost entirely a personal philosophy, not a religion like other religions. No, to me it's like a practical philosophy, which is also how I view consulting the *I Ching*. I'm attracted to this sort of spiritual activity because it seems to me do-it-yourself, something you only embrace insofar as it seems true to and proves helpful to you, in other words, a "faith" based entirely on personal experience as opposed to social intimidation. Thich Nhat Hanh, in chapter 62 of *Old Path White Clouds* quotes the Buddha as saying to a group of young villagers, "My friends, you are already qualified to discern which things to accept and which things to discard. Believe and accept only those things which accord with your own reason, those things which are supported by the wise and virtuous [i.e., persons whose values you admire, your heroes whoever they are], and those things which in practice bring benefit and happiness to yourselves and others. Discard things which oppose these principles." This to me is not "religion" but the antidote to the way religions are too often presented.

And since I'm an American writer, it shouldn't seem odd that I hear in this the same philosophy I believe I've heard in and learned from Emerson, Clemens, Ginsberg, Dylan, Vonnegut, Faulkner, Jefferson, and others. Just as I consider the Universal Declaration of Human Rights literature, poetry rather than politics, so I consider Thich Nhat Hanh's scribblings in Vietnamese and English—retelling texts written in Pali, Sanskrit, and Chinese—literature, belles lettres rather than religion. And most of all, I love Thich Nhat Hanh because when he gathered a tiny group of Buddhists to help deal with the circumstances of the War exploding all around them, he wrote some Buddhalike precepts or rules for the group to live by, and the first (and, he said, most important) rule was: *Do not be idolatrous about or bound to any doctrine, theory, or ideology, even Buddhist ones. Buddhist systems of thought are guiding means; they are not absolute truth.* That's the kind of disclaimer I want to read on any spiritual package, Christian or Moslem or Jewish or whatever it may be. TNH saw his country and its young and its old destroyed by ideology, so when he talks about the Buddha's life he's not offering you or me a set of ideas to live and die for. He's keenly aware how destructive "isms" can be. Rather, he wants to give others a chance to see Siddhartha the way he does, as a person just like you or me who woke up by looking at things differently from what his parents and peers had taught him, who found liberation (peace and freedom) in a way of being toward oneself and others that a) anyone can do, according to Siddhartha, and b) that makes possible happiness, even in wretched circumstances.

And the way Thay tells it, it's a fabulous story, an inspiration regardless of whether the reader chooses to "follow" the path or not. Giving your attention for the amount of time it takes you to read the book is enough. Nothing to get bound to. "Nothing to get hung about," as John Lennon once said.

Okay, let's return the discussion to the arts, which is what I intended this book to be about, and talk about the novelist's, I mean the biographer's, technique. The most important thing (and it makes you wonder where he learned to do this, what he does is so precisely the right thing to do) is the viewpoint. Who's speaking? Well, the author is. But as in many novels, he tells the story as much as possible from the point of view of one of the lesser characters, a child when we first meet him, the Untouchable Svasti, the young *bhikkhu* (aspirant/student) who used to be a buffalo boy.

When one learns TNH's own story, it becomes clear that Thay didn't choose to tell this story through the eyes of a young adolescent just because he intuitively (or wisely) knew that is the right way to tell a story when you want young people to be interested by it. Thay's story is that when he was nine, two years younger than Svasti at the start of *Old Path White Clouds,* he saw a picture in a magazine of a monk sitting on the grass and felt a keen, almost obsessive, attraction, and then when he went on a school field trip to a mountain, he wandered away from his group because he'd heard that a hermit lived on the mountain and he just had to see him, even it if meant getting lost in the woods or punished by his teachers. So we can understand Thich Nhat Hanh telling the Buddha's life from the perspective of the young buffalo boy who, according to legend, stumbled on the Buddha as a hermit sitting under a tree at the edge of the forest—a boy captivated by the wanderer's smile and his improbable kindness to an Untouchable child. Svasti then started bringing the hermit cut grass to meditate and sleep on. As a result, the boy is later the first person to see and talk with Siddhartha after his enlightenment.

"Teacher, you look so different today." What a viewpoint character! The *witness*. At this moment he stands in for all of us, the
whole non-Siddhartha world. Later, age twenty-one, Svasti shyly
accepts the Buddha's invitation to become a *bhikkhu*, or appren-
tice monk, and so for the purposes of Thay's elegant narrative he
has the opportunity to tell Siddhartha's stepmother his eyewit-
ness story of Siddhartha's awakening (Svasti and his young village friends are even credited with giving Siddhartha the name
Buddha, meaning "awakened one") while she in turn fills Svasti
in on details of Siddhartha's childhood.

Svasti makes friends with the Buddha's young son Rahula,
another aspirant monk. Throughout the book Svasti reappears as
occasional viewpoint character, as Thay unfolds the long story of
the Buddha's rock star–like success-by-attraction (everywhere he
goes, thousands of young people and successful merchants are
eager to become his students). Thay describes the circumstances
of the Buddha giving talks which were to become famous sutras
(his big hits) and tells us also of his difficulties with bickering
monks and political intrigues and the murderous jealousy of other
"enlightened masters." So we see the great man's life through the
eyes of a modest, faithful student, Svasti, who despairs at times of
his own ignorance and clumsiness as he tries to follow the Way.
The book that results is much more inviting and readable than if
it were told by a narrator who sees himself as a teacher. In other
books, of course, TNH gently and lovingly approaches his readers as a teacher, offering guidance on how to meditate when the
telephone rings or while turning the ignition key of an auto-
mobile. But in *Old Path White Clouds* the invitation is simply to
see the great man through the eyes of a simple, loving boy, or boy-
at-heart, who happens to have the opportunity to be around
Siddhartha from the days before and the morning after enlightenment until his death forty-five years later.

Mobi Ho did a fine job translating this masterwork (original
title *Dường Xua Mây Trang*) into English, and I daresay it is
already or will soon be available in many other languages. A
greatest hit? Not as measured by sales figures, but look back a century or two from now and see what the impact of this very

appealing yarn has been. No apprenticeship required for prospective readers. As with all the other entries in this book, you are already qualified to discern which things in this work of art to accept and which to discard. Beauty is in the eye of the beholder who knows she is observing with her eye and mind as she observes.

What interests me most is neither still life nor landscape but the human figure. It is through it that I best succeed in expressing the nearly religious feeling that I have towards life.
—Henri Matisse, December 1908

The "human figure" the artist is referring to in this quote (from his famous magazine essay "Notes of a Painter") is not what you or I might think of first when this phrase arises in reference to works of art. He isn't talking about a portrait of the human body in dramatic poses like the sculptures of his contemporary Auguste Rodin, or about a painter's exploration of the beauty and endless fascination of the female or male physique. No, the human figure he's thinking of, judging by the paintings he did in the months before and after he wrote the essay, is more like a cartoon. A greatly simplified image that recognizably represents a human being caught in some human action or mood. Look at *Dance*. This painting, certainly one of the most famous and familiar works of "fine art" of the 20th century, is a snapshot (courtesy of the color camera of the artist's imagination) of five naked women holding hands and dancing in a circle at the top of a grassy hill, women (well, several of

HIT

13

Dance by **Henri Matisse** (painted winter 1909–spring 1910)

them could be men) drawn so crudely that their nakedness could only be offensive in the most prudish of cultures (see below for the story of Matisse's problems with his patron). Indeed, one superb (but little-known, alas) mid-20th-century cartoon artist and humorist, Abner Dean (an American), made a career of drawing cartoons of not-distinctly-sexual naked people in imaginary contemporary situations, in a style almost certainly inspired or encouraged by Matisse's *Dance* and its companion piece *Music*.

Quick, think of a 19th-century painting famous enough and familiar enough now to be considered a "greatest hit" of its era. Perhaps Vincent van Gogh's radiant, madness-tinged landscape *Starry Night* (1889) comes to mind. Twenty years later, why is this Matisse guy—famous in 1909 only for having made a very public fool of himself four years earlier when he presented works full of shocking colors and seemingly sloppy technique at an important show, causing him to be ballyhooed in the press as leader of a new art movement, the "fauves" or wild beasts—why is he now offering us these cartoonish figures and seemingly childish colors and backdrop? The answers, my friends, are in the mind of Matisse and the history of modern art, the latter a process in which Matisse was indeed to be a leader, a hugely influential figure. He wasn't just painting what he saw, but what he *felt,* and he was using all of his considerable skill and intelligence and his awareness of painters before him and his willingness to work very very hard to find ways to allow himself (and, ultimately, others) to do that. History of art? Well, it isn't obvious what the style or content of *Dance* has to do with Van Gogh or Monet, but these peculiar naked figures of Matisse's have a lot to do with his keen appreciation of the work of a now-famous but then-obscure gentleman named Paul Cézanne, and the sometimes beautiful and lifelike but also sometimes cartoonish bathers (naked people in nature) that show up in a lot of his paintings done in the ten years before his death in 1906. To follow this thread (and get a glimpse of the mind of Matisse at work) take a look at Matisse's 1907–08 paintings *Luxury* and *Game of Bowls* and *Bathers with a Turtle* and especially his 1906 masterwork *Joy of Life* (which just happens to have, in the background behind its lounging bathers, a circle of dancers holding hands, like the figures in *Dance* already stirring in the artist's mind and awaiting their chance to leap into the foreground of his canvas and his consciousness).

Phew! you say, do I have to look at all these other paintings (and dig out a Cézanne book) just to appreciate this one? No no, it's fun to play this history-of-the-painter's-consciousness game, but it's not necessary. Not according to Matisse's theories of art. He wants to make you happy, and his intent is that the hard work be only his—you, his public, need only look at the painting and get direct nourishment thereby, analogous (as Matisse has very often said) to the experience of listening to music.

Another quote from 1908's "Notes of a Painter": "What I dream of is an art of balance, of purity and serenity devoid of troubling or depressing subject matter, an art which might be for every mental worker, be he businessman or writer, like an appeasing influence, like a mental soother, something like a good armchair in which to rest from physical fatigue." This is not what the good people of Paris in 1908 were expecting to hear from the "King of the Wild Beasts." But then Monet and Renoir and Degas were also described as radical and talentless upstarts by the press when they first showed their work in the Paris salons.

In any case, although the critics were at first unkind, Henri Matisse was fortunate, in his late thirties and at the start of his "career," to have a few wealthy and influential patrons, rabid art fans like the Russian Sergei Shchukin and the Americans Leo, Sarah, Michael, and Gertrude Stein, who expressed their interest and enthusiasm by spending their time, energy, and money buying new Matisse paintings and then hanging them in their living quarters where their friends (in the case of the Steins, the best minds of their generation) would see them and in some cases also become Matisse supporters. This was very helpful; Matisse's father, a grain merchant, was not pleased when his son dropped out of law school to pursue a sudden desire to "become an artist"—and Matisse at age thirty-four in 1904 was finding it difficult to support his wife and three children without abandoning his passionate commitment to expressing himself in art and to discovering or inventing visual languages that would make this possible. The man was following an intensely personal vision, and for ten very important years a few patrons and appreciators kept him going, and also laid the groundwork for the international reputation that would sustain him for another forty years of tireless invention and exploration and creation thereafter.

So the story of *Dance* starts at the beginning of 1909, when Russian businessman Sergei Shchukin brought up the idea of commissioning Matisse to paint one or two huge "decorations" for the stairwells in his Moscow mansion (he was interested in getting a large figure piece like the recent *Bathers with a Turtle*, which he'd seen). Before this, Matisse painted and sculpted whatever he chose, and if he was lucky sold the finished work to the Steins or Shchukin or another customer (Matisse was then his own "publisher"; he didn't sign his first contract with a dealer until later in 1909). Matisse responded by suggesting the themes "Dance" and "Music"; Shchukin had already seen the 1907 "sketch" (rough draft or work-in-progress) called *Music* and was pleased. Later in the winter, Matisse showed him a "sketch" for *Dance* he'd just done in the size Shchukin wanted—actually almost the same painting as the finished 1910 version, except for the all-important color scheme. You can see this early version, as I did last month, at the Museum of Modern Art in New York; the completed painting is still in Russia (at the Hermitage), and yes, I would love to see it in person (again; I don't remember much of my 1964 visit to the Hermitage).

In April 1909, shortly after Shchukin formally "commissioned" the paintings (committed himself, and agreed to a price), Matisse in an interview with a newspaper critic provided the following example of how he composes a painting:

I have to decorate a staircase. It has three floors. I imagine a visitor coming in from the outside. The first floor welcomes him. One must summon up energy, give a feeling of lightness. My first panel represents the dance, that whirling round on top of the hill. On the second floor one is now within the house; in its silence I see a scene of music with engrossed participants; finally, the third floor is completely calm and I paint a scene of repose: some people reclining on the grass, chatting or daydreaming. I shall obtain this by the simplest and most reduced means; those which permit the painter pertinently to express all of his interior vision. . . .

Matisse had a rough several months the following year, when, as Alfred Barr tells it in his definitive study *Matisse: His Art and His Public* (1951):

Shchukin lost his nerve and informed Matisse that he could not accept the two overwhelming canvases for his house in Moscow. He explained that he had just adopted two young girls whose presence in his house would make the nude figures even more unsuitable than before. He feared a scandal and asked Matisse if he wouldn't paint two smaller pictures for his bedroom for the same price, or, at least, retouch the flute player in *Music*. Matisse refused to do either. Furthermore he was so shocked and disappointed by Shchukin's change of mind that he found he could not work in Paris. By mid-November he had left for Spain and did not return until early in 1911.

Shchukin changed his mind again sometime before the end of 1910, and eventually *Dance* and *Music* hung in the stairwells of his mansion (with a little cover-up work on the flute player, not approved by the painter but what can you do?). Françoise Gilot, in her wonderful memoir *Matisse and Picasso: A Friendship in Art* (1990), says:

Whether Matisse was readily understood or not, he was not inclined toward bitterness, he was not keen on retaliation, and he was interested in neither fending off opposition nor competing for the affection of wayward friends. His only competition was with himself; each year he wanted to transcend what he had been able to achieve the previous year. His goal was always to surpass himself while remaining consistent in his approach. Yet he was not blind to the currents around him, and he was quite able to assimilate concepts that were foreign to his temperament if they enlarged his vision of the world and augmented his expressive power.

Dear reader, if you'll allow me to interrupt this story, which I'm afraid could go on for dozens of pages if I don't restrain myself. . . . After all, it is in the nature of "greatest hits" that there are almost always great stories behind them, and as I am a lover of the arts, it is not so strange I find it hard to resist collecting and sharing such tales. Of course, in some of these entries I feel a particular need to make the case for a great or momentous work that is not yet as well known or well acknowledged as I'm sure it deserves to be. That can even be a "minor" work by a recognized "great" artist, like "Things We Said Today" or *Girl Before a Mirror*. And then there are these relatively safe bets that help give my list some credibility or anyway solidity, that are useful for communicating to one and all what I mean by a "greatest hit" of the century—like *Dance* and *Pet Sounds* and *Winnie-the-Pooh* and Billie Holiday in her prime. And since I feel less need to "make a case" for these, they become instead my opportunity to tell fragments of stories about the kinds of vision and commitment and inspiration and good luck that go into the making of these marvelous monuments that human beings leave behind—which I argue are living beings, continuations of the bodies and minds and spirits of these great men and women, still able to soothe and enliven and enlighten us, now and in moments and centuries still to come.

Okay, end of interruption, on to a few more essential (I think) morsels of information about this marvelous painting, which is not necessarily the Matisse I would like to look at every morning for a decade but certainly a "hit" (look around, you'll start seeing it, and maybe its descendants, all over the place).

From a 1950 interview with Matisse:

I like dance very much. Dance is an extraordinary thing: life and rhythm. When I had to paint *Dance* for Moscow, I had just been to the Moulin de la Galette [in Montmartre, in Paris] on Sunday afternoon. And I watched the dancing. I especially watched the *farandole* ["A lively dance of

S. France, in 6/8 time, by a winding chain of dancers"].
The dancers hold each other by the hand, they run across
the room, and they wind around the people who are
milling about . . . it's all extremely gay. Back at home I created my *Dance* on a canvas of four meters, singing the
same tune I had heard at the Moulin, so that the entire
painting and all the dancers are in harmony and dance to
the same rhythm.

In a 1941 interview he said he and other painters were often
invited to come and work in the music hall, "but all I managed to
do was learn the tune of the *farandole,* which everyone used to
roar out as soon as the orchestra played it:

Let's pray to God for those who're nearly broke!
Let's pray to God for those who've not a bean!

I whistled it as I painted. I almost danced."

From the time he painted his first version of *Dance,* Matisse
worked on the painting, intently and anxiously, for a full year;
that time was entirely spent getting the colors (and therefore the
relationship between color and form) right. Matisse helps us
understand his working process as a painter when he explains, in
a 1935 essay:

For me, the subject of a picture and its background have
the same value, or, to put it more clearly, there is no principal feature, only the pattern is important. The picture is
formed by the combination of surfaces, differently colored,
which results in the creation of an "expression." In the
same way that in a musical harmony each note is a part of
the whole, so I wish each color to have a contributory
value. A picture is the coordination of controlled rhythms,
and it is thus that one can change a surface which appears
red-green-blue-black for one which appears white-blue-
red-green; it is the same picture, the same feeling presented differently, but the rhythms are changed. The
difference between the two canvases is that of two aspects
of a chessboard in the course of a game of chess.

Elsewhere (1936), he describes the intensity of his hours and months at the easel with one painting:

> My reaction at each stage is as important as the subject. It is a continuous process until the moment when my work is in harmony with me. At each stage I reach a balance, a conclusion. The next time I return to the work, if I discover a weakness in the unity, I find my way back into the picture by means of the weakness—I re-enter through the breach—and I conceive the whole afresh. Thus the whole thing comes alive again.

A 1929 Matisse comment specifically describes the color scheme in *Dance* and *Music* as:

> composed with a fine blue for the sky, the bluest of blues. The surface was colored to saturation, that is to say, up to a point where the blue, the idea of absolute blue, appeared conclusively. A bright green for the earth and a vibrant vermillion for the bodies. With these three colors I had my luminous harmony and also purity of color tone. For expression comes from the colored surface that the spectator perceives as a whole.

Alfred Barr tells us:

> Edward Steichen [the great photographer] followed with interest how the color and line of *Dance* changed gradually from something rather mild to its ultimate shocking power. Even Matisse himself, on more than one occasion, seems to have been alarmed by his own creation. Once he told Steichen rather uneasily how at a certain moment in the evening, as the light was fading, the painting *Dance* [8½ feet high and 13 feet wide] suddenly seemed to vibrate and quiver. Matisse was so disturbed by this that he asked Steichen, who at the time was deep in the scientific theory of color photography, to come out to Issy [M had the finished painting at his country place for a year before

shipping it off to Moscow] especially to observe this phenomenon and explain it, if he could. One evening shortly
afterwards Matisse and Steichen watched the picture as
the sun was setting. Steichen confirmed what Matisse had
seen and explained that, as the light faded and at the same
time grew warmer, the colors reached a balance point at
which a complementary reflex within the eye made them
jump and vibrate. Once he understood this, Matisse was
no longer disturbed.

Matisse had a lot of respect for the power of his paintings, not
as works of art or intellectual statements but something more
immediate. Lawrence Growing, in his book *Matisse,* reports,
"More than once, when people who were ill looked to him to
nurse them, he left a picture with them instead, and went off to
paint."

It's hard to stop quoting Matisse. He had a keen awareness of
what it meant to be an artist working in a particular century: "We
never realize sufficiently clearly," he said in 1931, "that the old
masters we admire would have produced very different works if
they had lived in another century than their own." And, later in
the same interview: "A painter doesn't see everything that he has
put in his painting. It is other people who find these treasures in
it, one by one, and the richer a painting is in surprises of this sort,
in treasures, the greater its author. Each century seeks to nourish
itself in works of art, and each century needs a particular kind of
nourishment."

And tends to get particular sorts of great artists. Van Dyke
Parks spoke eloquently of Brian Wilson's unique style as "saturat-
ing the tape with music." I have to think of this when I read of
Matisse needing to saturate his canvas with color. I also have to
think of Brian Wilson being alarmed by his own unreleased
recording "Fire" (he thought it was causing conflagrations) when
I hear of Matisse's twilight discomfort with *Dance*. And certainly
Wilson learned from and was inspired by studying Phil Spector's
works in almost exactly the way Matisse found his path by study-

ing Cézanne's paintings. And then there's this funny quote from Françoise Gilot about Matisse's art as a private and compelling universe that of course makes me think of Philip K. Dick:

> In the years 1908 to 1918, Matisse's work gained power and often extended to monumental size. Secure in his boldness, he further simplified both shape and color. His only concern was for the whole; any unnecessary detail was discarded. Nevertheless, thematically his own work evolved in sequence according to an inner logic. The garland of dancers that animated a middle-ground plane of *Joy of Life* was magnified and amplified to become the central theme of *Dance I* and *Dance II*, and parts of the group were also used in some other canvases to bring the activity of the human figure into some still lifes. Some of his sculptures appeared within other pictorial compositions, as did his ceramics, while significant parts of other paintings found their way into *The Artist's Studio* (1911) and *The Red Studio* (1911). Members of Matisse's family often permeated this parallel universe. Willingly or not, they became transfixed, and each acquired an archetypal persona. The painter's own work, environment, familiar objects, landscapes, and memories of travels were again and again put to the question; they had to enter the dance. Stable architectonic statements pulsated with life through vivid color interaction. At other times the dynamism came from the intensity of movement. In *Dance*, for example, the idea of motion was accentuated by the emphasis on the limbs, the joints, and the garland effect of swinging arms and hands clasping each other, except in the front plane, where they reached out but did not touch.

Matisse agreed with his friend Françoise years before he met her. In 1907 he told Guillaume Apollinaire: "I found myself or my artistic personality by looking over my earliest works. They rarely deceive. There I found something that was always the same and which at first glance I thought to be monotonous repetition. It was the mark of my personality which appeared the same no matter what different states of mind I happened to have passed through." Philip K. Dick couldn't have said it better (and it would be true of Brian Wilson if he were to say it). I'll close by noting that *Dance* first caught my attention when I saw it sitting there as an objet d'art in Matisse's *Nasturtiums and The Dance* (1912), I think in a museum in Paris. In such a painting, Henri Matisse himself seems to be a character in a Borges story.

HIT

14

2001: A Space Odyssey
by Stanley Kubrick
(released April 1968)

Just as Matisse, first as a student and then as a young artist, dealt with the problem that the public and the academic authorities and newspaper critics all were stuck in the idea that a painting should be a *likeness,* so Stanley Kubrick in the mid-1960s worked at a time when people who paid attention to film at all were mostly stuck in the idea that a movie should be a *story,* a narrative so lucid that the watcher believes he or she follows it, understands it, and, ideally, can recapitulate it, can tell a friend the next day what happened in this movie.

Film director/producer Kubrick evidently had (or was open enough to follow his muse to) a different idea of what could be done in and by means of this medium. Again, like Matisse. A 20th-century pioneer. Breaking a path. Also like the Beatles or the Velvet Underground, having fun creating stuff out on the aesthetic edge, where ideas take startling and very palpable—and sometimes, entirely beautiful—forms. *2001: A Space Odyssey* is such a creation. Not a story in the usual sense (although, importantly, the viewer can feel the presence of a story very clearly and powerfully, even if he or she can't be certain they understand it or even understand why it brings up such strong feelings in her or him).

Kubrick in *2001* gives us what now seems obvious: a series of powerful, often beautiful, always stimulating and inspiring *images*. And with a success quite a bit beyond what good filmmakers had achieved before, he juxtaposes, combines, counterpoints images and music. A visual symphony. With the all-important (and sometimes exasperating) illusion that there is a story being told here, however obscurely. Of course! Ask Matisse or Picasso—what else would one do with a medium like popular film? Flash one image after another at the watcher. And thereby make a statement. A statement that might require two hours to be received once, and days or months more before it could be digested (though certainly the visceral impact would be immediate). What fun for a visual artist! And how quickly can you name another 20th-century film (*all* films, so far, are 20th-century films) that is so spectacularly successful at this? Hey, *2001* is (was) a Cinerama film, okay? And very arguably the greatest (most awe-inspiring) of the genre.

It's an epic (as the Homeric title suggests): a remarkably grand and simple work of art. And yet people often say (admirers of the film as well as detractors) that they don't "understand" it. And that's appropriate. The artist's intent is to leave you feeling puzzled, struck by the awe of being alive at this historical moment (1968, when I first saw the film, or whenever in the next hundred years you happen to be watching it) when we can see and feel an enormous jump ahead of us, the transition from an Earthbound species to explorers and inhabitants of the greater Universe. Struck by the awe of the oncoming changes and the beauty of the extraordinary passage ahead of us—but not too full of very linear ideas about what forms this exploration of the galaxies is going to take. Epic story. Brilliantly told (by director Kubrick and his screenplay co-writer Arthur C. Clarke). But, very appropriately, not easily resolved into an "explainable" narrative. That's how myth is. Not too damned explicit.

Science fiction author and editor Lester del Rey, in his book *The World of Science Fiction: The History of a Subculture* (1979), acknowledges that he's in the minority in his distaste for this film, and sneeringly explains: "to most people, the mysticism of the ending in which mankind seems to need transformation into alienness or to require extra-human help was satisfying (just what the ending meant is something I never could learn from [his friend] Clarke)." In the same breath he says he's read Clarke's novelization of the screenplay (a novel written during the making of the movie and first published in July 1968). So apparently even the book version couldn't help del Rey understand the ending. I can empathize; I wasn't sure whether I liked the movie as a whole when I saw it the week it was released. I was charmed by the psychedelic ending, but wasn't too confident I understood it, and usually just let my enthusiastic friends burble their interpretations without any comment from me.

But this piece of art has really grown on me. I liked it better the next time I saw it, just after my first son's birth in 1973; but I like it hugely now that I'm seeing it again for purposes of writing this entry, autumn 1998. And the "meaning" of the ending now seems perfectly clear to me, and quite perfectly and wonderfully executed by an artist every bit as inspired and mystifying as Brian Wilson in his prime. I'm not speaking here of Kubrick's whole body of work, because I only really know his extraordinary films of 1964 and 1968, *Dr. Strangelove* and *2001*. What an artist he was then! Of course I have seen and been impressed by *A Clockwork Orange* (1971) and *Lolita* (1962). I think I saw his *Spartacus* (1960) when I was too young to notice the name of the director. But the more I watch and live with (like a painting) *2001*, the more I appreciate it, the more confident I am that it is indeed a masterpiece. Not that my opinion is all that important. But as I've said, this entry is fairly widely recognized as a great film of the century, and therefore a safe pick for a "greatest hit." I acknowledge that the phrase "greatest hit," as in the name of a record, *Greatest Hits of Pat Boone,* usually means the songs or records or pop art objects that sold the most units or scored highest on the "charts" that list record sales and book and movie sales. But obviously that's not the way I'm using it for the purpose of this book. I'm more gesturing in the direction of something that's always fascinated me, the consensus of popular or critical or academic opinion that allows certain novels or symphonies or plays or poems or sculptures to "survive" in the attention of human civilization for many years, sometimes even centuries, after the artist's birthing of the work. What will survive like that from the 1901–2000 era? This ain't intended to be the "definitive" list but a representative sampling, designed to a) tell the story of the century as reflected in its juiciest art, and b) encourage the reader to make your own list or in any case be an energetic champion of what you believe would most enrich the lives of many of our descendants should they ever discover these ancient records or movies or children's books.

Okay, okay. I'll tell you what I think (no, if I'm honest, what I now *know*) the ending of *2001: A Space Odyssey* means. But first I want to share some of what I've learned (and intuited) from my research about the process of collaboration that led to the work of art called *2001*. It would be natural to imagine the movie was made by director Kubrick working from ("based on") a novel by science fiction writer Clarke. No, as Clarke explains in his 1972 book *The Lost Worlds of 2001*, the project started with Kubrick (an American who worked, made movies, in Britain) in early 1964 writing a letter to Clarke (a British expatriate living in Ceylon, and a highly regarded science fiction writer since 1946, known for his scientifically accurate and evocative descriptions of space travel, and for his sometimes poetic, visionary, metaphysical writing about the human future, notably in his 1953 novels *Childhood's End* and *Against the Fall of Night*).

The letter, sent around the time that *Dr. Strangelove* was arriving in movie theaters, expressed Kubrick's wish to make what he called "the proverbial good science fiction movie." Clarke was invited to fly to New York to meet Kubrick; before he did, he says, "I had run through my published stories in search of a suitable starting point for a space epic. Almost at once, I settled upon a very short piece called 'The Sentinel'" (an early story written in 1948).

ACC and SK met for the first time on April 22, 1964, and: "after various false starts and twelve-hour talkathons, by early May 1964 Stanley agreed that 'The Sentinel' would provide good story material. . . . The rest of 1964 was spent brainstorming. As we developed new ideas, so the original conception [which had been to have the movie climax 'with the discovery of an extra-terrestrial artifact,' as in 'The Sentinel'] slowly changed."

At every step along the way the two collaborators discussed and tinkered with the plot and let it evolve. My only background source (there is a book called *The Making of 2001,* but I haven't seen it) is Clarke's *Lost Worlds,* but his brief recollections and diary extracts therein are enough to make it clear that the collaborator with the upper hand was always, of course, the director. Like Brian Wilson with Tony Asher, Kubrick just needed a sympathetic partner to play the game with, a companion in the process, someone to brainstorm with and react to. The story line of the movie is Kubrick's creation, based partly on an idea from a story Clark once wrote, and on ideas and suggestions Clarke offered in the course of several years of two-person story conferences, and also I suspect on some feelings Kubrick got from reading Clarke, very probably *Childhood's End* (that Kubrick had read it seems to be confirmed by Clarke's diary entry of May 25, 1965: "Now Stanley wants to incorporate the Devil theme from *Childhood's End*").

Clarke says in his memoir that when he and Kubrick met, K "had already absorbed an immense amount of science fact and science fiction," and "even from the beginning, he had a very clear idea of his ultimate goal, and was searching for the best way to approach it. He wanted to make a movie about Man's relation to the universe—something which had never been attempted, still less achieved, in the history of motion pictures." K, says C, was aware that even the few non-trashy space movies that had previously been made "were concerned more with the schoolboy excitement of space flight than its profound implications to society, philosophy, and religion." And he wanted to "create a work of art which would arouse the emotions of wonder, awe . . . even, if appropriate, terror." And so he did.

How ambitious: to use the rapidly evolving film medium to create a Homeric epic poem for the 21st century, in which Odysseus would be a new, very modern kind of Everyman, wandering dazed on a different sort of ocean. Clarke's diary, October 15, 1965: "Stan has decided to kill off *all* the crew of *Discovery* and leave Bowman only. Drastic, but it seems right. After all, Odysseus was the sole survivor. . . ."

About that ending. Odysseus (David Bowman) comes home, of course, but he looks a lot younger now. His visible form is that of a human embryo (with seeing, apparently conscious, eyes) in a globe, a flying globe. In the closing frames, he can be seen orbiting the Earth (or orbiting the Moon as it orbits Earth), back from a journey that took him (us) a lot farther than Jupiter.

The (memorable, often-debated) ending of the movie starts about five minutes into the movie's third "act" (there are only three segments in the film that get identified with a printed name at their beginnings, clearly analogous to the acts of a play: "The Dawn of Man"; "Jupiter Mission, 18 Months Later"; "Jupiter and Beyond the Infinite"). The first half of the ending is nine and a half minutes long, a "special effects" sequence, a psychedelic light show that gives the definite sensation of falling into an immense universe of stars, at faster-than-light speed. This certainly (and appropriately) inspired the slogan that appeared on most posters and advertisements for the new film (possibly the first mass-culture overt acknowledgment of the LSD or psychedelic sub-culture that had blossomed in America in the years leading up the film's release): "The Ultimate Trip."

The second half of the ending is nine minutes long and takes place in a hotel room. This hotel room sequence ends with the fourth appearance in the film of the tall rectangular solid known as "The Monolith." It appears to the old man lying in the hotel room bed—who is obviously Bowman, the protagonist or view-point character, who in turn is obviously all humankind, just as the apeman who picks up the bone in the opening sequence is clearly the whole proto-human species, learning something and changing forever because Everyapeman listened to some cosmic voice that whispered in his mind when the Monolith showed up in his clan's berry-picking grounds.

Okay, let's recapitulate. The story being told is the myth of the Monolith, and its rumored impact on or interference with humankind. (This monolith was a pyramid in Clarke's story "The Sentinel," found on a curiously smooth plateau by a geologist in the first human expedition to the Moon's Mare Crisium area. In that story the geologist realizes this object could only have been made and placed there by a species more "advanced" than we are yet and therefore extraterrestrial, maybe from far beyond our solar system, leaving markers that would sound an alarm in some far-off galaxy when creatures from Earth advanced to the point where they could travel to their moon and find the marker and set off the alarm.)

When the Monolith and the apemen have their encounter in the opening sequence, the black rock zaps the lead ape and he immediately invents tools and weapons (hammering at a pile of bones with a larger bone, like a hyperactive three-year-old). By the end of the sequence, the berry-pickers who just shoved and screamed the warthogs away from their grazing area because they were herbivores with no interest in warthog meat discover not only how to use a bludgeon but the taste of meat. Kubrick effectively suggests that nothing will be the same after this, and indeed the apemen start fighting each other violently. The electronic music and the screams of the apemen and the portrayed violence in these scenes are so jarring that the shockingly boring and banal (except when you look out the window) human future portrayed in the next scenes of the film seems welcome and restful (particularly thanks to Johann Strauss's "Blue Danube" on the soundtrack).

The viewer easily sorts the sections of the film in his or her mind: the apeman stuff, the space station and Moonbase segments, the long long Dave-and-Frank-and-Hal-in-the-*Discovery*-section, with the climactic confrontation with Hal that no one forgets. And then the weird ending. That's it. But as it happens, the space station/Moonbase/visit-to-the-top-secret-Monolith-site segments, about thirty-five minutes altogether, don't have their own printed section name, so if we divide the film into three acts, this stuff from the year 2001 (the "present" of the film) is the second two-thirds of "The Dawn of Man." The evident reason for this is that the segue between "Dawn" and "the present" (ape tosses his breakthrough bone in the air, and through the power of sequenced images the bone becomes a spaceship in the sky, soon joined by other space objects in a gorgeous waltz) is so wonderful. An absolutely exquisite visual segue, one of the many great moments in the film, and why should Kubrick lose it just to put the name of the segment where it belongs? Anyway, as I said, he doesn't mind confusing the overly mental viewer. He was something of a Zen director at this point in his creative career, and seems confident that small confusions can actually open the observer's receptivity and thus lead to clarity.

I'm getting lost in my recapitulation. Sorry about that. The second appearance of the Monolith is at the end of the 2001 part of Act 1, when the government visitor gets shown the site where they found this thing suspiciously buried in the soil of the Moon. During his visit, the Monolith comes alive. It doesn't zap him or try to alter human evolution at this point. Instead it sends a signal to Jupiter. We know this because we hear about it on the tape recording that speaks to Captain Bowman at the end of Act 2. Supposedly Bowman himself didn't know what his "mission" was until this moment. After we get this news, the film immediately moves into Act 3, "Jupiter and Beyond the Infinite." We are with Bowman as he arrives near Jupiter and sees the Monolith orbiting Jupiter or orbiting one of its moons. This is when the ending, the psychedelic "hyperspace" segment, starts. So that's three appearances of the Monolith; the fourth occurs when old man David sees it at the foot of his bed and as he stares finds himself (but he's used to finding himself going through abrupt stages in his life-cycle during this segment) a starbaby. The Monolith did it. And nobody's complaining.

Okay, Mr. del Rey, I know you could still say you don't know what it "means," but even though you're an experienced SF writer and reader, let me spell it out for you: When Bowman in the *Discovery* completes his mission by arriving at the location where NASA traced the Monolith's signal as having gone, he sees another one of these extraterrestrial objects and falls into a "stargate" that will take him to another part of the universe at faster than light (it's called "hyperspace," a science fiction writer's cliché and never so well portrayed visually), presumably for an interview with the species that placed the Monolith-sentinels.

I acknowledge that I was aided in this "interpretation" (though I'd like to think that I or anybody could have eventually arrived at it anyway) by the following phrases in Clarke's *Lost Worlds*: "By Christmas 1964, we [the co-writers] had managed to get Bowman into the Star Gate, but didn't know what would happen next, except in the most general way." Diary entry, October 3, 1965: "Stanley on phone, worried about ending . . . gave him my latest ideas, and one of them suddenly clicked—Bowman will regress to infancy, and we'll see him at the end as a baby in orbit." October 5: "Suddenly (I think!) found a logical reason why Bowman should appear at the end as a baby. It's his image of himself at this stage of his development. And perhaps the Cosmic Consciousness has a sense of humor."

Clarke is brainstorming here, and I know some critics think Kubrick in his finished work is just shoving vague or half-baked ideas at us. Because his movie-making style is so outrageous and free, like Matisse's painting style in his "fauve" period, critical minds reach for their guns and fail to see what seems quite apparent to me: that Kubrick in his slowly-arrived-at final cut is telling a story that is as well-thought-through and as attentive to the artist's relationship with observer as, say, a first-rate science fiction novel. As the intensity of the psychedelic section calms down, it's clear that we (Bowman) are still in motion but now within a solar system instead of in the vast emptiness between systems . . . and apparently landing on some kind of a planet. We (Bowman) watch helplessly this approach that we are not directing as captain or navigator, and when motion stops we look out at what turns out to be a hotel room that we can eat, sleep, and wander around in. Now, assuming an alien species advanced enough to mess with men's minds, which has just brought this Terran here via its own technology, how would they handle his education session or evolutionary treatments? Well, it wouldn't help to terrify the poor dope, so you put him in an environment that he can mentally project some kind of "normalcy" onto, at those moments when he "wakes" and looks around at his surroundings or even looks at himself from outside (called an out-of-body experience). Hey, I had already taken quite a few LSD trips when I first saw this film, and since then I've found myself living in a hospital bed after a serious brain injury, so I can absolutely attest to the accuracy with which Kubrick portrays the subjective feeling of the sort of strange mental-emotional experience that Bowman would be going through here if you grant the author's premise.

I love the way he notices himself as a boy or young man in a spacesuit, or as an old man at a table or in bed, and then finds that he is that person right now, is looking out from the body that a moment ago he was staring at in puzzlement. The look on Bowman's face through most of the hotel room sequence is a brilliant bit of direction. And absolutely haunting if and when you notice (hey, you do subliminally at least) that that curious gaze is exactly the same look on starbaby's face in the closing shot.

That music! The thundering of Richard Strauss's *Also Sprach Zarathustra* as we see starbaby Bowman rising from his old-man body to return from the stars to our home solar system, the adrenaline surge we get from the return of this bit of music, tells us unambiguously that this is a dramatic moment in this film, this epic, precisely equal to (or even bigger than) the moment when apeman started using tools and ceased being "an animal." This artist, this director, actually speaks so clearly to us his audience. I've already said *2001* is a triumphant use of the juxtaposing of music and moving images (as in ballet, for example). I love the simple freedom he gives himself here by writing his own soundtrack as a disc jockey, playing the snatches of orchestral music he wants to hear with each image and at each moment in the sequential experience of watching the movie.

I can certainly appreciate collaboration, but when it comes to movies I personally find the art form limited by the number of opinions that so often have the power to express themselves in the writing and making and editing of a film. To me it's like art-by-committee, something I'm very dubious about (although I do admire what Eleanor Roosevelt's committee wrote, the exception that proves the rule). So I guess you could say I'm into the auteur theory of filmmaking. Probably. In any case, it totally makes sense to me for a particularly great film to be made by an artist who manages to control the elements of his medium as surely as Matisse or Picasso controlled their paints and canvases and lights and shadows. Of course Kubrick made all the story line decisions, after listening carefully to Clarke . . . *of course* Kubrick chose every piece of music and every five-second fragment of music himself, just as he no doubt chose (and directed) every beautiful Chesley-Bonestell–like astronomical background painting himself. And every "special effect." He paints his masterpiece with every image, every edit, every sound-and-sight-and-dramatic-moment juxtaposition. You can see his characteristic brush strokes in every part of the work.

"Normally," of course, directors are thought of as properly focusing most of their talent on guiding and choreographing people, actors and actresses. And Kubrick is often criticized for the banality of the dialogue and the flatness of the people in the populated parts of this film. I remember that bothered me when I first saw the movie. I thought he was celebrating sterility—I didn't realize he might be acknowledging its inevitability or using it to make the future more everyday, more believable. I felt slapped in the face by his bold anti-Romanticism, I guess (though the nonhuman images in the film are certainly Romantic, as is the music). And I wasn't alone, if you read the critics' comments.

In an interview with the *New York Times* after the film came out, Kubrick stated clearly that he kept the dialogue wooden in order to avoid interrupting the mood of his carefully constructed epic poem:

> There are certain areas of feeling and reality that are notably inaccessible to words. Non-verbal forms of expression such as music and painting can get at these areas, but words are a terrible straightjacket. It's interesting how many prisoners of that straightjacket resent its being loosened. . . . I don't like to talk about *2001* much, because it's essentially a nonverbal experience. It attempts to communicate more to the subconscious and to the feelings than it does to the intellect.

Again, "A poem should be palpable and mute. . . ." Even more true of an epic, or mythic, poem. For sheer beauty, and mute profundity, I think one must compare *2001* favorably with any painting or paper poem of its century.

HIT 15

Concert Performance

by Umm Kulthum

(April 7, 1966)

Umm Kulthum of Egypt was the greatest Arab singer of our century. This is universally agreed. And most non-Arab appreciators of vocal music who are aware of her work will readily concur that she is one of the greatest singers of the 20th century of any kind. A major artist.

What is the unit of such art? (This book is a list of works of art, not a list of greatest artists.) In the case of the Beatles or the Beach Boys (or Hank Williams; see entry #40), it's a record, a recording, an "album" or a "single." Then there are great artists whose works are performances before a live audience. I am a passionate appreciator of this type of art, and have written a series of books about Bob Dylan as a performing artist in which I argue for the recognition of live performances, recorded or unrecorded, as works of art that can add up to a great and memorable body of work just as surely as artworks that endure as physical objects. So when I started this book—and the first thing I wrote was the list; I wrote it over the course of two days, like a poem—I wanted to include some live performances as units of art worthy to be honored as "greatest hits" of the century alongside paintings and novels and films and songs. These could just as well have been dance or dramatic theater performances, but I chose musical examples because, as limited as my knowledge of 20th-century art necessarily is (necessarily because it's too broad a subject for any individual to truly grasp or "know"), music is the performance medium with which I have the most experience as an observer/appreciator.

Umm Kulthum immediately came to mind, because I love the recordings of her performances I've heard and seen, and because it's hard to think of another modern artist who has touched and changed the lives of tens of millions of people primarily via live performances (Jack Benny, possibly . . . or the Grateful Dead, see entry #26). Umm Kulthum certainly did. Every year for thirty-six years, this woman performed a concert at a theater in Cairo on the first Thursday of every month for a season of five to eight months; these concerts were broadcast live on Egyptian Radio, and during those broadcasts the whole country stopped while people gathered in homes and public places (it was an important social event) to listen to the concerts together.

> Her concerts reached beyond Cairo into towns, villages, and camps, beyond the boundaries of Egypt, throughout the Arab world via the radio, and her audience consisted primarily of people who never attended a concert. These listeners, as much as the concertgoers, evaluated, compared, complained, raved, and glorified her. Not only her performances but talk about the performances became pervasive. The audience, their attention and their talk, created the space in which she became "the voice of Egypt."
> —Virginia Danielson, *The Voice of Egypt: Umm Kulthum, Arabic Song, and Egyptian Society in the 20th Century* (1997)

Naguib Mahfouz, winner of the 1988 Nobel Prize for Literature, has a scene in his 1967 novel *Miramar* in which the primary characters meet and interact during an "Umm Kulthum evening" at their boardinghouse. Afterward the young narrator recalls a comment made by his neighbor the thoughtful veteran of the 1919 Revolution:

> I really admired Amir Wagdi, sitting up so late, and thoroughly enjoying the singing and the music. It was almost

dawn when we got up to go to bed [her concerts sometimes ran that late].

"Was there ever in your day a voice like Umm Kulthum's?"

"No." He smiled. "It's the only thing today for which the past can provide no equal."

So which Umm Kulthum concert shall I put on my list, to stand in for the fact that her concerts taken collectively (and so why not any one of them to stand for the whole?) were indeed one of the greatest hits of the 20th century, in terms of popularity and in terms of substantial aesthetic accomplishment, in any popular art form? (And remember, when we say "popular art" we're talking about the medium of Shakespeare and Mozart and Dickens.)

One way to choose would be if I had been to one of her concerts, but I didn't become aware of her existence until 1978, three years after her death, so I never had that opportunity. Or if I had an audio or video recording of a particular five-hour concert, I could reasonably focus on that one. But so far, none of the Umm Kulthum recordings I've acquired has come with recording dates or indications as to whether they're "studio" or "live" recordings. (I believe many of them are a little of both, edited together.) None of the discographies I've found so far is helpful in this regard, except that one does give the debut date of "al-Atlal"— probably the most famous and most fondly remembered of the 286 songs she performed in the course of her extraordinary career.

"Al-Atlal" was introduced in a concert (presumably also broadcast on the radio) in Cairo on April 7, 1966. Memorable show! As it happened, this was her first concert after the death of her good friend Muhammad al-Qasabji, one of the first composers she worked with and the oud player in her band for decades (even after she stopped using his compositions). A great loss. And an interesting moment for her to first perform in public this poem of heartwrenching loss put to music in a structure based on and evocative of classical Arabic song form. "Al-Atlal" is an astonishing work of art that brings together past and present in deeply spiritual and evocative ways, thereby making a powerful and enduring statement about who the singer is and who we, the individual and collective listeners, are.

I first heard of and became interested in Umm Kulthum when Bob Dylan said in a 1978 interview that she was his favorite singer. I like the way some artists lead you to others. (It was in fact Philip K. Dick who first made me aware of the existence of Richard Wilhelm's translation of the I Ching, which he described in a 1962 novel.) Bob Dylan is a great lover of music, a collector of songs and of musical heroes and heroines. In a later interview (1984), he spoke of The Lady again, in the context of talking about his own approach to phrasing and the dynamics of singing:

> And there was this Egyptian singer Om Khalsoum [her Arabic name has a dozen different Western spellings], have you ever heard of her? She was one of my favorite singers of all time, and I don't understand a word she sings! And she'd sing one song—and it might last 40 minutes, same song—and she'll sing the same phrase over and over and over again, in a different way every time. And no U.S. or Western singer, I think, is in that kind of category, you know . . . except possibly me (laughs).

"Al-Atlal" is just one of, probably, three songs Umm Kulthum performed at the April 1966 concert we're celebrating here—which probably went on for five hours. I don't know what the others were, but "Inta Umri" was very likely one of them, and it likely lasted over two hours, and "al-Atlal" could have lasted slightly over one hour—although the officially released version I have is only forty-eight minutes long.

"Al-Atlal" means "The Embers" (also commonly translated as "The Ruins" or "Traces"). It's a sorrowful, aggravated song of lost love, edited by Umm Kulthum from two poems by Ibrahim Naji, a poet who'd died in the previous decade, and arranged and set to music by Riyad al-Sunbati, the most talented and boldly-innovative-while-still-rooted-in-glorious-tradition composer among the several she employed. The song belongs to (and indeed has helped keep alive) an ancient Arabic

form call *qasida*, in which it was common to have song-poems
that draw in the image of wandering in the desert and coming
upon the ruins or traces of someone else's camp, or a dying camp-
fire, perhaps left behind (actually or metaphorically) by the
departed beloved.

The words of the song are very important, as Umm Kulthum
tells us in a quick summary of her aesthetic: "The song depends
before all else on the words. If the words are beautiful, they will
inspire the composer and the singer, and the composition will
turn out beautifully and the rendition excellent." The words of
"al-Atlal" talk of love as "a dream-edifice that has collapsed" and
speak ruefully of "your glance which brings thirst to the one who
glimpses it." The climactic words of this love lament, which
became political in the way the singer sang them and the way the
listeners heard them, are: "Give me my freedom, set free my
hands! I've given everything and held back nothing. Ah, how
your chains have made my wrists bleed. . . ."

In 1966, according to Kulthum scholar Virginia Danielson,
these lines were perceived by some listeners as addressed to the
repressive measures of the Egyptian government at the time
against its own citizens. But after the Egyptian defeat in the
Arab-Israeli War of 1967, the phrases "took on a wider meaning,
suggestive of the bondage in which many Egyptians felt the entire
Arab world to be held." So as audience members cried out for
The Lady to repeat these words (a standard part of the relationship between her and her audience, so that the length and shape
of a song were determined by the crowd's requests for repetitions), they were bathing in the ecstatic pain not only of romantic disappointment but of other sorts of deeply felt defeats and
aggravations: "Give me my freedom!" Which brings us to the
important subjects of *tarab* and the live audience's role in the creation of the work of art.

I learned from Danielson's book in Arabic about Umm
Kulthum, "a good singer is a *mutriba*, one who creates an environment of *tarab* with his or her performance. Excellent rendition generates *tarab*, literally 'enchantment,' the sense of having
been deeply moved by the music." Billy Holiday was certainly a

mutriba, and I recommend Danielson's book to anyone (singer, scholar, or fan) interested in learning more about how great blues singers and soul singers do what they do. In Arabic, it turns out, there are words for it. A singer communicates all sorts of nuances of meaning by using *bahha* (hoarseness), *ghunna* (nasality), and falsetto, collectively referred to as vocal colors, and a further grab bag of vocal ornaments (*zakharif*) including of course trills, vibrato, harshness, and gentleness, along with repetitions, improvisation, and clarity of articulation (something Umm Kulthum learned from childhood classes in reading the Qur'an out loud). "Asked to explain *tarab,*" Danielson tells us, "Umm Kulthum said it was attained when the listener 'felt' the meaning of the words. It was frequently said that even one who did not speak Arabic would understand the meaning of a text from listening to her sing it."

In regard to the concert performance of April 7, 1966, it is helpful to know, as Ali Jihad Racy writes in an essay called "Creativity and Ambience: An Ecstatic Feedback Model from Arab Music":

> *Tarab* music itself can be emotionally experienced outside the immediate ecstatic and interactive ambience that originally led to its creation. Whether in the form of recordings of live performances . . . or radio broadcasts . . . *tarab* works become ecstatic codes capable of establishing a *tarab* ambience for the culturally trained and musically initiated listener.

In other words, you didn't have to be in the room. You can get a buzz from the vibe created by the Grateful Dead and their audience responding to each other, just by listening to the tape, because the vibe becomes part of the work of art. How this vibe was achieved in Cairo concert halls can be seen in Michal Goldman's fine documentary film *Umm Kulthum,* and is described by Danielson: "Umm Kulthum's performance of a song ultimately dominated its constituent parts. The effect of her varied repetitions [in response to ever-changing demands from the audience] and her shaping and reshaping of songs in performance was to create with and for the audience the mood of the poem she sang and to involve the audience completely in this mood."

Of course, as much as her performance was rooted in thousands of years of Arab musical and social and spiritual tradition, and shaped by her enormous willpower and discipline (she usually rehearsed and fussed with a new song for a year before debuting it, and she even made composers and lyricists offer her alternate versions of small sections of new songs, so she could choose which fragments felt best to her), there was also a space for spontaneity even beyond the question of which vocal flourishes to lean into at each moment. In Paris in 1967, at the only shows she ever performed outside the Arab world, a very inebriated admirer approached her as she was singing, in "al-Atlal," "Has love ever seen such intoxicated ones as we?" She responded by singing (and making it fit the song's meter,) "Have we ever seen such drunkards among us?" And no doubt managed somehow to work the audience's resultant laughter into the song's mood of enormous sorrow and anguish.

Umm Kulthum stands for me as perhaps the century's most striking example (even compared to Elvis or Piaf) of how much and how enduringly singers can be loved by the people who feel that this artist speaks for me, for us, in the voice of our place and history and moment. Her funeral brought four million mourners into the streets of Cairo, possibly the largest single gathering of human beings in one place for one reason in human history until now.

For a last comment on this phenomenon, and on the concert I'm proclaiming one of the more memorable art objects of our era, here is Jehan Sadat, widow of the former Egyptian president, from her memoir A Woman of Egypt:

Not before or since has there been a more popular singer in the Arab world. Um Kalthum sang of love and sorrow with such emotion that many people seated in the audience or in their own homes cried. Her voice was magical, her prowess extraordinary. She could hold a single note for a minute and a half. During her concerts she would sing only three songs, the first two lasting nearly two hours, the final song one hour. Over and over she would sing the same refrain, changing the nuance each time the tiniest bit.

Europeans found her songs repetitious, but we did not. To foreigners every dune in the desert looked the same as every other, but we knew that each grain of sand was different. And so was every one of Umm Kulthum's Thursday concerts.

It's all personal. That's the untold secret of our relationship with great works of art. Someone has to see the painting, hear the concert, watch the movie and read the poem, and how they/we respond is the determinant of whether this particular work gets a reputation that endures. This book is about the 20th century (an interesting place to visit, and I've loved living here) and works of art from this period that have a chance to (and deserve to) endure. How does such longevity occur? I don't know, but yesterday afternoon I was rereading "The Bear" with such intense delight that I found myself thinking about *Moby-Dick* and *The Adventures of Huckleberry Finn* and *Walden*, greatest hits of American literature that have touched me and enriched my life and that I certainly would never have encountered were it not for their reputations. Yesterday afternoon I was experiencing a personal connection with this story that was so pleasurable and felt so nourishing that I was glad I'd stuck it on the list and therefore given myself a reason to read the thing again. And very glad that I'd been introduced to this story and its author (by shotgun) in eighth-grade English class in 1962, only two decades after the story was first published. How'd the guy become Required Reading in American literature so fast? Not thanks to Americans (though at least two, Phil Stone and

Malcolm Cowley, deserve a lot of credit). Primarily thanks to a few Europeans (mostly Swedes) who gave William Faulkner the Nobel Prize for Literature only eight years after this story's publication and only twenty years after his first significant novel appeared, and at a time when Faulkner's reputation in the United States was quite modest (most of his books were already out of print and no publisher or arts foundation would pay him a living wage for writing what he wanted to write; instead he made the classic American journey from Mississippi small town and farm to Hollywood, California, and a "hack" writing job for the movie industry).

The personal part occurs when somebody on the Nobel Prize committee or some friend of theirs or an outside expert (like novelist Ralph Ellison, who once called "The Bear" "one of the most sublime stories in the language") has a personal experience like what happened to me yesterday afternoon. It probably helped that I was reading the first three sections of the story for the second time this year. At first I thought I'd just "skim" the part I recently read to refresh my memory before reading the rest, but instead I was caught by the story and the language and the characters and had to read every word. It all just started singing to me. Kinda wonderful, but what really reminded me of how personal this whole matter of evaluation—the word "great" as in "great art" is all about evaluation, right?—and reputation is, was yesterday evening when, after re-rereading those magnificent early sections, I got into the notorious section four and found myself furious at the author and seriously questioning whether I could stand to have such a frustrating and (I thought) careless and ultimately unrewarding piece of work on my greatest hits list. I started the section with enthusiasm for its out-there form and subject matter, confident that I would be able to unscramble the puzzles like a champ if I just read attentively and patiently enough, but after much hard work and disappointment I had a real bad attitude, even though hours earlier I was unexpectedly falling in love again, in a big way. So should I vote for this guy for the Prize? Depends on which personal experience I had, or which I had most recently—or how intimidated I am by his reputation, or how resentful I am of it, all that stuff, which is also ultimately personal, okay?

But look. Bill's still in the book. It's been a roller coaster ride. I was mollified by learning that Faulkner himself said:

> If he [the publisher] had told me he was going to print it separately [as in the book called *Three Famous Short Novels by William Faulkner*], I would have said, Take this [section 4] out, this doesn't belong in this as a short story, it's a part of the novel [*Go Down, Moses*] but not part of the story. The way to read the story is to skip section 4 when you come to it.

Now he tells me. But I do understand why Random House/ Vintage years later still hasn't followed his instructions. Partly because he didn't deliver them directly (even if the book in which he says this, *Faulkner in the University*, was published by Vintage). But mostly because even though the author and almost everybody else agrees the story reads better without section 4, nevertheless section 4 (almost as long as all the other sections put together) is a big part of what the story is "famous" for. And maybe Ralph Ellison wouldn't have endorsed the story so strongly were it not for the passionate revulsion expressed by the protagonist at his ancestors' treatment of their black slaves and former slaves, which is only expressed, however convolutely, in section four. My advice to my reader is read 1, 2, 3, and then 5 (the last section) and be happy. (And you will be, it's a terrific story read that way.) And then if you want to dive into section 4, take it as a footnote, like the extra material in the *Pet Sounds Sessions* box set—and don't be trapped like I was into thinking you can get to the point where you're sure you know who's talking when and what they're talking about in this paragraph. Really. You could have great, even sublime experiences reading section 4 (certainly you could have fun writing a paper comparing it to Bob Dylan's portrait of the South in "Blind Willie McTell"). And you could also be satisfied with "The Bear" as a greatest hit and Faulkner as a great writer without ever reading section 4 at all. Funny how these things work. And look, I didn't say you *have to* hear the particular Umm Kulthum concert I chose to write my essay about. The important thing is just to give yourself a chance to have the voice-of-Umm-Kulthum or voice-of-William-Faulkner experience.

So Faulkner's prize acceptance speech is here along with his big hit story because, like the story, it had a considerable impact on me and my eighth-grade classmates and I know has meant a lot to many other readers—a very timely purpose statement (in 1962 it felt as though he must have written it last week):

> It is easy enough to say that man is immortal simply because he will endure; that when the last ding-dong of doom has clanged and faded from the last worthless rock hanging tideless in the last red and dying evening, that even then there will still be one more sound: that of his puny inexhaustible voice, still talking. I refuse to accept this. I believe that man will not merely endure: he will prevail. He is immortal, not because he alone among creatures has an inexhaustible voice, but because he has a soul, a spirit capable of compassion and sacrifice and endurance. The poet's, the writer's, duty is to write about these things. It is his privilege to help man endure by lifting his heart, by reminding him of the courage and honor and hope and pride and compassion and pity and sacrifice which have been the glory of his past.

Matisse spoke of finding the mark of his personality repeating itself like a refrain when he looked over his earlier works. Such signature images and phrases also recur in Faulkner's oeuvre, so it's no surprise to stumble on bits of language in "The Bear" that seem to anticipate the Nobel Prize speech:

From section 3, about the bearing and physical presence of the wild dog Lion:

> Lion implied not only courage and all else that went to make up the will and desire to pursue and kill, but endurance, the will and desire to endure beyond all imaginable limits of flesh. . . .

From section 4 (also found in Bartlett's *Familiar Quotations*, as are parts of the Nobel speech):

> They [the Negroes] will endure. They are better than we are. Stronger than we are. Their vices are vices aped from white men or that white men and bondage have taught them.... And their virtues [are] endurance and pity and tolerance and forbearance....

Also from section 4:

> They were His [God's] creation now and forever more until not only that old world from which He had rescued them but this new one too which He had revealed and led them to as a sanctuary and refuge were become the same worthless tideless rock cooling in the last crimson evening....

Finally, I embrace "The Bear" (as Lion embraced the bear at the end and as Old Ben embraced Lion and as Sam and Old Ben embraced the Ultimate before the boy's very eyes) because it is such a resonant story of love (for example, the love of the mongrel human Boon for the great mongrel dog Lion) and anguish that every reader including me just naturally creates their own personal meaning out of it and carries it off with them as proudly as we carry what we've created out of The Lady's radio broadcasts. Great art strikes notes in us that resonate deeply. Worth the agony and sweat? My answer depends on whether you ask in the afternoon or the evening.

HIT 17

Renaldo & Clara
by *Bob Dylan*
(released January 1978)

First, I should explain to most of you who don't have any reason to know this already, *Renaldo & Clara* is not a musical album or a song; it's a movie, a rather obscure film that was only available for showing by movie theaters during the first year of its release, and which has not been formally available to the interested consumer in any form ever since (my copy is a copy of a videotape made by Bob Dylan fans in Europe when the movie was broadcast on British television not long after its original release).

I am not including *Renaldo & Clara* in this book because I think it is "greater" than Bob Dylan's better-known works. No, as with the Beatles' "Things We Said Today," it is here partly as an expression of my desire to avoid certain traps that are inherent in making a list of the "best" or "finest" of anything. I don't want this book/list to be taken as an assertion that this Matisse painting or this Beatles song or this Billie Holiday recording or this Bob Dylan construction is in my opinion his or her greatest achievement as an artist or as a human being. No, what I'm trying to say by my choices is that these forty disparate works of art from my century are worthy to be considered equal to each other and, taken together, can serve as a good cross-section of the best of what we (as people, and as artists) created while we were here this time.

Another angle to this list-making thing is that, in terms of what Bob Dylan once called "famiosity," it is arguable and even obvious that the greatest (most talked-of and therefore historic) concert performances of the 20th century include Igor Stravinsky's *Rite of Spring* debut (1913) and Bob Dylan's much-bootlegged May 17, 1966, acoustic/electric "Judas" concert. So why aren't these among the three concert performances included in this book as my acknowledgment of the significance of this art form? Because I insist that famiosity is not the same kinda greatness as the greatness of art that actually touches and moves the heart of one person. Those famous examples have done that too, of course; but the disadvantage of famousness as a cultural value is when it crowds everything else out, and we fail to validate our more private joys and discoveries.

Speaking of private joys and discoveries, I have to thank Bob Dylan, because not only did he first alert me to the existence of Umm Kulthum, but this weekend he again (this happened before, eight years ago) directly influenced me to give myself an extraordinary gift, the gift of seeing, experiencing, my (and Bob Dylan's) leading candidate for "greatest film ever": the 1944 *Les Enfants du Paradis*, also known as Marcel Carne's (and Jacques Prévert's) *Children of Paradise*. This is the marker Bob Dylan was reaching for, the trailblazing work of art he was inspired by, when he decided to spend a lot of time and money (and to risk his reputation and, perhaps, his sanity) making a movie intended to be as committed and energetic and fully realized a creative act as any song he'd ever written and recorded or any concert he'd ever given.

One greatest hit leads to another. Just as I know Matisse would be very pleased to hear that his work brought someone to Cézanne's paintings, so I am certain Bob Dylan is gratified every time he hears that another person—often a woman, I imagine, because twice in my life now I've had dear female friends testify passionately to me about how much *Children of Paradise* has meant to them—has discovered and fallen in love with Carne's film as a result of Dylan in interviews (around the time that *Renaldo & Clara* was released) saying things like, "I've only seen one other film [besides his own, which he was very happy with after finishing the final edit] that has stopped time—*Children of Paradise*." Dylan said this to Allen Ginsberg in 1977. In 1975, one of his first questions to playwright Sam Shepard when interviewing him as a possible scriptwriter for the film-in-progress was whether Shepard had ever seen *Children of Paradise*.

In autumn 1975, when the footage for *Renaldo & Clara* was shot, mostly in the course of a unique event called "The Rolling Thunder Tour," Bob Dylan was thirty-five years old, and two years into a series of separations from and temporary reunions with his wife (and the mother of his five children) Sara, who is the co-star of *Renaldo & Clara*. He's Renaldo the fox, she's Clara the bright light. In the view of many fans and critics, Dylan's greatest work—albums like *Highway 61 Revisited* (1965) and *Blood on the Tracks* (1975) and songs like "A Hard Rain's A-Gonna Fall" (1963) and "It's Alright, Ma" (1965) and "Visions of Johanna" (1966)—was behind him. The artist's own opinion, however, is clearly (and playfully) stated when the four-hour movie opens with him singing (on stage, wearing a transparent mask) his 1971 song "When I Paint My Masterpiece."

Speaking of Cézanne, as I was a moment ago, the closest Dylan comes to explaining what he means when he praises *Renaldo & Clara* and *Children of Paradise* for "stopping time" is in this comment in a 1978 interview in *Rolling Stone*:

> The movie creates and holds the time. That's what it should do—breathe in that time and stop time in doing that. It's like if you look at a painting by Cézanne, you get lost in that painting for that period of time. And you breathe—yet time is going by and you wouldn't know it, you're spellbound.

So he sees himself as a painter, using modern technology (and his bandleader's ability to lead and inspire other performers during an act of co-creation) to paint a moving picture. And to arrive at this result, he employs the same technique and principle that is at the heart of his success as a songwriter and performer, improvisation. In the end neither Shepard nor Ginsberg, though invited to join the Rolling Thunder Tour and film crew as scriptwriters, wrote dialogue that was used in the film. Instead they and everyone else in the cast of dozens improvised their lines while the camera was running. Ginsberg asked Dylan why he chose to do *Renaldo & Clara* as improvisation. The director replied:

> How else? Life itself is improvised. We don't live life as a scripted thing. Two boxers go into the ring and they improvise. You go make love with someone and you improvise. Go to sports car races, total improvisation. It's obvious everyone was acting in that movie for dear life. Nobody was thinking of time. People were told this, this, this—the rest of it is up to you, what you say in this scene is your business, beyond that the only directions you have are: you're going to die in a year, or see your mother for the first time in 20 years. So far as instructions to actors go, less is more. And I made it clear to the cameraman that it wasn't a documentary, and I told him not to shoot it like that. "Documentary" pretends toward objective reality, this pretends to Truth.

In other words, his film is about subjective reality, the truth of how it feels to be here in these bodies, listening with these ears, seeing with these eyes, thinking with these minds, and feeling with these hearts. Dylan told *Rolling Stone*, "What I'm interested in [as a filmmaker] is the struggle to break down complexity into simplicity." That's evidently what he loves in *Children of Paradise*, whose subjects are love and time and the world as a stage on which we play our parts, clumsily and brilliantly and, often, beautifully. *Renaldo & Clara* deals with the same subjects, and expands the canvas to examine the conflicts between being a lover and being a performer. Sam Shepard, for example, plays the part of a rodeo star who can ride a wild bull but finds it difficult to talk with his woman companion (played by Sara Dylan) about the future of their relationship. The improvised exchanges between men and women throughout the film seem to encourage the viewer to see every "actor" as Renaldo and every "actress" as Clara.

As with *2001*, the movie has no story except the one the observer creates out of what he or she sees and hears and feels while watching, and also as with *2001* it means more when you have watched it more than once. That's also true of Bob Dylan's songs (and William Faulkner's novels). But it shouldn't be a surprise that people who happily listen to a five-minute song over and over are resistant to the idea of watching a four-hour movie again and again in order to heighten one's appreciation of its thematic and musical and visual juxtapositions. It takes a lot of time and effort to make a movie. In this case (and in the case of the three-hour *Children of Paradise*) it takes a lot of time and effort to receive the work of art. We as audiences expect that from high art like Cézanne and Picasso. And we also find it quite natural and very pleasurable to spend a lot of time with favorite works of recorded music. But movies (and plays and musical concerts) are supposed to entertain us in one sitting. *Renaldo & Clara* does, with all its wonderful concert footage of Dylan and others performing on the Rolling Thunder Tour (a rather successful attempt to re-create the unique ambience of the post-Beat pre-Rock live folk music scene Dylan started out in, onstage and offstage). The many improvised vignettes (Ronnie Hawkins as "Bob Dylan" tries to talk Ruth Tyrangiel as a young farm girl into coming on the road with him, while she tries to talk him into coming to the farm to talk to her daddy about this) are also marvelously entertaining on first view. The problems arise when the viewer's expectations that he or she should be able to "understand" what's going on on the screen (like my expectations that I should be able to make sense of section 4 of "The Bear" if I just read slowly enough) start to overwhelm and frustrate him or her. Picasso's cubist paintings, great hits of the century though they may be, were never intended to be appreciated by a mass audience. So no surprise that *Renaldo & Clara* was probably Bob Dylan's "greatest flop" in the course of a career that included much success at reaching a mass audience. In 1974 he sold more tickets to a two-month concert tour than anyone in rock music history before that. But in 1978 his movie was ridiculed by critics and ignored by the public to the point that he had to withdraw it from the market and abandon his plans of making more movies in the future now that he'd found a way to do it that was so satisfying to him as an artist. So you could say that *Renaldo & Clara* is on my list not only because I love it and could watch it happily several times a year for a lifetime, but also because I suspect that a list of Greatest Hits of the Century that doesn't include at least one Greatest Flop is somehow lacking in what Bob Dylan or I would refer to as Truth.

Bob Dylan's 1978 idea that the documentary form actually contradicts or obscures truth by its allegiance to objectivity is not a new notion to the 20th century's world champion surrealist poet. He expressed it in the title of his first film, *Eat the Document,* in 1966. *Renaldo & Clara,* Dylan told me in 1980, was the continuation and completion of the work he and his friend the film editor and director Howard Alk had begun in 1966 when they explored their ideas of what film could be in the course of editing for a television film a batch of documentary footage that had been shot of Dylan and the Band on tour in England in May of that year. As Alk and Dylan would later do when they shot and edited *Renaldo & Clara* together, in 1966 they organized small units of footage by content (i.e., all shots of highways) and (shades of Matisse!) by color. Dylan devised an almost mathematical system for film editing by theme, by number, as though he were composing music or writing rhymed poetry. He has acknowledged the influence of Beat novelist William Burroughs's "cut-up" techniques of constructing narrative. (Maybe a touch of cubism also?) Those 20th-century artists kept experimenting with methods of creating by deconstructing. Probably an anticipation of and early resistance to the coming computer age, in which everything would be cut up and conveyed in tiny, uniform, objectively organized pieces. The artist intuitively fears a fully objective, digitized representation of reality. Dylan, 1978: "What we did was to cut up reality and make it more real."

Jonathan Cott in that 1978 *Rolling Stone* interview astutely noted the relationship between Dylan's approach and aesthetic values and those of the great Russian film pioneer Sergei Eisenstein. Cott: "Eisenstein talked of montage in terms of attraction, shots attracting other shots . . . Eisenstein once wrote: 'The Moscow art is my deadly enemy. It is the exact antithesis of all I'm trying to do. They string their emotions together to give a continuous illusion of reality. I take photographs of reality and cut them up so as to produce emotions.'" Dylan replied with the comment above.

What makes *Renaldo & Clara* a great work is what it does document, its success at portraying the human soul and the human heart, in the musical performances onstage, in the moments of inspired improvised dialogue between two people or among three, in portraits like the long beautiful monologues delivered by songwriter David Blue while playing pinball. This, Dylan states clearly, is the sort of art that deserves to be remembered for centuries, the way this guy talks and tells stories, the look in his eyes, totally private and known only to his friends and acquaintances but just as powerful as Shakespeare or Michelangelo. So Dylan collects for us these beautiful humans and these moments in which they express themselves, including strangers on the street in Harlem baring their beautiful souls to the camera and microphone as they answer the cameraman's questions about the case of imprisoned boxer Hurricane Carter. Dylan the director loves to let people talk and then freeze the shot on their faces in one expressive moment, and hold the shot until we the viewers have had a chance to broaden our knowledge of the human spirit by getting lost in this painting of this man's face.

And then far beyond all these momentary paintings of great beauty and soulfulness, there's the incredible power of the juxtapositions, the songs that play on the soundtrack at the same time that we also hear Allen Ginsberg or Anne Waldman reading poetry and at the same time that we watch and hear the film's characters interact with each other, and best of all the transitions from shot to music, from spoken sentence to burst of music and song lyric. Alk and Dylan spent two years editing *Renaldo & Clara*, and though Alk is dead now both men will live forever (as long as a print of the movie exists) in these cuts and transitions and sound-on-sound-on picture montages, all these glorious expressions of the particular human beings who put these hours and miles of reality back together with so much love and consciousness and humor and enthusiasm and compassion. If you can't find a copy of this film, follow the artist's example and find a way to shoot and edit together and improvise your own home movie telling truths that you know deserve to survive and be shared for centuries to come. Great art begins at home, and your audience, as Matisse would tell you, exists only when you are willing and able to feel their presence and trust the quality of their attention. With that trust, on a good day, you too can stop time.

HIT

18

Gravity's Rainbow
by Thomas Pynchon
(published 1973)

One greatest hit leads to another. In the introduction to *Slow Learner*, a 1984 collection of his early stories, Thomas Pynchon talks about influences on him and other college students at the end of the 1950s (he was born in 1937):

> We were attracted by such centrifugal lures as Norman Mailer's essay "The White Negro," the wide availability of recorded jazz [see entries #6 and #30], and a book I still believe is one of the great American novels, *On the Road* by Jack Kerouac [see #21].
>
> [TP continues] By the time I got back to college [from two years in the Navy], I found academic people deeply alarmed over the cover of the *Evergreen Review* ["a forum for Beat sensibility," in TP's words] then current, not to mention what was inside. It looked as if the attitude of some literary folks toward the Beat generation was the same as that of certain officers on my ship toward Elvis Presley. We were at a transition point, a strange post-Beat passage of cultural time, with our loyalties divided. As bop and rock and roll were to swing music and postwar pop, so was this new writing [see #10] to the more established modernist tra-

dition we were being exposed to then in college. Unfortunately there were no more primary choices for us to make. We were onlookers: the parade had gone by and we were already getting everything secondhand, consumers of what the media of the time were supplying us. This didn't prevent us from adopting Beat postures and props, and eventually as post-Beats coming to see deeper into what, after all, was a sane and decent affirmation of what we all want to believe about American values.

Gravity's Rainbow is a wonderful and strange and very rewarding work of art, but it could not be called a sane and decent affirmation of anything. It doesn't have to be, because, as Pynchon so eloquently acknowledges above, Ginsberg and Kerouac in "Howl" and *On the Road* had already done such a fine job of that and had thereby helped create a cultural and to some extent stylistic jumping-off place for Pynchon and his friend Richard Fariña and of course for Bob Dylan and Patti Smith and the Velvet Underground.

Funny how the entries in this Greatest Hits book are so interconnected. Is that because of the tastes of the listmaker and essayist? Well, partly. But mostly (I insist) it's because things that take place in the same era or in the same transtemporal consciousness zone do tend to turn out to be a lot more interconnected than most of us dare admit to ourselves. And that of course is the primary theme of *Gravity's Rainbow*.

In entry #12, *Old Path White Clouds*, there is a chapter called "Dependent Co-Arising," which tells how two friends who would later be among the Buddha's greatest disciples were enlightened when one of them, Sariputta, saw a monk begging in the city, was immediately drawn by his "relaxed and serene bearing" and asked him for the name of his teacher and if he would share a morsel of his teaching. The monk replied with a brief quote from his teacher, the Buddha: "From interdependent origins all things arise and all things pass away." Sariputta was blown away on the spot, and went home and told his buddy Moggallana. Upon hearing this bit of third-hand teaching, Moggallana "also felt a sudden flash of light illuminate his heart and mind. Suddenly he saw the universe as an interconnected net."

A standard routine in *Gravity's Rainbow* is a bunch of guys (and sometimes gals too) standing around—not actually, but inside their minds, viewpoint mysteriously shifting from one person's extended stream-of-consciousness to another's—trying so hard not to be too paranoid about their paranoia.

> There doesn't exactly dawn, no but there *breaks*, as that light you're afraid will break some night at too deep an hour to explain away—there floods on Enzian what seems to him an extraordinary understanding. This serpentine slag-heap he is just about to ride into now, this ex-refinery, Jamf Ölfabriken Werke AG, *is not a ruin at all. It is in perfect working order.* Only waiting for the right connections to be set up, to be switched on . . . modified, precisely, *deliberately*, by bombing that was never hostile, but part of a plan both sides—*"sides"?*—had always agreed on . . . yes and now what if we—all right, say we *are* supposed to be the Kabbalists out here, say that's our real Destiny, to be the scholar-magicians of the Zone, with somewhere in it a Text, to be picked to pieces, annotated, explicated, and masturbated till it's all squeezed limp of its last drop . . . well we assumed—natürlich!—that this holy text had to be the Rocket . . . What else? Its symmetries, its latencies, the *cuteness* of it enchanted and seduced us while the real Text persisted, somewhere else, in its darkness, our darkness . . . even this far from Südwest [SW Africa, where he and his tribe are from] we are not to be spared the ancient tragedy of lost messages, a curse that will never leave us. . . .
>
> —*Gravity's Rainbow,* p. 606 of the Bantam paperback I bought in 1974 and have now read twice

Two more greatest hits interconnections, please. Is it a coincidence that the closing scenes of *2001* and *Gravity's Rainbow* are, respectively, an infant or homunculus in a tiny, transparent spaceship apparently made of clear plastic, and a boy in a rocket, wrapped in form-fitting almost sentient plastic (the boy, Gott-fried, has been placed there by a mad technologist, German rocket scientist Captain Blicero)? No coincidence. Pynchon was in the midst of writing his huge, ambitious novel when the movie was released . . . and may have been shocked (and even, like one of his characters, frightened) by the resonant similitude between the film's closing shot and what he perhaps already had in mind as the concluding image, plot-twist, revelation of his rocket book.

Second intercon: It is certainly not a coincidence that Pyn-chon's career (and his lasting role as the most beloved-by-critics American experimental novelist of the second half of the 20th century) began with his winning the William Faulkner Founda-tion Award for best first novel of 1963—and that my emotional experiences in the course of rereading *Gravity's Rainbow* these past few weeks have been very similar to my already-recounted experiences rereading "The Bear": agonies of frustration, ecstasies of enthusiasm and self-realization, serious self-questioning as to whether I even *like* now this famous book which I absolutely loved when I first read it (after a few bored, frustrated, doubt-ridden false starts) in 1975. Certainly Faulkner more than any other writer in "the more established modernist tradition" gave Pynchon permission and encouragement to write in the extra-ordinarily lyrical, ambitious, self-indulgent, and difficult manner that he does and still be able to tell himself that what he was working so hard at could indeed be worthy to be considered liter-ature (an important permission, not because TP wanted to please "academic people" but because like all of us he had to address the skeptical critic inside himself).

So do I recommend *Gravity's Rainbow*? Um, you'd better have a lot of time and energy to devote to challenging and rewarding prose (hey, I unambiguously endorse section 4 of "The Bear" as a great experience for a reader who has consciously committed himself to the challenge). And also, you'd better have a strong stomach for descriptions of and allusions to peculiar (perverse? ah, but what does that word *mean*?) sexual activities of all kinds, plus a fair amount of scatology and a huge truckload of dope talk, descriptions of people using all kinds of recreational drugs and evidently enjoying themselves—not a book that's likely to be added to the curriculum of any American high school class in this or any foreseeable century. . . .

Is it a greatest hit of the 20th C? Unquestionably. Is it as good as *Moby-Dick*, as some critics have asserted? I love *MD* more, if I must be forced to make such choices (after all, a primary theme of *GR* is preterition, the condition, much contemplated by our Puritan ancestors, of being passed over, not chosen best in the class or finest of the era or most beloved by the Man in the Sky). And I can imagine more happiness for me stuck on a desert island with Melville's text than Pynchon's (though I'll take both, thank you), just as I am sure there is another Matisse I would choose over *Dance* to be part of the decor in my compartment on the long voyage to a different star system. And so what? What you learn from such choices, perhaps, is something about me, nothing about the artist or the merit of his or her creation.

But difficult choices aside, Thomas Pynchon's *Gravity's Rainbow* is better at what it does than any other book ever written—the runners-up being his two other studies of interconnectedness, *V.* (1963) and *The Crying of Lot 49* (1966)—except that it is done comparably well in the short work of the author who perhaps most inspired Pynchon, Jorge Luis Borges (see entry #32).

And what *GR* does is of tremendous value to us, the collective human consciousness (the art-consumers) of our era. It encourages and enables us to see, with self-conscious humor and awe, the interconnected net and our place in it and the nature of our relationship with our own trembling perception of that net. Most of all, *Gravity's Rainbow* helps us see through the myth of History—it may in fact be the only historical novel (did I mention the setting of the novel is World War II in Europe?) that truly questions our collective and individual relationships with the all-pervasive concept of history. History is a story which in its telling conveys all sorts of subjective information and, usually, propaganda about the way things and events are connected to each other. It isn't truth. We can only begin to know the truth of our own planetary and species history, ancient or recent, when we pierce through our concept of history, and know as we read it that what we're reading is one person's or one huge conspiracy of persons' narrative, necessarily full of assumptions—this is "England," this is "France," this is what category these concepts belong in and this is "time" and this is why what I'm gonna tell you happened between England and France in 1066 is Important—and concepts and implied interconnections and, therefore, misinformation. Usually pernicious misinformation. Small wonder some of us get paranoid. . . .

Although *Gravity's Rainbow* is a historical novel, there are very few historical figures among its cast of thousands. True, Adolf Hitler is spoken of by other characters (but surprisingly seldom). *GR* protagonist Tyrone Slothrop does "maybe even get a glimpse of that President Truman" when he's retrieving a stash of hashish buried on the grounds of the building where Truman, Churchill, and Stalin are having their Potsdam Conference (authentic "historical" event) in 1945. German industrialist Walter Rathenau does speak a few lines in the novel, though only as a disembodied voice from beyond the grave speaking at a séance where he is being consulted. But most of the time the reader, even the most educated and widely read reader, is left wondering whether perhaps there really was a historical Dr. Laszlo Jamf or Major Weissman, possibly under other names. Where does "actual" 20th-century history stop and the inventiveness of Pynchon's novel begin? There really was a Russo-Japanese War, so Tchitcherine's father really could have been a gunner on a boat that stopped in Südwest Afrika on its roundabout journey, making it possible for Tchit's dad to have also fathered Enzian . . . and there really was a Rapallo Treaty in 1922 in which the Tchitcherine that Pynchon's character is "no relation at all to" (p. 393) really did give Walter Rathenau and Germany the opportunity to secretly manufacture weapons in Russia. But you knew that already, right?

The authentic historical figure who comes closest to actually participating in *Gravity's Rainbow* as a fictional character is Malcolm X, known as Red during the part of his life when he encountered Tyrone Slothrop while he (the genuine Red) was working as a shoeshine guy and selling reefers at the Roseland

Ballroom in Boston. This made an impression on me because I also came of age in Cambridge, Massachusetts and used to carry around a blues harmonica I wanted to learn to play, just like Slothrop (well, in a novel with as many sparkling fragments of fine detail as this one, there's bound to be some spooky points of overlap for every reader), and also because, as somebody said, one greatest hit leads to another. And here I am confronted, via Pynchon's clever references to information contained in *The Autobiography of Malcolm X* (as told to Alex Haley, 1964), with an uncomfortable reminder that there are surely many works like this that would have been absolutely perfect for my Top 40 list (in this case, a book that had a huge impact on me when I first read it, arguably one of the most powerful and memorable works of its sort, autobiographies, of our era, and also of course a great essay about being alive in the 20th century) that I've overlooked although I would have included them in a hot minute if I'd just happened to think of them during that forty-eight-hour period when I composed the list like a poem in a muse-driven fury. My own preterites. Passed over by the list-maker. Ouch. And hey, I also missed the chance to give myself an assignment to reread *The Autobiography of Malcolm X* in 1998–99, an opportunity I regret missing as much as I appreciate having tricked myself into finally rereading GR, an item on the back-of-my-mind "to-do" list for more than twenty years. And the moral, ladies and gentlemen, is that the preterites, those who are not chosen, are often as much a part of the interconnected fabric of our being and our conscious-ness as the few who do, by accident or merit, happen to make the lists. So read Malcolm's book if you get a chance. You'll be glad you did. This is a memo to myself.

The most important lists are the unwritten ones that are im-plied (and made necessary) by the posting of other lists. You too, like Pynchon and Kerouac and Ginsberg, can be the champion of those who are passed over, left behind on the rubbish heaps. Just remember that all lists, even your own, have shadow lists. If this is true, how can there possibly be such a thing as objective truth, or history?

HIT 19

Concert Performance by Nusrat Fateh Ali Khan (September 16, 1995)

This time I get to write about a concert I did attend. There can be little argument that Nusrat Fateh Ali Khan of Pakistan (1948–1997) was one of the truly great singers of the 20th century in any form (opera, popular song, or qawwali) and in any language. Few people who care about singing and who are aware of the history of this art form in the 20th century and who have ears to hear the available recordings would deny Nusrat's stature as a great man, great artist, exceptional musician. So it seems eminently reasonable, if one wishes to honor the performing arts, to place one well-executed example of his work in his chosen art form on a greatest-works-of-the-era list. And since it is not easy to determine whether in fact audio or audiovisual recordings of the performing arts can be considered the equivalent (for purposes of making aesthetic judgments) of actually being present at a dance performance or musical concert, it makes sense that the judgment of the singers' live audiences (as individuals and collectively) must be considered by critics and commentators and curriculum committees identifying "great works."

So of course, what is really on my list is "*a* concert by Umm Kulthum," "*a* concert by the Grateful Dead," "*any* concert by Nusrat Fateh Ali Khan." Great hits of the era, indeed. But to mock the fact that critics and art historians must point to particular objects, specific paintings or novels or compositions, I chose for my list a few credible examples of concerts on specific dates by the aforementioned great artists. Concerts which you who are reading these words in another century surely wish you could have been present at. I apologize if I seem to be boasting of my good fortune—but it does seem appropriate to me that one of my selections be a concert I actually experienced directly as an audience member, someone standing or sitting before the performer in the actual time and space in which the work of art was created.

Okay, in order not to get trapped in trying to justify this particular Nusrat Fateh Ali Khan concert as an especially memorable work of art, let me point to the obvious: It is memorable to those of us who were there because we *were* there, and this is the universal rule for the performing arts. And let me repeat and quote what I wrote about this concert back then, in my quarterly music newsletter, shortly after seeing and hearing (and being part of) it:

> Saturday September 16 was a day I'd been looking forward to for weeks. For years—since good friends in Europe introduced me to his music and described the hysteria at his live appearances wherever there are Pakistani immigrants—I have wanted to see Nusrat Fateh Ali Khan in concert as much as I've wanted to see any living performer. And finally my chance came. Nusrat has been called "the Elvis of Pakistan." He's also the inheritor of a long (and sacred) musical tradition called qawwali—Sufi devotional music, "a dominant feature of Indian Islamic culture since the twelfth century." This is truly ecstatic vocal music (accompanied by tablas and harmoniums) about the love of God. Expressing and conveying the love of God.
>
> What can I tell you? If you haven't heard his records yet, he is one of the greatest and most expressive singers now alive on the planet. I would even describe him, if this makes any sense to you, as the person Jerry Lee Lewis and Little Richard have always wanted to be. God's singer. Who has the power to make us feel our oneness with

Divine Spirit by opening his musical mouth. Regardless of one's religious or cultural background. On the Indian sub-continent, he's also loved by Hindus and Sikhs and non-Sufi Muslims. He also, on his albums, speaks directly and convincingly to me of my God, as too few singers ever have. And it makes no difference that I don't speak his verbal language, because his musical language is utterly universal. I'm not talking about theory. I'm talking about ecstatic personal experience. Get yourself a copy of *Shahen-Shah* or any other Nusrat album. You too might find that this is something you've forever waited for.

So we went to the pyramid-shaped basketball arena at Long Beach State College to see and hear the man described on the ticket as "The Great Khan." My anticipation was keen. I really believed in this man's greatness, though I hadn't heard him live yet, and I knew that many others also passionately believe in and recognize him as a great soul, a star of a very special kind . . . I mean just slightly beyond even, say, Willie Mays or Jackie Kennedy in our culture (besides, imagine you were going out tonight to see *Willie Mays* play outfield!) . . . and I knew or expected that many people who felt that strongly would be present at this show tonight.

"Star" is an overused word in our culture, but in a certain context it can be understood to have a spiritual side. Sometimes a mere singer or athlete can shine forth as our brightest embodiment, a king but truly a man of the people. Nusrat is often referred to by his public as "Shahen-shah-e-qawwali" (the brightest-shining star of qawwali). I worried that we'd have trouble meeting up with our friends who had the tickets, not likely, but I mention it as an indication of this inner trembling I felt (something extraordinarily important may be about to happen to me tonight, unless something goes wrong somehow).

We did meet, got inside, and waited in long lines for Indian food being supplied by special concessionaires, because we were hungry but also perhaps because we all collectively knew that we were to begin this evening by eating together. Real (homeland) food. Meanwhile an opening act, maybe an Indian pop singer, was warming us up, but speaking for myself I was impatient. "When do we get to the real stuff? The Man?"

And as my own kind of warmup, while waiting in the curry line, I read to my friends from a xeroxed page of a book called *Qawwali* I'd grabbed from my files as we left the house:

> Like other forms of Islamic vocal meditation, qawwali transports the audience into another plane of consciousness. Regular attenders of qawwali sessions often use the concept of travel when they speak of their experience during a qawwali. They feel as if they are traveling to another domain or plane. The external manifestation of this transportation is the *hál*, literally meaning 'state of mind,' often used to denote musically induced ecstasy. This ecstasy can range from rhythmic moving of the head, dreamy dancing, to such extremes as violent convulsions of the body, depending on the person affected. This musically induced state of ecstasy is closely watched by the qawwal [the singers], who find the combination of music and content responsible for the state, repeating it with increasing intensity until a climax is reached, often creating enough resonance to pull in other members of the audience.

—*Qawwali* by Adam Nayyar, Islamabad 1988

We ate, found our seats on the arena floor, waited through the pop singer and her band, glanced around at the crowd, mostly Indian or Pakistani, some anglos but not many and, mysteriously, almost no college students. And then Nusrat Fateh Ali Khan took the stage with his party, other vocalists, tabla and harmonium players. I was not

disappointed. He sounded good, the sound of his voice
(and of the other occasional lead voice) was familiar to me
from the records, and though I wasn't sure yet that anything remarkable was happening, my feeling was more one
of acceptance, being lulled by the music and believing that
it would catch me up more and more palpably as the
chanted, droning rhythms repeated themselves. I was not
sure what was happening yet, but I believed I'd get to like
it a lot, and it was easy to give myself to the music, though
I wouldn't have called it a trance, yet. Just a warm happy
I'm-hearing-a-good-concert feeling. I wanted to get a little
closer, to see the singers and musicians, especially Nusrat,
more clearly. There were hired security people preventing
audience members from moving from the higher seats to
the floor, but I guessed that I could go forward for a little
while up the side row we were in without being stopped. I
did, and saw the musicians more clearly, and felt like
I brought that image of them back with me to our seats, I
could feel their presence better now. Good singing, good
music, good songs. But not tense. As though it just felt
okay to accept it and enjoy it gradually, naturally. Oh,
those highs and lows, those rhythms, those repetitions, felt
by my body and spirit, not so much thought about by my
mind. It was pleasantly easy to be mindless while grooving
with this performance.

I had heard from friends including one with us who had
attended a Nusrat concert before, that it's common at
these shows for men to rush up and show their enthusiasm
by giving money, currency, to the performer. And I'd heard
descriptions of the excitement of the men taking part, like
girls at a Beatles or Elvis show at the right stage in their
careers, keen in any case, caught in a kind of frenzy. And
I'd been told, maybe by a German friend, that the audience was an important part of the Nusrat experience, in
the right communities. I had the notion before the show
that I might like to do the money ritual if it turned out to

be not too bold or improper for a non-Muslim, and so I made sure to have a number of dollar bills in my wallet. I think I envisioned something like men sticking bills into a belly dancer's costume, or perhaps with more dignity leaving bills at the singer's feet.

It took time (things were building, naturally and wonderfully, with time), but I did see some men make money offerings in the second or third hour of Nusrat's performance, and what they did was shower the performer, tossing the bills into the air in front of him or over his head. I'd got up from my seat again, as the show went on and again it felt like it would feel good to get closer (well, don't I always feel that at a good concert?). I was standing in the side row near the front, and I'd watch the occasional man (once or twice a woman, we'd wondered if it was okay for women to do, but it seemed to be; the women in our party felt underdressed when they saw the great colorful finery the Indian or Pakistani women came in) walk past the front row and over to the floor space before the singer (he kneels or sits cross-legged on the low stage, as do the others) and look at him and then throw money. Nusrat would nod to the person who approached him, thus acknowledging the acknowledgement. I was watching, and an Indian man standing near me said, "Go ahead!" as if my eyes showed clearly that I was considering walking past where we were to the midstage area. I guess I had the bills in my hand, that was the other clue that I was considering it, despite my white skin. So okay (the security hadn't been restricting us at all, us who were standing somewhere near the front). I walked over, and by this time I was happily and naturally dancing, moving back and forth in place like at a Grateful Dead concert, to the unstopping pulse of the music, and that feeling helped take me right to the singer.

I met his eye and threw the bills in the air more or less over him. He nodded slightly to me, still singing, and I (feeling great) continued in the direction I was going, to before-stage-right, intending mostly to head back to my seat and friends, already with some feeling of pleasure at accomplishment (acknowledging and being acknowledged, participating). There were a lot of men standing and dancing, crowding the aisle of the left front section. One man grabbed my hands aggressively and I thought he was like a security guy telling me to go around and not walk down that aisle, but he didn't let go of my hands and in an instant of understanding and acceptance I suddenly realized he was dancing with me, so we danced, held hands and danced together happily. Another man danced with me, and one of them or another threw some bills at me and gestured that I should pick them up. I declined, not knowing if it was wrong to decline, but I was doing fine just doing whatever came naturally to me. People looked at me appreciatively, warmly, I felt good, knowing my own sincerity and enjoying this feeling of freedom and welcome and acceptance as I walked, danced, back to our seats. Before long my girlfriend and a male friend and I went back to that left front corner again and danced in the crowd. It felt great.

And when the four-hour performance (Nusrat and party, not counting the opening act) was done, we just all felt so high [with no alcohol or other intoxicant having been consumed]. People came up to me and said friendly things. At least two men, one in the auditorium and another at a convenience store a mile away, said, "I saw you dancing!!" One man told us with pride and pleasure that Nusrat was from his home town in Pakistan. The excitement of dancing and being danced with and of feeling so accepted and appreciated by the Muslim men and women, was a wonderful high certainly, but for me it was part and parcel with what I was feeling directly from the music. In hindsight, I could say that I did enter a kind of trance, and that it was not alien to me. I recognized it from, say, the Fillmore and Avalon Ballrooms in San Francisco in 1967 when I was 18 or 19. And, thankfully, many other music experiences. I've been similarly transported at a Violent Femmes concert in a club. Reading that trance passage again, now, I recognize more surely than I did then (I didn't want to "try" to have anything happen, just let it take place naturally) that I was in fact in a musically induced ecstasy, encouraged and pushed on by the performer, by each new verse or song, and supported by the friendship of and safe space created by the rest of the audience, all of us in this altered state together. It was absolutely fantastic. Okay, I got treated nice because I was an anglo and because I had so sincerely and genuinely participated (I guess), and that was a wonderful experience for me, but the main thing (and this is the basis of community) was that we had accepted each other. United by our common love. For the singer, for the singing, and for God. Singer as vehicle of God's spirit. And each other as vehicles of the singer's and song's spirit. Yeah. Something like that. We all had such a good time. Because the singing and the music truly were great, fulfilling needs too large for even a long-winded music essayist like me to articulate. Naw. It happened. Great good fortune. Just a matter of being here now. What else could be the secret of the live music experience?

I don't know. But I gotta tell you, it gets easier with practice. But at the same time there's something holy about being a beginner, as I was a beginner that evening in Nusrat's audience. Zen mind, beginner's mind. Different tradition. But the same ancient wisdom. Love of God. Love of music. Spontaneity. We don't have to be so afraid of these things. And I think of Patti Smith [at a club performance a week earlier—see entry #24] even sharing with us, from her experience, that we also don't have to be so afraid of death and loss. Love of life. What a teaching. Gosh, the things you can learn at a concert! School of love, school of awakening, school of community, and refreshing fountain of courage and health and spirit. Drink deep. That's what I've been doing. Who needs to drink spirits? I mean, it's okay, but for me drinking music is like drinking Spirit itself. And I sure have some great adventures. I'd like to thank the music for constantly calling out to me and getting me into these situations. I can't help it if I'm lucky. . . .

HIT 20

The Anatomy of Dependence
by Takeo Doi, M.D.
(published 1971)

This is a book of transcultural psychology by a Japanese psychologist. Its original title was *Amae no Kozo*, which means "the structure of *amae*" (pronounced *ah-ma-eh* or *ah-my-ay*). In 1968 I attended a lecture by Jorge Luis Borges (see entry #32) in which he said that as he grew older his ambition was to say more by writing less; he felt that if one really progresses as a writer he should be able someday to express everything in one sentence. And then perhaps, some fine day, in one word. This memory of that wonderful man talking to us in a room in New York City comes back to me now because *The Anatomy of Dependence* is on my list of the 20th century's greatest hits because it is an essay that succeeds ultimately at one simple and momentous task: introducing the non-Japanese reader to a single word, a word which, once you have read all the supporting text explicating and illuminating its usage and context, does indeed come to hold as much relevance and depth of feeling and insight into human nature as any poem or story or novel. All in one word.

A word that could change the world forever, and, I believe, for the better, if it could only find its way into all, or many, other human languages. What a legacy for the 20th century, if this should someday come to pass: "Oh yes, that was when Dr. Doi gave us *amaeru*!"

Amae is the noun, *amaeru* is the verb. I complicate things by mentioning the verb form because I believe the world of *amae* becomes recognizable to the non-Japanese reader as his or her (and everyone's) world only when he or she grasps what it means to *amaeru*.

I'll give a simple example that might be familiar to most of us. A married couple or two lovers who live together are at home and one of them is lying on a sofa on a rainy day, snug and warm and comfortable, and he says to his partner, in a funny, sweet, childlike voice, "Honey, do you think you could find my reading glasses for me?" It's an unreasonable request, he could easily get up and do it himself, but he doesn't want to disturb the comfortable nest he's made on the sofa, and because he knows it's unreasonable he does something funny to his voice to signal that he's asking a special favor that he could only ask of someone who loves him (or her) so much she or he is willing to be indulgent. Dear reader, isn't this familiar from your own life? In certain situations you find yourself screwing your voice up in a peculiar, private way, without thinking about it, because that's the way you've always talked when you want your mother, or in this case your living partner, to indulge you, to grant you a special unearned permission or kindness. That's called *amaeru*-ing. "Honey, I wouldn't ask this of you if I wasn't so sure of and grateful for your love. Won't you please spoil me tonight?"

To *amaeru* to someone means to indicate to them, verbally or silently, that you want them to indulge you or "spoil" you (in the American sense of "spoiling," i.e. indulging, a child).

Dr. Doi argues convincingly that *amae* feelings, and the concept of *amae* which is central to so many Japanese words and expressions, originate with the infant's feelings toward his or her mother—the feeling of security and well-being that comes from being loved and cared for unconditionally, just because you exist and are in a relationship with this being who is (almost) always there for you.

This book seems to me as important as the major works and insights of such turn-of-the-century authors as Freud and Jung, because once one recognizes the existence of *amae* in all human cultures and the universal wish to *amaeru*, one immediately has a matrix in which a great variety of common emotional circumstances and disturbances become more comprehensible and can be more easily described and responded to.

In entry #29, *God Bless You, Mr. Rosewater*, Kurt Vonnegut, Jr., observes that what science fiction stories and pornography have in common is "fantasies of an impossibly hospitable world." This is a helpful insight into the appeal science fiction has for its readers, and it is also a helpful phrase for understanding or recognizing the *amae*-related longings that are normal for most adults. We want to get back, not to the womb, but to the playpen, where someone will eventually pick us up if we're unhappy or bored or just wanting some friendly attention. Who among us doesn't sometimes find himself or herself longing for the world to be more hospitable? When we communicate that longing, usually to someone we trust or would like to be able to trust, we are *amaeruing*.

The frustrated desire to *amaeru* is a powerful force in many of our lives, but one that can only be talked about directly in Japanese, because, as Doi points out, there is no word for *amae* in English or any other language. The translated title *The Anatomy of Dependence* is not quite right, because the original title in Japanese is "The Structure of *Amae*," and *amae* is not dependence. The flavor of the two words in their respective languages is very different. Doi tells us how one of his patients gave him his first hint that *amae* could be considered a Japanese ideology in the modern sense of ideology as "a set of ideas, or leading concept, that forms the actual or potential basis for a whole social system":

> Not long after the patient's treatment had begun, he acquired a new awareness of his own desire to depend on others, and said one day: "When people are children, they depend on their parents, and when they grow up they begin to depend on themselves. Most normal people are the same, I'm sure, but I seem to have gone astray somewhere. I want to depend, but nobody lets me. For the past

six months or so, I've been wishing I had someone to act as a mother to me. Someone I could confide anything to, someone who'd take decisions out of my hands. But when you think about it, though that might be all right for me, it would be no fun for the other person. It's the same with you, doctor—I've just been using you lately to unload my gripes on."

Amae is not dependence but the desire to be loved, to feel free to depend on, lean on, another person or a group of people. Even the spiritual desire to depend on God or on the universe is a kind of *amae*, often frustrated by the feeling or the fear that God or the universe doesn't love me, I'm not worthy. What makes the Japanese different is not just that they have a word for it but that they are aware that this need to be loved unconditionally is normal, is a feeling or a set of feelings most adults (including, as Doi demonstrates, characters in novels) experience. Thus the great importance to the Japanese of the group (of friends, of family, of coworkers)—within the group the individual has a freedom (slightly different from Western concepts of individual freedom) to indulge himself or to act in a childlike or dependent manner or to ask or expect to be indulged. The individual can *amaeru* within the group that he belongs to, that has accepted and embraced him. Outside the group, something is missing.

Amae no Kozo was a best-seller (a big hit) in Japan in 1971, but its intended audience seems also to be outsiders, the rest of the world, members of other cultural groups. It is included on my Greatest Hits list as an act of advocacy, because I believe a keener awareness and wider discussion of the issues this book calls our attention to could be of great value in furthering the growth of human self-awareness, which I understand to be the purpose of psychology and philosophy and spiritual study. I like to imagine a future world in which the Universal Declaration of Human Rights and the Wilhelm/Baynes translation of the *I Ching* and Takeo Doi's introduction to the psychology of *amae* will be regarded as great accomplishments of our era. Along with Thich Nhat Hanh's modern retelling of the Buddha's story, and the music of Umm Kulthum and the Beatles, and the paintings of Matisse and Picasso. Great moments in the history of the evolution of our collective consciousness, obvious in hindsight in this future world I imagine in which every one of these hits has had a very palpable impact on later generations of artists, healers, leaders, and visionaries and, by way of them, on all the rest of us.

HIT 21

On the Road
by Jack Kerouac
(published 1957)

At the beginning of the 1998 movie *Kundun* (entry #38 in this book), a man is searching among the young children of Tibetan peasant families for the spirit of an ancient holy person (the immortal Dalai Lama of Tibet) reborn in our era. I wasn't searching—I was just sitting down to read again a beloved novel because a year ago I happened to include it on the list of 20th-century treasures I would celebrate in this book-length essay—but I have to report that I've "found" two old souls of great significance to two still-prominent spiritual traditions, present before my eyes and ears and heart and mind as I devoured again this exquisite tale of two young male friends, kind of like Butch Cassidy and the Sundance Kid or Roland and Oliver. A buddy story for the mid-20th century (you know, back when there were cars and roads). Two fictional characters vibrantly brought to life by a young novelist—both of them, as most of *On the Road*'s readers know, authentic historical figures who actually lived and did all this stuff a few years before *On the Road* (an autobiographical novel) was written and eventually published. Neal Cassady ("Dean Moriarty" in the novel) and Jack Kerouac ("Sal Paradise" in the novel). Ladies and gentlemen, the 20th century is proud to present, live in concert, this lifetime, tonight, the entities formerly known as St. Francis and Ananda Sakyamuni!

I was first struck by the uncanny resemblance between the characters and essential natures of Francis of Assisi and Dean Moriarty twenty-nine years ago, when I read *On the Road* for the first time (it was much too late for it to have a "bad" influence on me, I had already hitchhiked as much as two thousand miles in a two-week stretch, Boston to southern Wisconsin and back) the same year that I also happened to read G. K. Chesterton's delightful biography/book-length essay *St. Francis of Assisi*. Both Kerouac's Dean and Chesterton's Francis reminded me constantly of a good friend of mine who would swing through long manic cycles and spread lots of joy and cause lots of trouble (and break many promises) in surprisingly brief and surprisingly sustained bursts of energy. One day he was borrowing your car to pick up some sodas for the party, two days later he was calling collect from another state. Of course, the reader may wonder what such a fellow could possibly have in common with gentle, saintly, animal-loving Francis of Assisi? Read Chesterton's book! Or read Bonaventure or Celano or any of the classic biographies of Francis that Chesterton based his portrait on, with the thought in the back of your mind that this man you're reading about who had such an extraordinary effect on the people around him in his small town and everywhere he traveled in 1212, and who launched such a large number of enthusiastic enterprises, could possibly have been of the same personality type as the charming and untameable Dean Moriarty. Letting go of any judgments about whether that's "good" or "bad." Read these two texts (Chesterton and Kerouac) and marvel, as Dean and Sal and Francis and the Buddha did, at the wondrous nature of human beings and this human world we find ourselves in. And try to restrain yourself, after you read, from impulsively zooming off to try to convert the Sheikh of Araby or otherwise work miracles at the other end of the highway. . . .

Who's this other reincarnated spirit I claim to have found in the front seat of this great American novel? He's a character from entry #12, *Old Path White Clouds*. Ananda was the Buddha's closest companion, his personal attendant, the cousin/disciple to whom we owe every one of the Buddha's sutras, because they were talks the Buddha gave and Ananda is the freak who remembered 'em all word for word so they could be memorized by other students or, later, written down. Allen Ginsberg wrote an essay in 1972 in which he referred to Kerouac as "The Great Rememberer." Elsewhere (in the dedication to "Howl") Allen called Jack "the new Buddha of American prose." But I propose to you that, although the number of spontaneous comments and insights in *On the Road* that precisely articulate the Buddha's more advanced teachings is startling (all written several years before Kerouac first encountered Buddhist writings), and although there is certainly therefore reason enough to imagine the narrator of the book is Buddha reborn, I propose to you instead that the man Ginsberg called "The Great Rememberer" was more likely, if such things actually occur, the 1922–1969 incarnation of Ananda Sakyamuni, of whom (Thich Nhat Hanh tells us) it was said: "Ananda has the finest memory among us. No one else possesses his uncanny ability to remember every word the Buddha speaks. He can repeat the Buddha's discourses without leaving out one word." Like Sal for Dean. Okay, in a few cases Jack the author is quoting Neal the avatar so accurately because he's borrowing sentences or paragraphs from letters Cassady had sent him between road trips; but mostly the extraordinary Dean monologues are right out of Sal's astonishing memory banks, fueled by Benzedrine when he wrote the notorious "roll version" of *On the Road*.

   Is a rememberer a spiritual teacher? Not necessarily; in fact in *Old Path White Clouds* we are told that after the Buddha died, Ananda was having such a hard time coping with the loss that the Buddha's dharma heir, Mahakassapa, threatened to bar him from an important gathering because he had not yet attained true realization. After all those years so close to the Buddha! But Ananda responded to Mahakassapa's challenge appropriately; he didn't get mad, he meditated for three days and at the last moment (as his back touched his sleeping mat to rest) he attained the Great Awakening. So until then he was a rememberer but not a teacher. Is a rememberer a novelist? A fine question, which this masterpiece of Mr. Kerouac's raised and which was later taken up by Norman Mailer and Tom Wolfe and other blurrers of journalism and fiction. But although I consider *On the Road* a great novel, easily and obviously comparable to *The Adventures of Huckleberry Finn* (hey, Mark Twain fooled with those journalism/fiction boundaries himself!—it's an American tradition), my simple answer to any critic or scholar who is dubious that such an honest and factual autobiographical account can be properly called "fiction" is: *On the Road*, whether it fits your concept of a "novel" or not, is without any doubt one of the finer poems of the 20th century—possibly in any language.

I love this book. Rereading it at age fifty just now I found it as rewarding and nourishing and aesthetically pleasing as I did at age twenty-one. It's a poem because of its meter, its rhythm, its simplicity and clarity and the beauty of its singing. Before returning to this question of the true identities of Dean and Sal, I'd like to share with you what I've been able to piece together about the circumstances of the composition of *On the Road*. Yes, it was written on a roll of paper. No, it was not left completely unrevised according to the Kerouac theory of spontaneous writing (that theory came later). Yes, it was the product of a series of vectors or circumstances that wouldn't necessarily come together again, for Jack Kerouac or anyone. Just like the Beatles' job was to show up at the right time and be themselves, Jack (or Ananda) had a similar assignment. He did it well. Of course, Jack, since he died unhappily of his alcoholism, cannot be said to have attained the Great Awakening this time around. But he did shout out this book/poem, mostly in 1951 though it wasn't finished or published till 1957, and for that we owe him much gratitude.

On the Road takes place in North America (New York City, Denver, San Francisco, Mexico City, and the roads and towns between those places) from the end of 1946 to the beginning of 1951. Most of the novel as we know it was written April 2–22, 1951, in Manhattan, barely two months from the living of the novel's last scene. Kerouac typed it single-spaced without paragraphs (all one huge nonstop paragraph) on long sheets of paper that he'd taped together to form a roll so he'd never have to pause to put a new page in the typewriter. He was under the influence of amphetamine (Benzedrine), as Philip K. Dick was when he wrote *Martian Time-Slip* and most of his other books. He was also under the influence of Neal Cassady (as Sal is in various ways throughout the novel), because a month before Neal had sent Jack and Allen a forty-thousand-word letter telling the story of his relationship with a woman in Denver in a nonstop, breathless style, written in three Benzedrine-filled evenings. Kerouac biographer Dennis McNally says: "To Jack it was a godsend, a click of recognition in his inner ear that told him that *this* was the way to tell a story—just spontaneously tell it, allow it to flow out, assume its own shape, to use the infinite accretion of details as a form itself." Another influence on Jack—who'd been trying for two years to write a novel with the working title "On the Road," and was still dissatisfied with the approaches and styles he'd attempted—was reading the manuscripts of his friend William Burroughs's first-person autobiographical narratives *Junkie* and *Queer*.

Kerouac unwisely or self-destructively scared the editor who'd published his first, more conventional novel by bringing the unparagraphed novel-on-a-roll into the man's office and asking him to buy it, in May 1951. By October the first very minor revisions on the manuscript were made, as Kerouac began typing it onto single sheets of paper, adding paragraphs and changing the names of the characters and cutting or changing a word or a sentence here and there. Probably it was at this point that he started inserting sentences from Neal's letters as dialogue or monologue spoken by Dean and recalled by narrator Sal. It seems unlikely that the guy who was rapping out a story of four years of cross-country travels so intently that he didn't want to have to pause to put paper in the typewriter would have stopped to search his own journal entries or his friend's letters for raw material . . . so much easier to just narrate from memory, go with what comes into your mind as you're talking. Later, however, those sources would be invaluable for fixing up perceived gaps or weaknesses in the narrative.

The manuscript, even in non-roll form, was rejected by publisher after publisher until finally after five years Jack's champion Malcolm Cowley (who'd edited *The Portable Faulkner*, see entry

#16) convinced Viking Press to formally accept the novel. A few more minor revisions were made by the author and by anonymous copy editors, and a version of *On the Road* very similar to the early '51 "roll version" was published in September 1957. It was also very different from the replacement book about Neal, *Visions of Cody*, that Kerouac had written and assembled because he'd lost all hope that *On the Road* would ever be accepted and anyway was no longer so sure himself that he'd found the right way to tell the story.

My inquiry into the details of this process convinces me that we're actually very lucky that the book as we know it did somehow survive and eventually get published (made available to us, the public) in this form. Coulda easily never happened. The poor book was heavily buffeted by the publishing world's skepticism and the author's disappointment and self-doubts. But as Dean often exclaims in the course of the story, "Look here, we all must admit that everything is fine and there's no need in the world to worry. . . ." In part two, chapter 6, he goes on to exhort:

> "Listen will you to this old tenorman blow his top"—he shot up the radio volume till the car shuddered—"and listen to him tell the story and put down true relaxation and knowledge."

This is the voice of the Buddha, or of St. Francis, or of Jack's lost brother Gerard—who Jack thought might have come back as Neal since Gerard died the year Neal (who was five years younger than Jack) was born, and whom Jack thought of as a saint; indeed in Jack's mind, McNally tells us, "Gerard was St. Francis of Assisi as well, gifted with an almost supernaturally tender love for all living creatures"—the voice of Dean Moriarty reassuring Sal Paradise in paradise or nirvana that he did in fact succeed at his ambition of becoming a great writer worthy of comparison to Lester Young and Sal and Dean's other favorite improvisational music makers. Amen. Read *On the Road*, friends, and listen to this young/old tenorman blow his top.

It's not just a book about lifestyle, though that is its well-earned reputation. It's also a book about "the problems of the human heart in conflict with itself which alone can make good writing," to quote the Nobel Prize speech that Jack's friend Malcolm's friend William Faulkner delivered just four months before this twenty-nine-year-novelist blew his top on the roll he'd taped together out of Chinese paper left behind by the former occupant of his apartment.

There's a lot more to the story and essential nature of St. Francis than his tender love for birds and all living creatures, and the more one learns about Francis the more strikingly he resembles Neal Cassady as vividly portrayed in *On the Road,* and vice versa. To start with, of course, Kerouac's novel makes the point in nearly all of its little chapters that the essence of Dean Moriarty is his extraordinary and inspiring (so people want to follow him, want to share his vow of poverty and roam the countryside with him) tender love for all living creatures, particularly human beings of all ages and sexes and races and cultures. His *Enthousiasmos.*

From *St. Francis of Assisi* by G. K. Chesterton:

How early the plan [launching a Merry Prankster–like movement of peripatetic God-intoxicated monastics] appeared in Francis's own mind it is of course impossible to say; but on the face of events it first takes the form of a few friends who attached themselves to him one by one because they shared his own passion for simplicity.

More Chesterton on Francis:

He swore before God that he would never all his life refuse help to a poor man. . . . Never was any man so little afraid of his own promises. His life was one riot of rash vows, of rash vows that turned out right. . . . Over and above his main ambition to win fame as a French poet, he would seem to have most often thought of winning fame as a soldier. He was born kind; he was brave in the normal boyish fashion; but he drew the line both in kindness and bravery pretty well where most boys would have drawn it. . . . He had the love of gay and bright apparel which was inherent in the heraldic taste of medieval times and seems altogether to have been rather a festive figure. If he did not paint the town red, he would probably have preferred to paint it all the colors of the rainbow. . . .

[Regarding a story of young Francis chasing after a beggar:] In this there are certain notes of his natural individuality that must be assumed from first to last. For instance, there is the spirit of swiftness. In a sense he continued running for the rest of his life, as he ran after the beggar. Because nearly all the errands he ran on were errands of mercy, there appeared in his portraiture a mere element of mildness which was true in the truest sense, but is easily misunderstood. A certain precipitancy was the very poise of his soul. This saint should be represented as angels were sometimes represented in pictures, with flying feet or even with feathers. . . . With all his gentleness, there was originally something of impatience in his impetuosity. . . . Some might call him a madman, but he was the very reverse of a dreamer . . . he was very emphatically a man of action. At every turn of his extraordinary career we shall find him flinging himself round corners in the most unexpected fashion. . . .

Francis was one of those people who are popular with everybody . . . a sort of romantic ringleader among the young men of the town.

Francis had all his life a great liking for people who had been put hopelessly in the wrong.

On the Road, Part Three, chapter 3:

"I think Marylou was very, very wise leaving you, Dean," said Galatea. "For years now you haven't had any sense of responsibility for anyone. You've done so many awful things I don't know what to say to you."

And in fact that was the point, and they all sat around looking at Dean with lowered and hating eyes, and he stood on the carpet in the middle of them and giggled—he just giggled. He made a little dance. I suddenly realized that Dean, by virtue of his enormous series of sins, was becoming the Idiot, the Imbecile, the Saint of the lot.

"You have absolutely no regard for anybody but yourself and your damned kicks. Not only that but you're silly about it. It never occurs to you that life is serious and there are people trying to make something decent out of it instead of just goofing all the time."

That's what Dean was, the HOLY GOOF.

I longed to go and put my arm around Dean and say, Now look here, all of you, remember just one thing: this guy has his troubles too, and another thing, he never complains and he's given all of you a damned good time just being himself, and if that isn't enough for you then send him to the firing squad, that's apparently what you're itching to do anyway. . . .

Chesterton, *St. Francis of Assisi*, chapter V:

It was a solid, objective fact, like the stones in the road, that he had made a fool of himself. He saw himself as an object, very small and distinct like a fly walking on a clear window pane; and it was unmistakably a fool. And as he stared at the word "fool" written in luminous letters before him, the word itself began to shine and change. . . . When Francis came forth from his cave of vision, he was wearing the same word "fool" as a feather in his cap; as a crest or even a crown. He would go on being a fool; he would become more and more of a fool; he would be the court fool of the King of Paradise.

Near the end of Kerouac's novel *Desolation Angels*, his friend Cody (Neal) shows up unexpectedly just as Jack is opening a box containing the first copies he's seen of their book *On the Road*, and Jack sees a mysterious golden light surrounding the man. "I don't even know what it means, unless it means that Cody is actually some kind of angel or archangel come down to this world and I recognize it. A fine thing to say in this day and age! And especially with the wild life he was now leading. . . ."

A-ha, Jack, I recognize both of you! In Thich Nhat Hanh's *Old Path White Clouds*, the character of Ananda is distinguished by his loyalty to his master and also by his self-doubts and his great fear of being misunderstood, and a sort of reluctance to act that arises in him when he's asked to be the Buddha's attendant, a great bashfulness very reminiscent of Sal Paradise's character as sketched by nonstop typist Jack Kerouac. *On the Road*, Part One, Chapter 1: "I shambled after as I've been doing all my life after people who interest me, because the only people for me are the mad ones, the ones who are mad to live, mad to talk, mad to be saved, desirous of everything at the same time, the ones who never yawn or say a commonplace thing, but burn, burn, burn like fabulous yellow roman candles exploding like spiders across the stars. . . ." Other intriguing Sal Paradise comments from the same little chapter: "Dean reminded me of some long-lost brother." "Dean just raced in society. . . ." "A western kinsman of the sun, Dean."

Ihave a friend, an Italian publisher, whose father first became famous (and wealthy) by publishing a novel by an obscure Russian poet that became an extraordinary popular success around the world: *Doctor Zhivago* by Boris Pasternak. Pasternak couldn't find a Russian publisher, but Giangiacomo Feltrinelli's belief in the book quickly led to editions in eighteen different nations and languages and a sudden Nobel Prize (a year after first publication) and—getting to the point of why I've raised the subject—enormous spontaneous public enthusiasm and interest, across languages and cultures. As in the case of the Beatles and *Winnie-the-Pooh*. Why does that happen? It isn't just a matter of striking the universal chord, but also, I'm certain, of good timing. A "hit" in pop music is always the right song, the right feeling, the right message, the right public image, etc., at the right moment. The world didn't know it, but it was very ready to respond to just this sort of story from a writer whose situation in relationship to the present Soviet government was like this guy's. The moment was right for *Dr. Z.*

That was 1957. Seven years later, another Italian entrepreneur with an enthusiasm for the arts had another very surprising (though hardly as noble) global "hit," as a result of extraordinary response from the public all over Europe and Asia and Africa and the Americas to a low-budget film he hired a young di-

HIT

22

For a Few Dollars More

by *Sergio Leone*

(filmed summer 1965)

rector to shoot for him. That film was *A Fistful of Dollars* (1964), the first spaghetti western (or the first to become a huge international hit), and the entrepreneur was Arrighi Columbo and the director Sergio Leone (thirty-five years old).

For a Few Dollars More was the "sequel," the second world-famous spaghetti western starring young American "discovery" Clint Eastwood as "The Man with No Name." It's in this book because it's been one of my favorite movies since I first saw it and *Fistful* in 1971 (both films were first released in the United States in 1967, after they had already had enormous popular success in most of the rest of the world). This is what I put in my time capsule because this is what I want from a movie:

Great music, great faces, incredible landscapes, breathtaking intelligence in the timing and the camerawork and the story-telling, flattering the watcher's mind and his aesthetic senses and tastes. Juxtapositions of sights and sounds that challenge and awaken and linger. Story? Well, of course I like a good story (see entry #31, *Stranger in a Strange Land*). But I admit that I'm a funny kind of moviegoer who doesn't mind a relatively superficial chess-game-like plot line as long as it mainly serves to engage my attention while I'm being bathed in all this superb aural and visual music, this dance of sounds and men's eyes and terrain. Yeah, I do delight in the stories *For a Few Dollars More* tells me, over and over as I watch it again and again, but those stories are communicated to me by the music and the direction, so that the two-hour movie is actually for me a series of two-minute vignettes (like *Renaldo & Clara,* but see, everybody has their aesthetic predilections in any art form, and these are the sorts of movies I like, so I'm bound to argue for them as greatest-hits-of-the-century contenders). The big story—this guy gets killed eventually and these two guys survive, the older one gets even and the younger one gets rich—is of no consequence. But the tiny stories, even looks exchanged between strangers on a train, are full of mysterious but very gratifying profundity. Especially the stories told by Ennio Morricone's music in tandem with Sergio Leone's directing and editing. Wow. Morricone alone doesn't equal the drama and profundity and pleasure-giving of Beethoven, but

Morricone together with Leone is a genuine example of multimedia art worthy of comparison with Ludwig's greater hits.

As for that enormous spontaneous global audience response to this film and its predecessor the previous year . . . it was a happy surprise to everyone involved (as *Zhivago* no doubt was to Feltrinelli and Pasternak). Leone and Morricone were the same age and had known each other as children, but had never worked together before. They were both relative novices at their jobs, had only been making or scoring films for about three years each. Clint Eastwood was two years younger (thirty-three when *A Fistful of Dollars* was made) and hadn't starred in a movie before. He had a little film experience and a regular job as the second lead in an American television series, but when he agreed to spend six weeks playing the hero in this low-budget western to be shot in Spain by an Italian director, he had no reason to suppose that in addition to his $15,000 fee he would receive worldwide celebrity and, as a result, millions of dollars and a career as an actor that would last for the rest of the century, and a public image that would always to some extent refer back to the way he presented himself or was presented in these "Man with No Name" films.

What was the artist's intent? Leone wasn't trying to make a hit, and as far as we know didn't have a message he consciously wished to impart to the young moviegoers of Europe and the rest of the world. He was following his Muse. He followed her very well. These two films are inspired works of art. But does that have anything to do with their huge success? Good question to provoke a late-night argument or discussion in an urban bar or coffee shop. Do great art and great popularity have anything to do with each other? When they intersect, as in the case of Dickens or Bob Dylan or Picasso or Jack Kerouac's brief and agonized celebrity, is it always just a lucky or unlucky accident? Is there cause and effect ("Hey, these Beatles guys are geniuses and will probably change the world, so how about giving them a recording contract?") or just rolls of the dice? Do Mortimer (Lee Van Cleef) and Manco (Eastwood) survive because they have outthought Indio, or just because they're not smoking dope all the time like he is and aren't quite as treacherous to their friends and associates (if any)? The Eastwood character is definitely *cool* (ask any audience member on any continent). Colonel Mortimer is pretty damn cool too in his own way. Does that have anything to do with their "victory"? Over the audience, yes; over Indio, probably not. But enough philosophizing. . . .

A few helpful clues to the director/auteur's intent, found on the Internet—where all knowledge (a modern Library of Alexandria) is cross-indexed today—from Cenk Kiral (Turkey)'s 1998 interview with Christopher Frayling (England, author of a new biography of Sergio Leone):

> All of Leone's films are about a European's relations with the American dream. He grew up in the late 1930s, and for him American movies were like a religion. He grew up watching gangster films. The films he particularly remembers seeing were the films of James Cagney, Edward G. Robinson, Humphrey Bogart, and westerns of the late '30s like the films of John Ford and many others. Then these films were banned under Mussolini's regime . . . and became even more magical.
>
> In 1944 the allied armies came to southern Italy. That was young Sergio's first encounter with real life Americans. . . . He said to me that he got very confused because they (American soldiers) weren't like the heroes in the movies, or like the heroes in the books. . . . From then on he had this double attitude towards America. He loved it but he also hated it.
>
> What he wanted to do is to make films that recapture that magic that he was feeling when he was a child, with big music, big action with an almost childlike view of the world. . . . And at the same time, the theme is that 'none of these myths are true.' . . .
>
> Leone loved paintings. He was a collector of paintings. . . . He showed his cameraman the paintings and engravings of Rembrandt before shooting *Once Upon a Time in the West*. The monochrome darkness and portraits

of faces. . . . Rembrandt invented the physiological portrait. In that film you can read the person's history on his
face.

Elsewhere on the Internet, John Nudge (USA, I think)
describes *A Fistful of Dollars* as "What was essentially supposed to
be a throw-away film. This violent, cynical and visually stunning
film introduced The Man With No Name, the anti-heroic gun-
slinger for whom money is the only motivation and the villains
are merely obstacles to be removed. Leone's unique style, artistic
camera angles, extension of time and raw, explosive violence presented a skewed view of the West, making his film different from
any Western that had come before. Critics panned it for its brutal
depiction of an unromantic West, but audiences loved it. . . ."

When I fell in love with Sergio Leone's movies in 1971 (especially *For a Few Dollars More* because of that music box pocket
watch, and the way little bits of music tied everything together,
and the faces of the bandits), I was at war with America myself,
on my way back to the U.S. East Coast from a wilderness com-
mune in western Canada, where some of us were draft dodgers
but all (even the Canadians) thought of ourselves as deserters
from a corrupting civilization and economic system—we wanted
to prove that individual North Americans could live completely
self-sufficiently and therefore independent of the Central Econ-
omy. I don't remember seeing these movies or the Eastwood persona as having anything to do with our struggle with Amerika. I
just knew that they were not the kind of film I thought I would
ever like or be interested in, but a fellow communard dragged me
to the theater and it was love at first sight and listen. Something
connected. In almost every frame, and certainly in every fifteen
seconds of music, to the point where even the silent moments in
the film were full of drama because I'd hear the absence of the ongoing musical commentary and it would speak to me and give me
gooseflesh.

So how did the Eastwood character, who is called Joe in the
first film and Manco in the second, get almost immediately identified as "The Man with No Name?" A movie poster? I don't

know. And how did the artistry of this director and this composer and this cameraman and these actors combine to cause viewers all over the third world (and second, and first) to feel instantly and with great satisfaction that these "Dollars" movies and the faces of these actors/heroes were an expression of their most urgent and perhaps unspoken passions? So much so that Clint's face itself, like John Kennedy's a few years earlier in the decade, became an icon uniting the Earth's scattered individuals? An "antihero" icon, whatever that may mean. Good riddles to chew on. It will be interesting to see how the universal "man on the street" responds to a videocassette or floppy disk of *For a Few Dollars More* in 2171. When we don't know why a piece of art works its magic on us and others at its birthing moment, it's hard to guess whether that power and impact will endure into other centuries. But if I were a betting man, I'd bet that this portrait of man versus man or versus himself in a beautiful and brutal universe that is and is not of his own creation will endure and will still speak powerfully to people years from now of a mythical, romantic, and antiromantic borderland on the edges of New Mexico and Texas and old Mexico—somewhere in the badlands of Sol III—inhabited by Clint Eastwood and Lee Van Cleef and Gian Maria Volonte and whatever these archetypes evoke in us, a mythical realm probably slightly different to every viewer from every life-situation . . . but always evocative. I'm also certain this music will cause powerful physical/emotional responses in viewer-listeners for centuries without end, as long as the Library of Ancient Pop Culture and the hardware to decode it aren't destroyed by the Barbarians. . . .

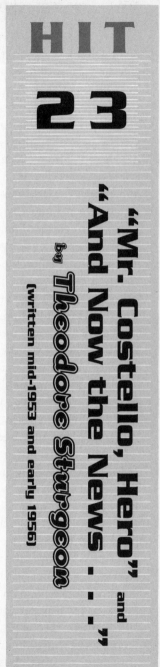

HIT 23

"Mr. Costello, Hero" and "And Now the News . . ."

by Theodore Sturgeon

(written mid-1953 and early 1956)

I think the corpus of Sturgeon's stories ranks with de Maupassant's. I think it is superior to O. Henry's, superior to Damon Runyon's, superior to Ring Lardner's, you know, the great short story writers of . . . I think it is superior to Hemingway's short stories (if you take the Hemingway novels, you may be into something else). I think one is dealing with a writer of that stature. To the extent that the short story is an art, Sturgeon is the American short story writer. The fact that he happens to be writing in science fiction is a glorious accident.
—Samuel R. Delany (1975)

I include these two stories by Theodore Sturgeon on my list of the 20th century's greatest aesthetic hits because I am absolutely sure that my friend Mr. Delany ("one of science fiction's most important writers and critics," according to the *New York Times Book Review*, 1995) is right in his assessment of this particular author's role in his nation's literary and cultural history. If *the* American short story writer of all time so far lived and worked in the 20th century, often not unreasonably called "the American century," then it follows that he belongs on any such list as surely as Faulkner or Joyce, even if he's not yet been officially embraced by all the "literary" poohbahs.

The important thing, anyway, is not how he gets ranked by the poohbahs or me or anyone. The important thing, if he really is as superlative at his craft as Delany and I believe, is that readers get the news. Paintings are to be looked at; stories are to be read and heard. The purpose of a century's greatest-hits list, mine or yours or anybody's, is to call attention to and preserve and make available these treasures of our heritage. Art is a form of nourishment with a singularly long shelf-life. Oh ye future eyes—read these two extraordinary and quintessentially 20th-centurian short stories! The passage of time cannot wither beauty and truth of this fine a quality. We have a lot to learn from these two stories today (1999) and so will you, eyes of 3001 and 4050. Too bad Sturgeon's a well-kept secret, except in the rather small world of the true science fiction aficionado—but you and I can change that, right? In your case, if you're discovering his stories for the first time, I envy you the thrills and pleasures and even, probably, revelations that will soon be yours.

See, I do know lists like this and assertions like these make a difference. I remember in high school reading and discussing selections from an assigned anthology of "great American short stories," and being impressed when the editor or annotator or my English teacher told me that many people consider Stephen Crane's "The Bride Comes to Yellow Sky" possibly the finest American short story. I personally was more ready to hear such claims on behalf of his "The Open Boat," but anyway I had to at least consider what it was about the Yellow Sky story that might lead someone to think that. I didn't agree—but the assertion did get my attention, and I guess I enjoyed the process. Similarly, I hope you're having fun with this book (and that you understand I will forgive you if you don't rush out to find and read these two stories—though I hope a few of you will pester your libraries enough to ensure that "News" and "Costello" become available to at least some future seekers after literary nourishment from this late, great century).

There's a rather unusual story behind each of these two great

short stories. First, the context: Theodore Sturgeon was born in
1918, began writing science fiction and fantasy for pulp magazines in 1939. His early stories had a huge impact on other science fiction writers starting at the same time or a few years later,
including Ray Bradbury, Isaac Asimov, Robert Heinlein, and
Arthur C. Clarke. His second novel, *More Than Human*, made of
three connected stories, won the International Fantasy Award in
1954. In 1952 and 1953, after the birth of his first son, he broke
one of his recurrent "writer's block" episodes with a remarkable
succession of powerful and very well received magazine stories.
But in 1954 his writer's block returned, and, quite frustrated, he
mentioned this in a 1955 letter to his (already very successful) fellow sf writer Robert Heinlein (see entry #31). Heinlein replied:

> I will do the best I can at this distance [H in Colorado
> Springs, S in Congers, New York]. I must say what I am
> flattered at the request. To have the incomparable and
> always scintillating Sturgeon ask for ideas is like having
> the Pacific Ocean ask one to pee in it.

Heinlein's "return airmail" letter, as Sturgeon later told the
story in his Guest of Honor speech at a science fiction convention, offered "twenty-six story ideas, ideas some writers would
give their left ear for . . . I had told him my writing troubles, but I
hadn't told him of any other troubles, but clipped to the stack of
story notes was a check for a hundred dollars with a little scrib-
bled note, 'I have a suspicion your credit is bent.'"

One of Heinlein's story notes provided the idea and almost the
full plot-line for what was to become "And Now the News . . .".
Heinlein wrote:

> Once there was a man who could not stand it. First he lost
> the power to read and then the headlines did not bother
> him any longer. Then he lost the power to understand
> speech and then the radio could not bother him. He
> became quite happy and the wrinkles smoothed out of his
> face and he quit being tense and he painted and modelled
> in clay and danced and listened to music and enjoyed life.
>
> Then a clever psychiatrist penetrated his fugue and made

him sane again. Now he could read and listen to the radio and he became aware again of the Cold War and juvenile delinquency and rapes and rapacity and et cetera ad nauseam.

He still couldn't stand it. He killed quite a number of people before they got him.

Thus Theodore Sturgeon became the first modern storyteller to call attention, in an eerily resonant fable, to the enormous impact on Everyman, on the individual human being, of the rapid evolution of our communications media during the 20th century. The way it has changed and continues to change our sense of ourselves in relation to society, the world. What a scoop—the story of the century, really, mass murder after mass murder and all of them far more comprehensible (and even sympathetic!) after one reads "And Now the News . . .". And it turns out the visionary responsible for the fable's prophetic story line is science fiction grandmaster Robert Heinlein. Which is not to diminish Sturgeon's triumph in fleshing out the details of the fable in language and imagery and psychological nuance as memorable as what Crane added when he fictionalized the true story of his own 1897 shipwreck in "The Open Boat."

The story behind the other modern masterpiece of short fiction here celebrated, "Mr. Costello, Hero," was told by its author in a 1977 interview:

I had a deadline, and *Galaxy Magazine* editor Horace Gold called me up and said, "Hey, where's the novelet?" And I began to cry a lot over the telephone. This was the time of the McCarthy hearings. The whole country was in a grip of terror that, not having been through it you just would not understand how awful that was. It was a *frightening* thing. It crept into all the corners of the houses and everybody's speech and language. Everybody started to get super-careful about what they said, what they wrote and what they broadcast. The whole country was in a strange type of fear, some great intangible something that nobody could get hold of. A very frightening thing.

I became aware by that time that I had a fairly high calibre typewriter, and I became alarmed by the fact that I wasn't using it for anything but what I call "literature of entertainment." I don't want to knock entertainment at all, but I felt I had the tool to do something but I didn't know what to do with it.

Horace listened to me with great care, and he said, "I'll tell you what you do, Sturgeon. You write me a story about a guy whose wife has gone away for the weekend, and he goes down to the bus station to meet her, and the bus arrives and the whole place is full of people. He looks across the crowd and sees his wife emerge from the exit talking to a young man who is talking earnestly back to her. And he is carrying her suitcase. She looks across the crowd, sees her husband, speaks a word to the young man and the young man hands her her suitcase, tips his hat, and disappears into the crowd, and she comes across to him and kisses him. Now then, Sturgeon, write me that story, and by the time you're finished the whole world will know how you feel about Joseph McCarthy."

For the moment I didn't know what the hell he was talking about, and it comes right back to what I said earlier. If a writer really and truly believes in something, if he is totally convinced, if he has a conviction, it really doesn't matter what he writes about. That conviction is going to come through. At that point I sat down and wrote a story called "Mr. Costello, Hero" which was as specific and as sharply edged a portrait of Joe McCarthy as anyone has ever written. Not only the man himself and his voice and his actions and his speech, but his motivations, where he was coming from, what made him do what he did, which I had never analyzed before.

Actually the story does more than that. It is one of the most valuable (*and* entertaining) pieces of political fiction ever written, because it gives us a diagram, it demonstrates in much detail precisely how an Adolf Hitler or Joe McCarthy or Jim Jones or Charles Manson or Slobodan Milosevic can charm and seduce a handful of people who become his lieutenants so that they and soon whole nations start jumping to his tune and even believe they wrote it themselves. The more insight we gain into how this is done, the more opportunity we have to protect ourselves and others from this human peril. "Mr. Costello, Hero" is a great story as a story, as a narrative and a work of language, but more than that it offers direct insight into the methodology by which psychopathic and power-hungry personalities manipulate other persons by engaging their fears and hatreds, even of people or things they never thought of fearing or hating until the manipulator caught them in his web.

But along with the value and power of the message/information/insight is the power of the storytelling, the artistry. A story by Sturgeon is the equal of a painting by Van Gogh, and the pleasures it offers are just as immediate and the new perspectives and insights just as enduring.

When he awoke the following morning he sprang out of bed, feeling years younger, opened the door, scooped up the morning paper and glanced at the headlines. He couldn't read them. He grunted in surprise, closed the door gently, and sat on the bed with the paper in his lap. His hands moved restlessly on it, smoothing and smoothing until the palms were shadowed and the type hazed. The shouting symbols marched across the page like a parade of strangers in some unrecognized lodge uniform, origins unknown, and the occasion for marching only to be guessed at. He traced the letters with his little finger, he measured the length of a word between his index finger and thumb and lifted them up to hold them before his wondering eyes. Suddenly he got up and crossed to the desk, where signs and placards and printed notes were trapped like a butterfly collection under glass—the breakfast menu, something about valet service, something about checking out. He remembered them all and had an idea of their significance—but he couldn't read them. . . . He requested of himself that he recite the alphabet. "A," he said clearly, and "Eh?" because it didn't sound right and he couldn't imagine what would. He made a small foolish grin and shook his head slightly and rapidly, but grin or no, he felt frightened. He felt glad, or relieved—mostly happy anyway, but still a little frightened.

—from "And Now the News . . ."

That was the trip we shipped the crazy man. His name was Hynes. He was United Earth Consul at Borinquen [a planet] and he was going back to report. . . . He came busting in [to the narrator's room on his spaceship] and said, "I hope you don't mind, Purser, but if I don't talk to somebody about this, I'll go out of my mind." Then he sat down on the end of my bunk and put his head in his hands and rocked back and forth for a long time, without saying anything. Next thing he said was "Sorry," and out he went. Crazy, I tell you.

But he was back in before long. And then you never heard such ravings. "Do you know what's happened to Borinquen?" he'd demand. But he didn't want any answers. He had the answers. "I'll tell you what's wrong with Borinquen—Borinquen's gone mad!" he'd say.

He said, "You wouldn't believe it if you hadn't seen it done. First the little wedge, driven in the one place it might exist—between the urbans and the trappers. There was never any conflict between them—never! All of a sudden, the trapper was a menace. How it happened, why, God only knows. First, these laughable attempts to show that they were an unhealthy influence. Yes, laughable—how could you take it seriously?

"And then the changes. You didn't have to prove that a trapper had done anything. You only had to prove he was a trapper. That was enough. And the next thing—how could you *anticipate* anything as mad as this?"—he almost screamed—"the next thing was to take anyone who wanted to be alone and lump him with the trappers. It all happened so fast—it happened in our sleep. And all of a sudden you were afraid to be alone in a room for a *second*. They left their homes. They built barracks. Everyone afraid of everyone else, afraid, afraid . . ."

—from "Mr. Costello, Hero"

My youth/An unripe plum./Your teeth have left their marks on it," Thich Nhat Hanh (see entry #12) wrote in a poem while Patti Smith was still a teenager. "Fire consumes this century," he wrote, "and mountains and forests bear its mark. The wind howls across my ears/While the whole sky shakes violently in the snowstorm."

The Vietnamese monk called his poem "The Fruit of Awareness Is Ripe." Patti Smith's album *Horses* is the outcry of a similarly passionate human, in the midst of the same century. Her album could just as well have been called *Teethmarks*. Nhat Hanh's poem resonates with exactly the feeling of Smith singing, "Suddenly Johnny gets the feeling he's been surrounded by horses, horses, horses, horses, coming in in all directions . . . !"

The beat that runs behind the extraordinary verses of the "horses" section of "Land" (the tour de force title track of the poet/rock singer's first album) is very important. It is exactly the beat at the dramatic heart of the equally powerful opening track of the album, "Gloria." Why is this beat so important? Ask any mid-20th-century teenager. "At the other end of the hallway a rhythm was generating. . . ." "Jesus died for somebody's sins, but not mine . . . !"

That last line is from "Gloria," of which Smith wrote in 1998:

"Gloria" gave me the opportunity to acknowledge and disclaim our musical and spiritual heritage. It personifies for me, within its adolescent conceit, what I hold sacred as an artist. The right to create, without apology, from a stance beyond gender or social definition.

Patti Smith was twenty-eight when she recorded *Horses* with producer John Cale (ex–Velvet Underground, see entry #2) and with her band the Patti Smith Group: Lenny Kaye, lead guitar; Richard Sohl, piano; Ivan Kral, guitar and bass; Jay Dee Daugherty, drums; Patti Smith, vocals. Creating a great 20th-century hit—in the footsteps of her heroes Bob Dylan, Allen Ginsberg, and Anonymous Garage Band—was pretty much what Smith had in mind. She wanted to *become* the wind that howled across her ears. And she did. You can hear it and feel it yourself. It's in the grooves (obsolete terminology, now it's in the coded digital information), for as long as there's appropriate playback equipment. And for as long as the English language (mid-20th-century variant) survives enough to allow a few curious listeners to guess at the meaning of its shouting symbols. "HORSES! HORSES! Coming in in all directions . . ."

In order to be a greatest hit of any century, a work of art must have the ability to survive—to speak evocatively and stirringly to listeners/readers/observers in other centuries, with an enduring and surprising freshness. As, for example, is the case with Beethoven's concertos, Thoreau's *Walden*, and Hiroshige's Tokaido prints. They speak of and beyond their immediate time and space locations. Can Smith's *Horses* pass this test? It may be too soon to say, but yes, I'm quite certain it can and will, and that's why it's on my list and in this book.

What do we have here? Forty-three minutes of words and music, a "rock and roll" "record" (or "album" or "CD") by a young poet-singer and her amplified band. Eight "songs." Sorry for all the quote marks, but that's what "they" (we) called this kind of music, this kind of art object. By summer 1975, Patti Smith had had three books of poetry published in "small press" editions, and had gotten some attention in the "art world" of New York City for her poetry readings, and for a few years had been experimenting with singing her poems to accompaniment and becoming a rock-and-roll performer of some kind (some kind that hadn't ever quite existed before—like Bob Dylan and many others, including the Velvet Underground and the Beatles, she spontaneously and without much premeditation invented a unique new form to work in which fit her talents and her creative nature and her times and milieu quite perfectly).

Putting it another way, we have here a work of art, a greatest-hits entry, which is quite closely related to #15 (Umm Kulthum concert). And to #17 (*Renaldo & Clara*) and #2 ("Sister Ray"), #21 (*On the Road*), #26 (Grateful Dead concert), and #30 (John Coltrane pieces). An improvisation. The music and words and structures of these songs changed unpredictably from one performance to the next—onstage and in the recording studio—because singer and musicians were always improvising, making it up spontaneously within presupplied frameworks (like the actors and actresses in Bob Dylan's movie). Smith has said of "Land":

> We went through all kinds of voyages [the song had its origins in a much shorter, published poem, and in two fairly obscure rock-and-roll songs from years earlier]. . . . Usually there were Mexican boys and space guys, weird Burroughs stuff like Arab guys and Christian angels fucking in the sand, pulling out each other's entrails. Or like, there's Johnny in a blue T-bird going off the cliff while "Thousand Dances" is playing on the radio. People used to come to CBGBs night after night to find out what was gonna happen to Johnny next. And I was curious to find out what was gonna happen to him on the record. . . . On the second take something weird happened. The Mexican boys and spaceships were gone; instead there was a black horse, and all those electrical wires and a sea—a "sea of possibilities"—I didn't know what direction the song was taking, there was all this strange imagery I didn't understand. . . .

The power of improvisation is the power of performance. The artist/musician/dancer is given (gives herself) the opportunity to hear divine spirit speaking through her voice, her gestures, her improvised language and imagery. "Wow! Where did that come from?!" After a while an Umm Kulthum gets used to it, comes to expect that if she does her job impeccably she will be allowed to be a vehicle for something much larger than herself. In Umm Kulthum's case, she knows it's the voice of Allah and the voice of her ancestors, because she thinks of herself as singing (creating, sometimes even co-composing) the music of Allah and of the Egyptian people. In the case of a Patti Smith, she knows it's the voice of the Muse because she has a relationship with what she calls the Muse that's as conscious and deliberate as Umm K's relationship with her God and her Nation. In this instance (the performance of "Land" that ended up on *Horses*), she finds herself spontaneously naming the Muse and defining the technique: "The sea . . . sea of possibilities . . . seize the possibilities!"

"Land" is the second-to-last track of the original *Horses* album (the 1996 "remastered" CD is the same except that fittingly, a 1976 live performance of the Who's 1965 mock anthem "My Generation" has been appended). The third song on this great record is called "Birdland." Like "Land" and "Gloria," it's a tour de force. Three on one album!—no wonder it's a greatest hit. And the other five songs are as modest as these are ambitious—and as successful. "Kimberley" and "Free Money" and just about every track on this record is worthy of long remembrance even apart from the powerful role it plays as a part of this remarkable whole, this rock suite not completely separate from *Pet Sounds* or *Blonde on Blonde* (Bob Dylan) or *The Dark Side of the Moon* (Pink Floyd), other memorable examples of the genre.

"Birdland"—even more than the unforgettable "Land"—is Smith's strongest bid to locate herself in the aesthetic tradition of that 18th-century great-hit-writer (also emulated by Allen Ginsberg) William Blake, notorious visionary mystic eccentric (and songwriting poet). "Birdland" starts, "His father died . . . ," and tells the story of a little boy who falls asleep after a funeral and sees "his Daddy behind the control board" of something like a flying saucer. The boy ends up beseeching, "No, Daddy, don't leave me here alone!" (one thinks of an earlier son: "Father why hast thou forsaken me?"). "Take me up, Daddy, to the belly of the ship. . . ." As Smith acknowledges very fleetingly in the album's credits, the story told in "Birdland"'s lyrics is taken almost literally from an obscure and wonderful autobiography by Peter Reich, Wilhelm Reich's son, called *A Book of Dreams* (1973). Smith herself "at the age of four came down with scarlet fever and malaria and subsequently suffered periods of hallucinations, which stayed with her well into her adolescence" (according to punk music historian Clinton Heylin). "Birdland" is fairly clearly the singer/writer's passionate expression of identification with Reich's half-real-but-possibly-quite-real adventures, based on their similarity to her own childhood experiences.

The power of improvisatory singing is evident at more than four key moments in this nine-minute song-story, when more is communicated by the tone and feeling of the singer's voice than could ever be said by words alone: "and he started to *drift, drift*" (one minute in), then "*he was not human*" (1:57 and again with a different pronoun at 4:40) and "*take me up! take me up!*" (2:45 and again at 5:31) and the climactic, indeed orgasmic, "*up, up, up, up, up, up*" at 7:53. The brilliant doo-wop ending is a perfect denouement and also our clue that the song title does not refer primarily to the legendary jazz nightclub but to an airy land where one flies with the birds as felt and intuited in a childhood vision. This comes through powerfully whether or not the listener understands English or can follow the singer's diction. Like Umm Kulthum (and, if we can accept the poems we have as "recordings," William Blake).

"Birdland" and *Horses* as a whole seem to me to be successful and memorable, "great," for many of the same reasons as Joyce's *Ulysses*. They inspire and reward the attention of the reader/listener. Smith is as full of allusion as Joyce. For example, the Mexican boys she tells us often inhabited the changing narrative of "Land" were surely related to Cannibal and the Headhunters, four young Mexican-American musicians from Los Angeles who hit the national "Top 40" with "Land of 1000 Dances" in 1965, a year before Wilson Pickett's Top 10 version. And just to express her admiration for the songwriter who wrote "1000 Dances,"

Chris Kenner, the poet/songwriter/rock critic segues very sleekly from "1000 Dances" into a pre-hip-hop rap of "and the name of the place is I like it like that" in reference to the 1961 Top 10 hit recorded by Kenner himself.

You can go almost as deep into *Horses* as you can into *Ulysses*, and get almost as much pleasure from the sheer language and performance. I like it like this, obviously.

In order to locate ourselves we need an excuse. The "we" in this statement refers to *my* "we," 20th-century Americans. The statement is true for many other peoples, but it does not apply, for example, to the 19th-century American protagonists of Edith Wharton's novel *Ethan Frome* (1911), who, as I recall from reading the book in school long ago, were lovers doomed by their inability to even imagine the possibility of moving to another town. They, like many people all over this world right now, were located by their births and circumstances and couldn't conceive of changing their addresses for any reason, not even to save their love or their lives.

But consider, please, the characters in Monte Hellman's well-loved but little-known 1971 film *Two-Lane Blacktop*. Where they find themselves, like the characters in Jack Kerouac's novel, is on the American road, in this case a 1970 version (very different from, say, the 1999 or 1942 versions) of the southern route from California to Tennessee by way of New Mexico and Texas. Why are they there? Presumably because they want to be, because they enjoy or are attracted to or love the road. In the case of The Driver (James Taylor) and The Mechanic (Dennis Wilson), their excuse is that this is how they make a living, or anyway is the game/hobby/pastime they're addicted to—they're hot-rodders, drag-racers, they've got a rebuilt 1955 Chevrolet to which they've added a stronger engine, making it possible for them to win money regularly in races against cars that look more like the commonly accepted image of a fast car, whose owner-operators are easily roped into betting that their beloved chariots will of course be able to beat this dumpy-looking '55 Chevy driven and maintained by these arrogant out-of-towners. The excuse, in other words, is a way of life. You get in an argument with a likely prospect at a local gas station and then meet at an illegal "drag strip" (a short, preferably little-used segment of paved road—"two-lane blacktop") out on the outskirts of town somewhere. Betting drivers each give $200, say, to a third party who holds the money till the end of the race and then hands it to the winner. If the cops don't break up the contest before it's decided. Why are these guys on the road? Because they live for and in their car, and are looking for the next race, next opportunity to repair or improve the engine, next chance to make or lose some money, have some fun, express themselves.

For The Girl (Laurie Bird) who climbs into the backseat of The Car while its Driver and Mechanic are eating in a roadside diner, her excuse is she has dreams of following this Road to someplace better, more fulfilling, and she's bored with the guy (apparently a hippie boyfriend with a funky van) she was traveling with until a few minutes ago.

So this movie is about the road, the great American location, and it's also about our excuses. The other protagonist, GTO (Warren Oates) (named after the late-model vehicle he's driving), is wonderful because he seems not to know what his excuse is even though his favorite pastime is making up new versions of who he is and why he's here, and trying these out on every person he meets—usually hitchhikers he picks up, all of whom see through his bullshit soliloquies, which of course doesn't slow him down. Another American archetype. He's here to make up stories about why he's here, in hopes that he'll find one he can believe himself or be accepted for.

In order to locate *Ethan Frome* or some other novel or work of art on the Required Reading (or in the case of a movie, Viewing) list of a high school or college class or whatever other sort of list successfully motivates readers and viewers, we need an excuse. My excuse for putting *Two-Lane Blacktop* on my list and in this book is that it's my favorite road movie and I can't think of a better genre to represent my era, my time-and-space location. Never was movies or paved highways before this century, and as fast as everything is changing there may not be any such critters in future eras, or if there is they'll be radically different from anything we would have recognized as a "highway" or a "movie" in 1971. Very appropriate object for a time capsule, therefore. But a "greatest hit"? Stand by for another excuse.

And I'll demonstrate that my excuses are as shifty as the stories GTO tells his road companions by admitting that Barry Levinson's *Rain Man* (1988) is in many ways a better movie than *Two-Lane Blacktop* and could possibly end up as high on my personal list of favorite movies, if that's what I was up to here. Or not. See, there are lots of reasons (excuses) that affect inclusion and location on any kind of list of "important stuff." I say *Two-Lane Blacktop* is well loved but little known because I do know a few people who love it as fiercely as I do (and I have found evidence on the Internet that there are others out there) and I know it's an obscure film because it wasn't a "hit" the year it was released and has never been reissued or made available on videocassette and has hardly ever been shown on television since then. That gives it an advantage over *Rain Man*, which won an Oscar and is definitely well known as well as well loved. Like lotsa people, when I'm making a public assertion that a particular record or movie or novel is "great" or just boasting that it's a personal favorite, familiarity (popularity) breeds contempt. I don't wanna put *A Hard Day's Night* or "Like a Rolling Stone" on my lists, much as I love them; I get more satisfaction, make more of a personal statement, by going for "Things We Said Today" and *Renaldo & Clara*. Just like you might feel a lot more satisfaction owning and racing a '55 Chevy than a late-model GTO.

And there's more to it than that. *Rain Man* has it all over *Two-Lane Blacktop* in terms of compelling narrative, story line, and also in terms of portraying relationships between fathers and sons, between brothers, and between outcasts of various sorts and normal people. There aren't any fathers and sons or brothers in *Two-Lane Blacktop,* and hardly any "normal" people—except insofar as we the viewers may recognize the Girl or Driver or Mechanic or the GTO in ourselves, or in everyone. It's about the universality of non-normalcy (as is *Rain Man*). But although a sizable chunk of *Rain Man* is a long road movie sequence, and that sequence does the genre proud, it still must be said that *Rain Man* isn't primarily a "road movie," and therefore not half as good a time-capsule example of the genre as *Two-Lane Blacktop.* Besides, though I love the human relationships and the involving story line of *RM*, I equally appreciate how *TLB* makes such strong statements about the human condition and about being on the road in circa-1970 USA by stripping away all kinds of details about the pasts or the inner lives of its characters. Indeed, its triumph is that we learn huge amounts about the inner lives of The Driver and The Girl and The Mechanic and GTO and ourselves just by watching their faces and movements and hearing what they say and don't say to each other; the absence of details actually makes these inner lives more vivid, more affecting, it universalizes them and fills every face and every film-frame shot of these people sitting or standing around with as much beauty and feeling as is in the landscapes. Inside the car and outside the car—both types of shot are portraits of the Road. And filled with beauty, again like the everyday-life paintings of Cézanne. A portrait of a moment and a place and of the people who inhabit(ed) that moment. A mobile place, yes, but what better subject for a "movie"?

One peculiarity (but by now you realize I want every one of my choices to be idiosyncratic) about *Two-Lane Blacktop* being in this book is that it wasn't a "hit" in any commercial sense. True, neither was *Renaldo & Clara,* but Bob Dylan certainly was. Monte Hellman is not a name to conjure with. He hasn't made many movies, and none of the others can even be regarded as having a "cult" following, although there was a bit of a "buzz" in Europe about two of his earlier films, enigmatic homemade westerns (one of them written by Jack Nicholson, who did become a name to conjure with). Warren Oates is a character actor, beloved by those who love obscure character actors, and Leonard Maltin in his *TV Movies and Video Guide* says Oates's performance in *Two-Lane Blacktop* "is about as good as you'll ever see and should have had the Oscar." But the only other fairly well-known films Oates was in were *In the Heat of the Night* and *The Wild Bunch,* and his roles in both were minor. So anyway, this greatest-hits entry can be said to stand in for other superb and certainly memorable works of art made by artists who haven't otherwise publicly distinguished themselves. The point is, such works can be just as valid. There are great rock-and-roll records that weren't made by the Beatles or Bob Dylan or even the Velvet Underground, and if only the works made by the people with deservedly Big Reputations survive a century, I believe the resultant picture people have of that century and its great art will be distorted. Thus in my book *Rock and Roll: The 100 Best Singles,* I hold out for the greatness of the Bell Notes' "I've Had It" and the Only Ones' "Another Girl, Another Planet," even if you can't find those artists' names in the index of almost any other reference work. *In Obscuro Veritas.* In obscurity there is truth. Sometimes. Don't overlook the seemingly overlookable.

The screenplay of *Two-Lane Blacktop* was written by Rudolph Wurlitzer (though a guy named Will Cory gets part credit because his very different script about different guys crossing the country for a different reason is what the producer started with). Wurlitzer had already written two novels, *Nog* and *Flats,* portraying young people in the 1960s not so much as hippies but as a sort of blank generation. He was ahead of his time in that respect. Director Hellman's enthusiasm for the characters Wurlitzer created and Taylor and Oates and Bird and Wilson brought to life can be seen in a 1971 interview, wherein he tells the British Film Institute reporter:

I've always seen The Driver as the same character as Aznavour in Truffaut's *Shoot the Piano Player.* It's a guy who is so involved with his own existential dilemma, in just dealing with himself as a person, that he throws away the thing he wants most, which is love. He can't deal with those needs in time—realizes too late—and that becomes his tragedy.

Not that *Two-Lane Blacktop* is a tragedy. Just that its protagonists are all lost souls, not exactly drifting but actually racing across America. As Wurlitzer has The Driver explain, "You can never go fast enough."

The Driver and The Mechanic are played by two young stars with no acting experience. Pop music stars. Dennis Wilson, twenty-five years old when this movie was filmed, was the singing drummer and primary sex symbol or "cute guy" of The Beach Boys, whose early-1960s string of hit songs were about hotrodding when they weren't about surfing. James Taylor, twenty-two when *Two-Lane* was made, was oddly enough just enjoying his first hit records (the single "Fire and Rain" and the album *Sweet Baby James*) in September 1970. "Enjoying" may not be the right word. The pressures (mostly internal, as in "existential dilemma") of musical fame and success drove Taylor back into heroin addiction before the movie's release in spring 1971 (he'd recently been on the cover of *Time* magazine, which oddly enough did not seem to help *Two-Lane* at the box office). Anyway, Hellman made sure his actors, professional and otherwise (Laurie Bird, seventeen when the film was shot, had not been in a movie before) didn't look like they were enjoying themselves too much; he kept them weary and on the edge of frustration by not letting them see the script except for today's page and by insisting that the whole crew keep moving across country for every day's work, even though a lot of the shots were done inside the cars. The director had a Vision, in other words. The extraordinary thing is that the performances he gets from his non-actors are every bit as riveting and extraordinary as the tour de force performance delivered by *Gunsmoke* veteran Oates. Taylor *is* The Driver, Wilson *is* The Mechanic, and Bird, God help her, *is* The Girl. Somebody (okay, the producer, Michael Laughlin, certainly deserves some credit) brought exactly the right people together at exactly the right moment. And the result, like any true thing of beauty, is a joy forever. May it never pass into nothingness.

As *Two-Lane Blacktop* articulates, we 20th centurians have to work at locating ourselves because we are blessed with, suffer from, such a plenitude of freedom. Odd that James Taylor made this film right between his two big hit pop music statements: "I've seen fire and I've seen rain . . ." and "You've got a friend." The public loved both statements. But somehow the existential humor of "You can never go fast enough" never quite caught their attention. Even though the film he says it in may outlive his two fine hit singles.

Wait a minute!" says Conscious Reader. "Isn't that *three* concert performances?" And I say, "Nah, more like four or five because I didn't stick Feb. 11, '69 up there (and that's really two)." Okay, I'll start this entry by attempting to explain myself (as usual).

In considering live performances as listable greatest hits of the century, we've been wrestling in this volume with the question of whether the object (tree falling in the forest, Feb. something 1969) exists only if the observer can claim to have been there at the event, or if there's an available recording (but is that the same?), or just if we know the event occurred (Umm Kulthum really did sing "al-Atlal" for the first time at a Cairo concert on April 7, 1966). And now with the Grateful Dead, thanks to the wonders of psychedelic technology, we get to have it all three ways at once. February 19, 1969, I attended a GD concert at the Fillmore West in San Francisco. Sometime in 1970, the band released a much-loved two-record album called *Live/Dead* which approximates a GD concert at the height of their early power by cleverly splicing together sets from 1/26/69 and 2/27/69, along with some less spectacular material from another show on 3/2/69, all at "psychedelic ballrooms" (concert halls) in San Francisco, California, USA. As I write, that album is and likely will continue to be on sale and available to the curi-

HIT 26

Concert Performance
by *The Grateful Dead*
(January 26, February 19, and February 27, 1969)

ous almost anywhere on our planet. And if you object that it can't really be a "greatest hit" concert unless it's a recording or a first-person memory of an entire performance, then you might want to check out a 1997 CD from Grateful Dead Records (manufactured and distributed by a huge "legitimate" corporation whose owners live in Germany) called *Fillmore East 2-11-69*. On this double-CD you get a complete Grateful Dead concert from New York City—twice, because the band played an afternoon show and an evening show. Now all you need is the proper sacrament (that's a mid-20th-century joke, a reference to LSD, a consciousness-altering chemical frequently ingested by Grateful Dead fans before or during concerts, then and now and perhaps eternally).

Lest you grumble about having to trust my aging and human and fallible memory cells regarding the excellence or greatness of a performance I saw and heard thirty years ago, I can quote here an exchange between me and Timothy Leary (notorious LSD researcher and proponent) two days after the February 19 performance. Leary: "Rosemary and I were with Jann [publisher of *Rolling Stone* magazine] for dinner the night the Celestial Synapse Festival was being held at the Fillmore West; and Jann and Jane were planning to go with us but that's when he had to go see his business manager. So Rosemary and I went down to the Fillmore, and of course several thousand acid tabs were passed out; the place was just reeling with psychedelic energy. The Grateful Dead have never played as well in their life. Many people stripped naked on the stage and the whole thing turned into a . . . It happened, and God just radiated the room with loving energy."

I said this was an exchange; I was the interviewer (on assignment from *Rolling Stone*) and mostly I just listened, but a few days later as I typed up the transcript I interpolated this comment after Tim said the GD "have never played as well in their life": "I've never seen them play that well indoors before, anyway."—PW. This observation carries some weight, because at that time I'd seen the Grateful Dead perform, indoors and outdoors and in many different circumstances, even in two different countries, quite a few more times than Mr. Leary had. So you can take my twenty-years-old psychedelicized 1969 word for it: It was about as great a Grateful Dead performance as any observer could hope to encounter. And huge numbers of (mostly American) music lovers and art appreciators alive between 1966 and A.D. 2000 agree emphatically (and have expressed their conviction by voting with their feet—this is the *only* U.S. rock group ever to build a truly large audience year after year for its live appearances without a hit record or other major media exposure) that a first-rate Grateful Dead concert is about as worthy and memorable and valuable ("great") a work of art as our era has produced. The real thing.

And fortunately, you didn't have to be at the Celestial Synapse Festival (just a fancy name for one more Wednesday night at the Fillmore)—you can listen to *Live/Dead* or *2/11/69* right now in, um, A.D. 2525, and hear a performance as good as and very similar to what Tim and Rosemary and I were experiencing.

In that 2/21/69 conversation, Leary went on to say: "And as I was sitting there, completely stoned, I thought of Jann and felt that it would have been very important for him to have come there, as thousands of the rest of us had done, and have dropped acid under this holy circumstance, reminded once again of how it all began, this particular electronic movement, and where it got its energy, and how God infused it, and how it's being lost." This is relevant to our discussion in this volume, because the question always is, *who* is assessing the "greatness" of these human creations, these works of art, these Beethoven concertos and Van Gogh paintings, and determining that they do or do not deserve to be taught or preserved or sought out and experienced in centuries to come? *Rolling Stone,* then a San Francisco–based rock-and-roll newspaper, would naturally seem a good place to look for contemporary assessments of what was being created in this art form and cultural environment. Yet already in early 1969 the question could be raised of whether the editor and editorial policies of this magazine (venue and after-the-fact archive for contemporary criticisms and commentaries) were still willing or able to be as one with the artists and their audience. The question always arises: When the tree falls in the forest, *who* is the observer reporting to

us about the event, and aesthetically speaking was he or she willing or able to be as one with the new painting, the poem, the dramatic performance, and the artist-audience relationship within
which the work was created? No easy answers, please. The question so discomfited music-and-pop-culture magazine publisher
Jann Wenner that he never did publish the interview in which
Leary said, clearly, "I recommend as a yogic exercise that anyone
in the rock and roll business, artist or publisher, take a powerful
LSD trip once a month at a rock concert and renew his insight
into the electronic revelation."

What I would like to have said about the Grateful Dead just now is that their particular talent lay in the realm of creating—and allowing themselves to be created by—their audience. They were uniquely successful at this. This accomplishment is at the heart of the question that underlies this text: What is art? And what is our proper or desired relationship with it?

George Herriman's *Krazy Kat* comic strip is a 20th-century work of art that has already passed the test of time in ways I expect the Grateful Dead's music will someday (unproven however until fifty years from now, when recordings of the Dead's performances from 1966 and 1969 are as old as the reproductions of 1916 and 1920 *Krazy Kat* strips and Sunday pages are today).

Ever since these primitive yet sophisticated words-and-pictures sequences first appeared in the *New York Journal* and other Hearst newspapers, they have demonstrated before countless consciousnesses their remarkable ability to educate and create and seduce their own private audiences, who quickly find themselves reading this comic in a way not quite like how they've ever read any other comic or picture-story before—reading it like they've just learned a unique visual and narrative language so well that this place never feels like a strange land to them (nor they a stranger), except in the positive sense that it always fasci-

HIT

27

Krazy Kat Sunday Page

by George Herriman

(published June 13, 1920)

nates, and inspires wonder and humor and curiosity. *Krazy Kat*, like the Grateful Dead in concert, teaches its observers how to participate in a unique art-and-audience relationship. "Let me show you how to do this dance. It goes like this. . . ."

The mouse throws a brick at the cat, the cat is happy when it bounces off his head because he or she receives it as an expression of affection—in fact Krazy mopes when a few hours have gone by and he hasn't been beaned; does Ignatz not love him anymore? Ignatz Mouse on the other hand is unhappy when circumstances prevent him from throwing his daily brick at Krazy, because he gets his chief satisfaction (even seems rather addicted) from this specific expression of what to him is hostility, annoyance. The other corner of the triangle, the dog, Offissa Pupp, regards it as his duty to prevent these assaults and apprehend the perpetrator—particularly because the dog feels a romantic attraction to Krazy not quite as poetic as what Krazy feels for Ignatz but still compelling and inescapable. That's the dance. It's not your ordinary love triangle. Possibly because it takes place in a unique setting, the "enchanted mesa" of "Coconino County," an alternate reality, a desert village inhabited by talking animals. All three star-crossed lovers live happily, not exactly ever after but in a kind of eternal present moment that goes on forever like the desert vistas so wonderfully drawn by the inspired hand of Krazy and Ignatz's creator, George Herriman, a Los Angeles–based journalist/cartoonist of African-American descent, born in New Orleans in August 1880, thirty-nine years old when he drew this particular June 13, 1920, Sunday page, which I will now describe in words (as inadequate as trying to summarize verbally *Girl Before a Mirror* or Lady Day's "God Bless the Child"):

Krazy is sitting on a rock near one end of a page-wide panel; the left end contains introductory text amidst hints of wispy clouds on or over the desert horizon-line: "There comes to 'Krazy Kat' a day of direst desolation." Over on the right Krazy, head in hand, is saying or thinking: "Oh Death!! Come fourth and sting me—I'm a wery, wery unheppy 'ket.'" Next panel down, an oasis with palm trees and what could be a shallow pool appears on the left; Krazy stands with hands humbly clasped before him and soliloquizes, "Ah, beauty comes among me—I see a scenery of great loveliness before my eye." Next panel, Krazy is walking with arms outstretched toward the oasis, "I go to you, sweet wision, I go to you—." Another character appears (just walked into the panel) on stage right, a bee with a hobo's stick (bandana-bundle of belongings suspended from the tip) over his shoulder, saying, "Halt!!!"

Next panel down, Krazy stops with heels down and toes up in a comic skidding gesture, "Who calls at me?" "Tis I, 'Bum Bill Bee.'" Below this, they stand together surveying the oasis, and the bee, pointing, says, "That's only a 'mirage', it is nothing, it doesn't exist, it ain't, it isn't—you only think you see it—it's a mirage deceiving your eye." Next panel, the bee is walking off stage left with a serious, satisfied I-said-what-I-had-to-say look on his face. Where the oasis was is only a few cloud wisps. Krazy, toward the right, leaning back in shock and beating his brows, beads of sweat flying from his head, says, "It's gone!!!" Ignatz Mouse appears behind him, climbing over the horizon line to get into the panel, saying, "Ahh—there he is."

Next panel, cloud-punctuated emptiness in the left half; in the right half Ignatz quickly throws a brick (we see the word "Zip" in its trail) which hits Krazy's head forcefully with the sound "Bong!!!!!" Bottom panel, still clouds over empty desert on the left (artist's signature added in lower left corner); Krazy on the right is sitting on his rock with head in hand staring at the brick fixedly and saying or thinking, "It's only a 'mirage,' it's nothing, it dun't exist, it ain't, it isn't, I only think I see it. It's a 'mirage' deceiving my eye—"

We the readers understand that he wants to be happy because he's been beaned by his loved one's brick, but he's dutifully trying to apply what Bill the bee bum just taught him, i.e. that material things can't bring happiness, that's only an illusion. So as Krazy's mood of desolation tries to reassert itself, he or she innocently (of course) and enthusiastically engages in a Hume-ian mental dialogue about whether the chair (brick in this case) is really there or only *seems* to be there. Quick and willing student, Krazy.

Pablo Picasso (see entry #3) was a keen admirer of *Krazy Kat,* as were such other creators of great 20th-century art as Charlie Chaplin, F. Scott Fitzgerald, W. C. Fields, e. e. cummings, James Joyce, and Frank Capra . . . alongside such otherwise distinguished figures as art patron Gertrude Stein and American president Woodrow Wilson. *Krazy* was a hit, definitely. This, however, did not make Herriman a public figure in his own time as happened to other characters in this book like Milne, Ginsberg, Holiday, Dylan, and Picasso himself. The audience George Herriman created and still creates with *Krazy Kat* is a self-elected elite. That's part of the attraction, I remember from when I first became aware of *KK* as a ten-year-old: Just by your spontaneous ability to enjoy and appreciate *Krazy* you immediately join an inner circle, the "cool" crowd, and you know it. You feel it. You are at home in (as one with) Coconino County. How does he *do* that? Ain't it wonderful? Why do you suppose seventeen-year-olds in the 1980s so readily became [Grateful] Deadheads? And elected to spend their summers following the golden road? Greatest Hits are often tickets to ride. Or membership cards in exclusive clubs.

Art Spiegelman observes in a 1999 *New Yorker* article that: "comic strips like *Krazy Kat* and *Little Nemo* have long been welcomed into the canon of twentieth-century cultural achievement—right up there next to Picasso's paintings and Joyce's novels." Indeed, this welcoming began as early as 1923—ten years after *KK*'s first daily strip appeared and seven years after the first Sunday page—when critic Gilbert Seldes wrote in *Vanity Fair*.

> *Krazy Kat*, the regular comic strip of George Herriman is, to me, the most amusing and fantastic and satisfactory work of art produced in America today. With those who hold that a comic strip cannot be a work of art I shall not traffic. It happens that in America today irony and fantasy are practiced in the major arts by only one or two artists, producing high-class trash, while Mr. Herriman, working in a despised medium, without an atom of pretentiousness, is day after day producing something essentially fine. It is a result of a naive sensibility rather like that of Rousseau; it does not lack intelligence, because it is a thought-out,

a constructed piece of work. In the second order of the world's art it is superbly first-rate—and a delight!

A canon is "an authoritative list of books accepted as Holy Scripture," or, as in the Spiegelman quote above, works of art accepted as great cultural achievements of an era, a century. My point of view, as readers of this book know by now, is that as individuals we do well to question authority—which means, we gotta make our own lists. So if you prefer *Pogo* or *Peanuts* or *Li'l Abner* or even *Garfield*, don't be intimidated by us *Kat*-lovin' elitists. And on the other hand, as you know, my point of view is that the weird process of cultural canonization can be a blessing when it brings Thoreau or Beethoven or Pushkin or Herriman or Lewis Carroll (and their achievements) into our lives across the miles and centuries even though "our" circumstances and tastes and cultural interests and life-situations are inevitably so different from those prevailing back then, or over there. Which brings us to the mysterious issue of universality. The popularity of Beethoven and the Beatles and Shakespeare in cultures and eras so far from their points of origin attests that there is such a thing. So does my intuitive and unwavering appreciation of *Krazy Kat* when I was ten and ever since. Another subtext of this book: What is universality? How do they *do* that?

One thing the history of Herriman's *Kat* reminds us of is that universality, even canonized universality originating in popular culture, is not necessarily as welcomed and loved by the public as the authors of "Things We Said Today" were in their era. From the beginning and for twenty-eight years the *Krazy Kat* Sunday pages were only published—and thus created, because it's hard to create a Grateful Dead concert in an empty auditorium or a *KK* Sunday page with no newspaper offering to pay for the work or anyway put it in front of readers—thanks to the patronage of one stubborn and powerful admirer. According to Bill Blackbeard, preeminent Herriman scholar:

> William Randolph Hearst did everything in his power to get George Herriman's magnum opus, the Sunday *Krazy Kat*, on the American record for almost thirty years. Dur-

ing the same period, however, from 1916 through 1944, Hearst newspaper editors and the Hearst corporate officials did everything in their power to eliminate the strip from the newspaper chain. Both opposing factions worked hard, but the Hearst editors and the corporation eventually won . . . Almost.

Blackbeard reports that when the Hearst comics syndicate first sent out samples of the new Sunday comic to all American papers, it got by far the poorest response of any comic they'd ever offered. No takers.

Mr. Hearst, of course, was not deterred [continues Blackbeard]. He wanted the Sunday *Kat* published. By 1916 he owned nine major Sunday newspapers from Los Angeles to New York. These papers got their orders: print *Krazy Kat* every week. Don't argue; the old man wants it in. . . . Most readers simply could not fathom the strip. They quickly paged past it. Advertisers complained. And so, by the end of World War I, the various Hearst editors began to seek out new reasons to deep-six the *Kat* page whenever possible. For a while, Hearst fought back. Finally, continuing editorial resistance and his own new interest in making movies in Hollywood wore him down. Through the 1920s and the early 1930s, he settled for the regular appearance of the Sunday *Kat* in the one Hearst paper where the editor seemed to actually like the strip—the Seattle *Post-Intelligencer*. . . . Thanks largely to Mr. Hearst's largesse, Herriman remained nonetheless well-paid during those decades in which he drew largely a public void. Herriman's small but critically prestigious following gave him a vital sense of an audience that both knew and cared.

The moral is, dear reader, whether you're the owner of a newspaper chain or not, your committed dedication to and support of a contemporary artist whose greatness you (perhaps alone) recognize, may make a difference. Allen Ginsberg certainly did that for

Jack Kerouac. And Cézanne and Philip K. Dick only got by thanks to the help of a few friends.

So okay, in spite of the Beatles and *Winnie-the-Pooh*, great universality does not necessarily mean great popularity, does not necessarily show up in the bean-counting types of greatest-hits charts. But the question remains: Why are George Herriman's imaginary "Coconino County"—based on a real place, the Arizona county of that name that encloses the Painted Desert and parts of Monument Valley, frequently visited by an appreciative Herriman—and the characters who people it as real to this reader as the settings and interactions evoked by Bob Dylan in his songs "Mr. Tambourine Man" and "Desolation Row" and by Philip K. Dick in his novels? How do they know so much about me? They don't—it's just that we humans really do live in the same collectively and privately perceived reality, and these artists happily stumble on ways to paint or draw or write or sing that touch essential elements of this common realm and allow us to recognize it and ourselves in it via their works of "art."

What is art? Something too "highbrow" for the readers of the funny papers? Not necessarily. God, the author of this volume even sees spaghetti westerns as "art"! Anyway, art is both the way Ignatz throws the brick and the way Krazy receives it. And the way you and I observe this interaction against those stunningly simple and gorgeous Herriman desert backgrounds. And where we go from there.

It's pretty obvious where Walt Kelly and Al Capp and Walt Disney (another Herriman admirer) went from there, even though I said earlier that it's difficult to imagine *Pogo* or *Calvin & Hobbes* having been invented and drawn without *Pooh* first blazing the path. *Krazy* precedes *Pooh* (and of course has influenced all "serious" comic art ever since), so that blows that theory. Where do we go from Coconino County? Anywhere, that's the beauty of it. In one 1919 Sunday page Herriman sheds light on the origin of the relationship between Krazy and Ignatz by depicting a past-life in ancient Egypt where Krazy was Kleopatra Kat's daughter and Ignatz a noble Roman rodent, Marcantonni Maus, who could only express his frustrated love by having a love message chiseled into a brick so he could toss the note up to the pedestal his beloved rested upon. Now, this is before Herriman illustrated a collection of Don Marquis's *Archy and Mehitabel* poems and drew those wonderful portraits of Mehitabel the cat explaining how she used to be Cleopatra. Hmm. Of course, the brick hits the Egyptian Kat's head accidentally and gives her an experience of being loved by a mouse that she would not forget for many lifetimes.

Art is fun, mostly. At least, it can be. And our relationship with it is that we learn from it and are entertained by it and find ourselves in it. By the way, at George Herriman's request his ashes after he died were scattered over the Painted Desert. So he is, was, always has been as one with it. And has given the rest of us the opportunity to be hit on the head by the same sort of revelation. Small wonder Jack Kerouac, another Herriman admirer, has written that "*Krazy Kat* was an immediate progenitor of the Beat Generation and [*Krazy's*] roots could be traced back to the glee of America, its wild, self-believing individuality." Bong!!!!!

"Smokestack Lightning"

by Howlin' Wolf

(recorded January 1956)

You've probably heard the quote before, but if you're like me you'll always be glad to hear it again—the greatest twenty words of music criticism spoken by any person in the 20th century, Sam Phillips (best known for "discovering" and first recording Elvis Presley, Johnny Cash, and Jerry Lee Lewis) describing his feelings when he first tuned in Howlin' Wolf's KWEM West Memphis radio show in 1950:

"When I heard Howlin' Wolf, I said, 'This is for me. This is where the soul of man never dies.'"

Phillips invited Wolf to record at his Memphis studio; soon they recorded Wolf's first hit single, "Moanin' at Midnight," released on Chess Records in 1951. "I tell you," Phillips told journalist Robert Palmer, who himself recorded Sam's great quote above, "the greatest show you could see to this day would be Chester Burnett [Wolf's name when he was born on a Mississippi plantation in 1910] doing one of those sessions in my studio. God, what it would be worth on film to see the fervor in that man's face when he sang. His eyes would light up, you'd see the veins come out on his neck, and, buddy, there was *nothing* on his mind but that song. He sang with his damn soul."

And it wasn't only the singing. "Smokestack Lightning," Wolf's second hit record, was recorded in

Chicago in 1956 with Hosea Lee Kennard on piano, Willie Johnson and Hubert Sumlin on electric guitars, Willie Dixon on bass guitar, Earl Phillips on drums, and Howlin' Wolf on vocals and harmonica. What made this recording a "hit" with the black Americans who bought many thousands of copies of the single after they heard it on "rhythm & blues" radio stations in 1956 and with young white Americans and Europeans—many of them future "rock and roll" stars—when we heard it as a track on Wolf's first LP (long-playing record) a few years later was of course the extraordinary presence and power of Wolf's voice, but it was also something paradoxically separate from yet inseparable from that voice: a *sound*, a combination of wondrous elements all adding up to one singular and endlessly provocative experience: the sound of this recording. A sound that will live forever in the hearts and minds and consciousnesses of almost every human who encounters it, the sound of Howlin' Wolf's (and Hubert Sumlin's and Hosea Kennard's, etc.) "Smokestack Lightning." "Oh, don't you hear me crying?!!"

In the history of art, the 20th century marks the first time it was possible to create an enduring art object, like a painting on canvas, out of recorded sounds. As a result there is not much language yet in which to describe the remarkable aesthetic triumph of the guitar riff that frames and characterizes "Smokestack Lightning." Tone is a large part of it, as surely as it is in the relationship of colors in a Matisse painting. Relationship is vital here, too: the position (and tone) of the bass-and-drums combination in relation to the riff, and to the voice. The sympathetic listener senses (often is overwhelmed by) the precise location and texture of each sound within a palpable sonic space as well defined as if it were framed like a Rembrandt. A space where artist and audience meet.

They get into the bloodstream, those rhythms and tones, while the Wolf's voice enters the listener's mind. In this case a 20th-century listener's mind, one that is busily learning how to inhabit this space: the three-minute recording. Words and music and voices and instruments together. Powerful noncognitive spir-

itual information. In compact secular containers. Universally
available. "Oh, don't you hear me . . . ?"

"So," you ask (old-fashioned mind hasn't left us altogether):
"What do the words say? What's the song about?" It's about a
train (familiar 19th-century object). And about the anguish that
men and women normally cause each other just by being men
and women (i.e., sexual beings). "Ohhh, smokestack lightning,
shining just like gold, oh don't you hear me crying? woo-oooh,
woo-oooh." This can be understood as the speaker addressing the
train as though it were some spiritual apparition or presence, seen
and felt across the farmlands at night. A far-off inspiration, a
friend to share intimate feelings with. And without missing a
beat, the speaker addresses his lover (in his mind while standing
alone outside at night? or face to face in her cabin?): "Well . . .
Tell me baby, what's the matter here? Oh don't you hear me crying? Woo-oooh." After some evocative harmonica bursts, we
learn more clearly what's on his mind: "Tell me baby, where did
you stay last night?" The next two verses manage to bring the
train and the anguished lovers together (but only thematically):
"Well, stop your train, let a poor boy ride!" Now he's speaking
to the trainman, unless he's possibly, on his knees, speaking to
his lover. Next verse is unambiguously to the woman, with
the speaker imagining himself already on that train: "Ohh, fare
you well, never see you no more, oh don't you hear me crying?"
But the last verse indicates you don't escape anguish so easily:
"Ohhh, who been here baby, since I been gone? Little bitty
boy? To go beyond . . ." Okay, I don't quite understand that last
part, never know if I'm hearing it right, but that's okay because
mystery is the primary message of this recording—the atmos-
phere of which it's so "atmospheric." The quality that makes
us listeners fall in love with it so indelibly, usually with no idea
of what words he's singing or what they could possibly mean
apart from all this musical feeling we're being washed with:
"Woo-oooh . . ."

Every entry in this book, and every one on your own alternate
list of great hits of the century, is a window onto a glorious chain

of history, history of art, history of consciousness. An intercon-nected net. Howlin' Wolf's vocal style, though inimitably his own, was primarily influenced and inspired by the singing of the great blues pioneer Charley Patton (whom Wolf met and learned from on the Dockery Plantation when he was eighteen and Pat-ton thirty-one) and secondarily by the yodeling of another great 20th-century American singer, Jimmie Rodgers. Rodgers belongs in this book, of course, as does the immortal Robert Johnson, who was a traveling companion of Chester Burnett's in the 1930s in the Mississippi Delta long before the Wolf abandoned farm-ing to move to Memphis and form a (possibly the first) rock-and-roll band. Another contender for the title of Founder of the First Rock and Roll Band is Rice Miller, aka Sonny Boy William-son II, another traveling companion of Wolf's from the 1930s, and the first blues kid on the block (in the United States) to get his own radio show and a sponsor (King Biscuit Flour; Wolf's West Memphis sponsor was House of Bread). The story of Wolf's link to London's Rolling Stones will be touched upon in entry #35.

But the chain of history that made this century and its art what it was and is naturally goes as far back as we the species do, as demonstrated in this helpful comment by Gordon McGregor from an Internet site called BluesNet—helpful for those of us who wonder where all this mystery feeling we're being delighted by comes from:

> It is maintained by some blues writers that Delta blues artists, of which Wolf is an example, came from a tribe in Africa which communicates microtonally, that is, in har-monic increments that are smaller than those in the Euro-pean 12-tone scale. In addition to the polyrhythmic playing, it is what sets these blues apart not only from other types of music but also from other types of blues. The feeling produced can often be very eerie and "magical" as if the music somehow escapes time and the harmonic con-straints of European music.

Don't rule out the possibility that listening to Delta blues (including of course his hero Howlin' Wolf) is what (besides Cézanne) first got Bob Dylan (see entry #14) interested in stopping time.

Let a poor boy ride. . . .

God Bless You, Mr. Rosewater,
or Pearls Before Swine

by Kurt Vonnegut, Jr.

(published April 1965)

Under "normal" circumstances, this novel surely would never have found a publisher. It's not a novel according to almost any definition embraced by critics or academics or editors or the public at the time of its writing. To make matters worse, it doesn't fit into any genre (specialized market—e.g., "mysteries," "westerns," "horror," "romance," "thrillers"). It isn't remotely a "science fiction" novel, even though the author had previously published two slightly science-fictional novels (*Player Piano*, 1952, and *The Sirens of Titan*, 1959) that were close enough (and fortunate enough) to find paperback publishers who were willing to foist them on the public via the science fiction sections of bookstores and drugstore racks.

No publisher usually means no public and therefore little chance to be remembered as a major work (notable exceptions, from the consensus greatest-hits list of 19th-century art: the poems of Emily Dickinson and the paintings of Vincent Van Gogh—also worth noting within this parenthesis are great hits of the 19th-century published in tiny and obscure editions that eventually found large publics anyway by virtue of their critical reputations and the passage of time: *Walden, Moby-Dick, Les Fleurs du Mal*).

All of which is mentioned here by way of calling the reader's attention to the inevitable fact that placement on any greatest hits list, or in any highfalutin "art" or "literature" curriculum, depends on circumstances as well as or as much as on merit.

The funny thing about circumstances, of course, is that there are no normal ones, in the sense that they vary hugely from year to year and context to context—thousands of different factors affect every little event (including the publication or nonpublication and success or nonsuccess of any book). And at the same time it is not too absurd to speak of "normal circumstances," as I did above, because there are bulges of probability, waves rising and falling and sometimes enduring for decades or longer, whereby we can say that it's normal in book publishing circles for a marvelously funny and ambitious and original and well-executed literary effort by a writer who's already had several novels published to find some kind of publisher, but not at all normal for that to happen if the book in question is absurdly remote from almost anyone's professional idea of what a "novel" or a book-length work of fiction is supposed to be like, in terms of narrative structure, style, content, tone, and emphasis. That's *God Bless You, Mr. Rosewater*, in both cases, and the special circumstances that gave rise to its publication in book form by Holt, Rinehart & Winston in April 1965, when Kurt Vonnegut, Jr., was forty-two years old, are largely the same as those for entries #1 and 2: It was the 1960s. And the arbiters of taste in the overdeveloped Western nations were the young: the unwashed and collectively rebellious and surprisingly affluent teenagers and college students and ex-teens and college dropouts of the era. They ruled. And they identified with Eliot Rosewater, and, most of all, with his creator, Kurt Vonnegut, Jr.

True, the whole miracle of GBYMR's publication probably couldn't have happened in the first place without a couple of surprisingly favorable reviews in the "establishment" press for Mr. V's previous novel, another highly idiosyncratic and, if you were young, gloriously lovable work, *Cat's Cradle* (1963). What circumstances caused *Cat's Cradle* to get this break, when equally weird and equally superb earlier Vonnegut novels like *Mother Night* and *The Sirens of Titan* caused no blips whatsoever on the media's radar screens? The easy answer is, "timing." See my accompanying seven-volume text: *A Closely Documented Look at Elements of Timing, and Related Circumstances, in the Success and Nonsuccess of One Hundred of the Finest Paintings and Novels and Films and Musical Recordings of the Years 1901–2000* (Encinitas: Holt, Rinehart & Williams, 2002).

Surprisingly, *God Bless You, Mr. Rosewater* can be read now as an intuitive but almost unerring metaphor for the history of the '60s Generation, the "baby boomers" conceived in North America and Europe and Japan when mothers and fathers reunited after the end of World War II, who then came of age in the rock-and-roll, antiwar, free-loving, anti-authority, psychedelic-drug-taking, underground-press-reading, "countercultural" years of the mid-1960s. No sex or drugs or overt hippie philosophizing in this book (though you can find the latter in *Cat's Cradle* and *Sirens of Titan* if you wish). Even the antiwar theme is understated, very secondary until or unless it occurs to the reader as the novel ends that in fact Eliot Rosewater's remarkable idiocy and his keen sense of purpose are the direct result of his suffering from what was not yet in 1965 called "Post-Traumatic Stress Syndrome," due to injuries suffered by his conscience and his consciousness in wartime military service.

The relationship between Eliot and his father, right-wing, money-loving, outspokenly-contemptuous-of-the-poor, Republican congressman Lister Rosewater, as portrayed in marvelously comic (and teeth-gratingly accurate) dialogues between the two throughout the novel, is probably (along with anthropologist Margaret Mead's 1968 book on the subject) the definitive portrayal and description of what came to be known as the "generation gap" between parents and children in many postwar nations in the middle of the 20th century. According to Mead, this was a direct consequence of the explosion of the first atomic weapon, so that there were sharp divisions between survivors from the world that had existed before August 6, 1945, and the newcomers who were born in this newly created world and therefore natives to the place. Neither could comprehend or accept or respect the values and worldview of the other. GBYMR portrays this, as if written decades later when one could achieve such a perspective, but in fact written four years before the first use of the phrase "generation gap."

It's a comic, sometimes tragicomic, novel about values that gains its punch because the philosophical and ethical dilemmas it wrestles with are sincere, are very real to the author and utterly recognizable to the book's readers (when it was published, and ever since). He's really trying to figure it out—and so are we, as if we were voters in any modern nation sincerely trying to make up our minds between well-articulated "liberal" and "conservative" arguments about a political decision involving the well-being of the "have-nots" and the responsibilities of the "haves." Hilarious satire. But simultaneously (as has often been the case in literature) a stimulating and effective discourse on ethics, an argument made directly to the public, to the human collective consciousness. This is what a poet or novelist or essayist is supposed to do. And *GBYMR* is here on this list because it does it in a way that is likely to endure, due to its merit, and due to a large set of circumstances that catapulted Kurt Vonnegut, Jr., from "unsuccessful pulp novelist" to "enduring literary figure" rather rapidly and dramatically, and due to the fact that the maker of this particular list loved *God Bless You, Mr. Rosewater* when he read it the year it was published and still loves it thirty-four years later and believes it's worth bringing along on the spaceship/time machine voyage from the 20th century to the Future. And finds himself wondering if this is why he later joined and spent ten years in a small-town volunteer fire department.

Yeah, but. "Yeah, but, are you *sure* GBYMR is the right Vonnegut novel for your list? What about—," ask my friends and my readers (who are, I hope, the same people). And I reply patiently that this list is not intended to pronounce judgments as to "the best Beatles song," "the best Kubrick film," "the best Faulkner work," "the best Billie Holiday performance." I don't believe in preserving great art Noah's Ark fashion, with one or two of each animal. One Picasso painting to remember him by. But which one? That's not the mind-state I'm choosing to function in or wish to encourage in my readers. It's more like: quick, name forty works of art you'd take with you to a desert island (isolated in space and time, no Internet, so you gotta choose earnestly and sincerely). (But not too carefully, because my aesthetic puts a high value on spontaneity.)

Which Kurt Vonnegut novel is my personal favorite? In 1964 it was *Cat's Cradle*. In 1969 it was *Slaughterhouse Five*. In between, and out of sequence a few years later, it was *Mother Night* and then *Sirens of Titan* and, briefly, as I read it, *Player Piano*. So it went. And if I don't name any novels written after *Slaughterhouse Five*, that's not a judgment on my part regarding merit so much as it is an acknowledgment of diverse circumstances that changed my (Vonnegut) reading habits. Anyway, the question reasonably arises, since characters and perspectives recur throughout this man's work, is this another metanovel, like Philip K. Dick's? Yes and no. Dick's novels (and a few of his short stories) are all one big book and tend to be received or appreciated as such. In Vonnegut's case, his first six novels, 1952–1969, are indeed a metanovel, and ironically the seventh novel, *Breakfast of Champions*, which playfully explores this possibility, and the many KV novels that follow, are not part of the same construction.

Critic Jerome Klinkowitz cleverly points out that Vonnegut sort of acknowledges that his first six books and first twenty years of writing can all be perceived as an effort to write a single book when he says, at the end of the introductory chapter of *Slaughterhouse Five:* "I've finished my war book now. The next one I write is going to be fun." And we mutter, "Yeah, Boss, but the pieces of your war book (and that wartorn decade when the last three were written) were the most fun for *us!*" Why is that? For answers to questions like that, you gotta read Vonnegut. And I'm reminded of how much I loved the next sentence of *Slaughterhouse Five* (which makes sense because the one quoted above is preceded by "People aren't supposed to look back") back when I first read it: "This one [this book] is a failure, and had to be, since it was written by a pillar of salt."

Like Eliot Rosewater, Kurt Vonnegut, Jr., is a traumatized World War II veteran. Like Eliot's lower-middle-class-trash cousin

Fred, Kurt is also the son of a suicide (mother in K's case, not father). Little wonder *GBYMR* is a remarkably compassionate book. Little wonder Sylvia Rosewater is possibly the most sympathetic and human character in the novel. I love the scene where she says quietly to her wickedly didactic father-in-law, "as her doctor would have wanted her to," "'I don't want to argue.'" And he forces her to argue anyway and she acquits herself (and Eliot) magnificently. It's in Chapter 5. Heart of the novel. Another priceless scene (to name two out of dozens) is the Senator at the very end finding himself sincerely and enthusiastically sharing his son's appreciation of Kilgore Trout, the crackpot science fiction writer, who is certainly partly KV, Jr., albeit partly named after KV's friend Theodore Sturgeon (see entry #23).

Which is my favorite, out of the top 40 greatest hits of the 20th century? The one that I'm reading or listening to or experiencing right now. Which just could be all of them simultaneously.

HIT

30

Impressions, side one

by *John Coltrane*

(recorded November 3, 1961, and September 18, 1962)

During the year 1957, I experienced, by the grace of God, a spiritual awakening which was to lead me to a richer, fuller, more productive life. At that time, in gratitude I humbly asked to be given the means and privilege to make others happy through music.

—John Coltrane, 1964, in the liner notes to his long-playing record *A Love Supreme*

Dear friends, readers of these words, I would like you to meet, and experience the intimate friendships between and the creative interactions among, six men, all North Americans of African descent and all musicians: John Coltrane, tenor saxophone and soprano saxophone; Eric Dolphy, bass clarinet; Elvin Jones, drums; McCoy Tyner, piano; Reggie Workman, bass guitar; and Jimmy Garrison, bass guitar.

It is the nature of art, a deeply spiritual nature as Coltrane would be the first to tell you, that you can indeed meet these men and spend intimate time with them (and, by extension, with the other persons and forces in their lives) as soon as you wish, and for as long as you wish, simply by experiencing (in this case, listening to) an example of their collective artwork.

Here it is. Two songs, seventeen minutes, one side of a vinyl LP released in 1963 called *Impressions*. I first encountered it at age twenty in a college dormitory in Vermont, where I was visiting a young woman I'd met on an airplane. I went back to California, went shopping, and soon was spending a lot of intense and happy (and psychedelic) time with the above-mentioned gentlemen (plus a horn player named Pharoah Sanders and a percussionist named Rashied Ali, because I'd also picked up another Coltrane LP a Velvet Underground fan had raved at me about months earlier, called *Meditations*).

So of course I see a lot of interconnections between side one of *Impressions* and most of these other great "hits" that I propose to keep with me through a few more lifetimes as mementoes of a fabulous century (and as reliable friends and guides in my present life regardless of what they meant to me back then). Trane himself, after his first LSD trip (in Seattle, with another musician, before a recording date in 1965), reported: "I perceived the interrelationship of all life forms." Sounds like Moggallana (see entries #18 and 12), who "suddenly saw the universe as an interconnected net." Because it is. And when you get a jolt of awakening, you tend to see things as they really are. Either side of this album is certainly capable of delivering that jolt (lovingly) to the receptive listener, whether you speak jazz or not. I didn't, and still don't, though I do, happily, speak Coltrane—he and Elvin et al. taught me in a flash via these two songs ("India," "Up 'Gainst the Wall").

In case it's not obvious why Trane called his album *Impressions* (maybe you're thinking those darting sax solos are a little more edgy than any part of Monet's *Water Lilies*), let me remind you of the Emerson lines I quoted in the *Pet Sounds* chapter about how "great works of art teach us to abide by our spontaneous impression then most when the whole cry of voices is on the other side." I don't know if Coltrane was familiar with this quote, but when he and his record company released this album based around two tour de force performances from his quartet's legendary nights at the Village Vanguard in New York City in November 1961, he had already endured, within the small but incestuous world of jazz musicians and critics and listeners, a whole cry of voices so outspokenly hostile to his autumn 1961 experiments that his best friend and primary collaborator Eric Dolphy left Coltrane's group after six months because of his discomfort at the criticism. And Coltrane certainly did abide by the spontaneous impressions he and Eric and Elvin set down in those months. As Coltrane's biographer John Fraim reports, "Even more than representing a particular period in the Coltrane music of the sixties, Dolphy set the tone, the energy level, for much of the amazing music soon to follow. In some respects he was an Elvin Jones of the horn as he kept pushing Coltrane higher and higher during those extended solo flights so common to this period."

Why just one side of an album? Because it's a genuine experiential unit. If I go with the whole album, which is certainly as deserving of a place on my list, my mind (and maybe yours too) would immediately start in with, "Are you *sure*? What about *A Love Supreme, Giant Steps?*" Or if I just go with "India," which makes up fourteen of those seventeen minutes, my mind starts arguing that when you're picking *one* Coltrane song/performance as his (or a) greatest hit, you simply can't overlook "My Favorite Things." And what about "Africa"? "Alabama"? "Naima"? etc., etc. . . . And by choosing the whole first side of *Impressions*, I'm actually being true to my own experience, which is: *This* is what got me and still does get me, these two together as a complete listening experience. I love the way "'Gainst" works as a further coda to "India," as if it had been perfectly planned that way. Very gratifying. And just as effective as the trick endings accidentally built into "Sister Ray." And it is remotely possible that it *was* planned that way, because Trane did a lot of recording in 1962, and if his producer said, "I want to put out an album with a Vanguard '61 'India' on one side and an 'Impressions' from the same dates on the other side," Trane might have thought for a moment and said, "There's a tune I have in mind to fill out the rest of the time [to arrive at "normal" album side time] after 'India.' . . ."

And you already know I'm not trying to say, "This is JC's best performance" or "This is KV's best novel." I'm saying, "This is it!"—not in competition with or instead of those other great works, but a perfect expression for my purposes, for this list's purposes, of what I think should (nay, *must*) be remembered from our era. And also, if you're not already a happy Coltrane listener, I'm confident this is a good place to start. Sure worked for me. And all those critics who reviled the fall '61 Coltrane-and-augmented-Quartet performances, their problem was they knew too much. Their ideas about what jazz is *supposed* to be or what John Coltrane (or Brian Wilson or Henri Matisse) is *supposed* to do are interfering with their ability to receive and enjoy the great power and beauty of this new (to them, and to John and Eric) magical music.

Oddly enough, here is an indication that song two on this memorable album side, the one that was recorded in a Manhattan studio in September 1962, "Up 'Gainst the Wall," might actually be a reference to such misunderstandings, in the form of a recollection from the great flautist Rahsaan Roland Kirk (quoted in J. C. Thomas's 1975 book *Chasin' the Trane*):

> One night we were down in the Village listening to Max Roach, and John talked about how he felt "up against the wall" in his music because a lot of musicians had told him that what he was doing "wasn't hip enough." Talk like that used to give John a bad case of the blues.

Regarding the title of the other painting, I mean performance, on this album side, Bill Cole, in his 1976 biography *John Coltrane*, writes, "In the same year that he composed 'Africa' he also composed 'India,'" which served to honor both the country and the name of the daughter of his great friend Calvin Massey." Several significant Coltrane compositions are celebrations or evocations of specific people; "Naima" is the name of his first wife. But in this case, as Cole tells us, the title and composition serve a double purpose, because there is no doubt that Coltrane in 1961 was attempting to incorporate into the "free jazz" idiom the structure and feeling of the classical Indian music he'd encountered in recordings of Ravi Shankar and others. Later (1965) he named his second son Ravi. But the long-lasting nature of the inspiration behind this 1961 performance is indicated by David Amram's recollection (quoted by J. C. Thomas) of a conversation with Trane back in spring 1956: "He said that one of the things he was trying to do was to take music beyond the 32-bar song form, to constantly develop and improvise on an idea or a simple line, as Indian musicians do with a raga." Contemplating this, and realizing that the reason Coltrane used two bass guitar players on this performance was to reach toward the drone effect of the tamboura in a raga, one is struck by the geographical and cultural feat Jones and Coltrane achieve by successfully replacing Indian tabla with African drumming (on an African-American jazz drum kit), as though space and time and centuries of cultural history need not be obstacles when the medium is music and the quest is sincere and earnest and the searchers are possessed of genius.

And please remember, though information about the artists' intentions and influences and contexts is intriguing, the essence of great painting and music and other arts is that their beauty and profundity speak directly to and of the observer. Knowing nothing about jazz or Indian ragas, I was (and still am) overcome by the beauty of this performance and how much it has to say to me about invisible matters that are of tremendous personal importance to me. Like a Monet painting that captures a particular late-afternoon glow and the spiritual implications thereof that I'd thought were mine alone until I saw this painting, the Coltrane sextet's "India" captures a particular New York City sound, and the feelings that sound evokes, with compassionate intelligence and humor and a profound understanding of the oneness of human experience from the ancient African bush to the modern western metropolis. And no guidebook is required. To understand "India," you need only listen to "India" (and "Up 'Gainst the Wall") at the right moment. You'll be glad you did.

What is spiritual about this music is the intensity and sincerity of John Coltrane's quest for understanding, his heartfelt and palpable need to follow the directions that music and his relationship with music keep opening for him. The only difference between this side of Coltrane's *Impressions* and the Nusrat Fateh

Ali Khan qawwali performances I experienced in concert in 1995 is that in the latter case the performers and most of the audience are certain that the purpose of this evening's gathering is to share an ecstatic experience.

And I'm happy to tell you that although "India" from 11/3/61 followed by "'Gainst" from 9/18/62 is quite enough and complete in itself, if you want more of this particular moment in Coltrane's search there is, as an addition to the huge body of wonderful work left behind by this artist when he died at age forty in July 1967, a set of recordings now commercially available called *The Complete 1961 Village Vanguard Recordings*, four CDs of music performed live over the course of four nights, and including four different takes of "India," with different improvised solos within the same compositional structure. Snapshots from the expedition.

In the liner notes of the original *Coltrane "Live" at the Village Vanguard* album, Nat Hentoff quotes Coltrane on the subject of his friendship and collaboration with Eric Dolphy: "For a long time Eric and I had been talking about all kinds of possibilities with regard to improvising, scale work, and techniques. These discussions helped both of us to keep probing. Having him here [in the band now] all the time is a constant stimulus to me."

The six men playing on "India" and the four on "Up 'Gainst the Wall" are a constant stimulus to one another. In this sense, another subject of this particular work of art is friendship and the experience of journeying or creating or just being together with other human beings.

John Coltrane was thirty-five years old when he performed "India" in November 1961. His collaborators' ages ranged from twenty-two (McCoy Tyner) to thirty-four (Elvin Jones). This music they made together is full of the energy and enthusiasm of young men enjoying and appreciating life. Men on a mission. The spiritual awakening Coltrane refers to in his *Love Supreme* notes came when he was thirty, and it was the direct result of a conscious decision to stop using heroin and alcohol and other drugs. John Fraim tells the story very well in his fascinating book *Spirit Catcher: The Life and Art of John Coltrane*:

He awoke one morning and told Naima and his mother that he wanted to stop using drugs and asked for their help. . . . He then retreated into his room, where he would battle the terrible pains of withdrawal for the next few days. . . . About four days later, he announced to his family that he was no longer addicted to heroin or alcohol. There was a certain look of tranquillity on his face, a certain awestruck expression. He was extremely quiet. Naima asked him if something was wrong. . . . He told her that he had a dream in which he heard this droning sound. "It was so beautiful," he told her. She asked him to describe it and he tried but found it impossible.

Fraim tells us John attempted to play it on the piano and gave up after a few minutes. "With this event, the search for the mysterious sound began. It was a search that would cause him to create some of his most intense and emotional music."

Elsewhere in his book Fraim says of late 1961: "At clubs during this period Coltrane would often play an extended solo on his horn for upwards of an hour." Of course this made me think of Umm Kulthum. What gets into the artist/performer? Enthusiasm. *Enthousiasmos*, the state of being possessed by, or full of, God.

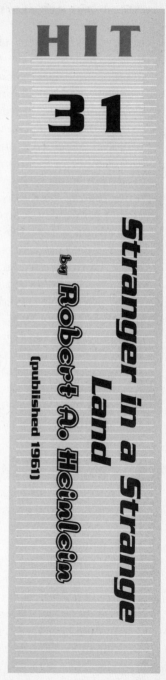

HIT 31

Stranger in a Strange Land

by **Robert A. Heinlein**

(published 1961)

Speaking of being full of God, did you ever hear the story about the Martian named Smith? If not, you're in the minority. *Stranger in a Strange Land* is one of the best-selling and most-read novels of the 20th century. Robert Heinlein's working title for this book, when he wrote to his literary agent in January 1955 to say he was on page 68 of the first draft, was "A Martian Named Smith." At other times he considered calling it "The Heretic," or "The Sound of His Wings," or "The Man from Mars."

There is, by the way, a geological formation on Mars, a crater probably formed by the impact of celestial debris, officially named the Heinlein Crater (by act of the International Astronomical Union on Earth, 1994). This had nothing to do with Mr. Smith's popularity, but was done as an acknowledgment of the tremendous role that Robert Heinlein's 1940, 1941, 1947, and 1948 science fiction stories— about near-space exploration in the near-future—played in making the American (and world) public supportive of the idea of undertaking an expensive and risky "space program."

Robert A. Heinlein was a science fiction writer, born in Butler, Missouri (hence the frequent comparisons between Heinlein's life and work and Mark Twain's), on July 7, 1907. So he was fifty-four years old in 1961 when *Stranger* was published, and forty-one in early 1949 when he started writing this novel (thinking about it, contemplating its premise and story line and making notes on questions and ideas generated by that premise). In many ways Heinlein can be, and often is, credited with originating or anyway defining the 20th-century concept or role of "science fiction writer." Bob did it. Did it by doing it so well and so much and with such confidence and imagination and popular appeal that lots of other people wanted to be "science fiction writers" too. And even more chose to be science fiction readers after encountering their first few Robert Heinlein novels or short stories.

But *Stranger in a Strange Land* is not a space story. Unlike Dick's *Martian Time-Slip* or Heinlein's own 1949 masterpiece *Red Planet*, it does not take place on Mars. Mr. Smith is *from* Mars but he's of Earth ancestry, and his story, as told in *SIASL*, takes place on Earth. And it's a great story about life on Earth. Mark Twain wrote a creditable candidate for the Great American Novel, and his fellow Missourian R. A. Heinlein may well have written, in *Stranger in a Strange Land,* a reasonable candidate for the Great Earth Novel. Um, I'm not suggesting it has the sort of literary strengths found in Tolstoi or Dickens or Mann or Cervantes. But it is an extraordinary (and very original, despite the plot similarities to the New Testament) evocation of physical and mental life on Earth that because of the inherent timelessness of its premise may last and may continue to be enjoyed by many millions of readers per century into the unforeseeable future. What a yarn! What a mind stimulant! (Yeah, but not the sort of mind stimulant science fiction readers are used to and go to science fiction for. Don't confront crossword puzzle buffs with a Rubik's Cube if they've never seen one before and were expecting a new and challenging but not too unfamiliar crossword puzzle! *SIASL* was not well received by science fiction critics and commentators, although it did win one of R.A.H.'s four Hugo Awards for best science fiction novel of the year . . .)

Kurt Vonnegut (see entry #29) reviewed *Stranger in a Strange Land* in the *New York Times Book Review* in 1991 when the "original uncut" version of this novel was released posthumously by the same publisher who thirty years earlier had required Heinlein to cut sixty thousand words (27 percent) from his manuscript before they would publish it. Vonnegut's essay is (methinks) very much in the spirit of this Greatest Hits book you're reading now. He describes a recent literary event, a dinner party at the home of a London publisher, where the host asked his distinguished guests, "What is the best novel ever written?" KV reports: "I nominated *Madame Bovary*. A majority went for *Anna Karenina*. Afterward, as I sat alone in my hotel room, I marveled that none of us had celebrated a story that took place in the world at large rather than in a stratified and codified little society."

Vonnegut goes on to say of *SIASL* that "an enormous number of readers have found this book a brilliant mind-bender, and yet I doubt that Heinlein's name was ever uttered at a meeting of PEN or in the halls of the American Academy and Institute of Arts and Letters." He points out:

> The name of the leading character in *Stranger in a Strange Land* is as familiar to millions of literate persons as Oliver Twist or Holden Caulfield. He is Valentine Michael Smith . . . raised by Martians on Mars without ever having seen another human being. And to those who get to say which novels are serious and which are not, professional critics and teachers of literature in the company of authors of novels about the rise or fall of ordinary people in provincial societies, he is absolutely intolerable. And I say that their rejection of not only Valentine Michael Smith but his creator, too, is an act based on social prejudices, and that intellectual and esthetic standards have nothing to do with it.
>
> In the Soviet Union before *glasnost* the Writer's Union regularly said that some writers weren't really writers, no matter how much and how well they had written, since they were politically incorrect. In this country the same thing is done to writers like Robert A. Heinlein because they are socially incorrect, because their stories are about places members of the literary establishment do not care to visit

and about characters, many of them not even human or humanoid, they simply do not care to befriend.

Truth be told, the establishment, on the same grounds, isn't all that fond of *Candide* or *Gulliver's Travels*, either, both of which I should have championed at Tom Maschler's house. I should have at least mentioned *Stranger in a Strange Land* as well, a wonderfully humanizing artifact for those who can enjoy thinking about the place of human beings not at a dinner table but in the universe.

Amen. Eliot Rosewater couldn't have said it better. As for those deleted sixty thousand words, dear reader, it sounds scandalous, but be assured that if you can lay your hands on one of those millions of pre-1990 copies of this novel, you'll be missing nothing; in fact, in my opinion the pre-1990 trimmed-by-the-author-under-duress version is the preferred text. Same great story and all the same scenes and conversations, with none of the "good parts" excised. In fact Heinlein's self-editing (tightening) is so skillful that a comparison of any few pages of the two texts would be an excellent exercise for any aspiring writer. Behold how a motivated author can tighten sentences and paragraphs in a well-formed narrative so that every paragraph contains fewer words and the whole thing reads that much faster, without ever losing or being untrue to the voices of his characters or of his narrative. Impressive stunt! By way of example, compare the first ten paragraphs of chapter 27 in both versions. The released-in-1990 "original uncut" text contains 418 words here; the 1961 originally published first ten paragraphs contain 271 words (a reduction of 35 percent). The content is unchanged. Every original paragraph or bit of dialogue is recognizably present in the shorter, first-published version. The flavor throughout is exactly the same; it just melts in the reader's mind a little faster.

This is a testament to the power of the gentleman's storytelling. It almost always has that mark of the creator's personality which Matisse was startled to notice looking over his own work. Picasso's or any master's underpaintings, early drafts, tend to be just as full of that artist's greatness as the "finished" or official works. Editing and revising, even under duress, can be part of the author's process. In this case, the proof of the pudding is in the eating, the reading. It always was a great novel, a great entertainment and a powerful provocation ("mind-bender") and still is, and if there's to be a schism in the future between adherents of the separate "versions," that's certainly appropriate for a spoof on both human religions and human religious texts. . . .

As for that premise: Heinlein's greatness as a storyteller rests primarily on his unusual skill at developing a fictional (or science fiction) premise, with rigor and freshness and insight and imagination and marvelous attention to detail. He is an inspired artist in this particular realm, yarn after yarn. And never more so than in *Stranger in a Strange Land*, though some readers of course find the implications of this particular premise and his development of it overwhelming and thus distasteful. So it's not for everybody. But neither is *Moby-Dick* or *Crime and Punishment* or *Gulliver's Travels*.

The premise of *SIASL* was suggested by Virginia Heinlein in 1949, less than a year after Robert and Virginia's wedding:

> Robert was looking for an idea for a story he had promised to write John Campbell for a special issue of *Astounding*. We approached this task in a fashion today known as brainstorming. I would put up an idea and Robert would knock it down. I suggested it might be possible to do something like the Mowgli story [Kipling, 1894]—a human infant raised by a foreign race, kept apart from humans until he reached maturity. 'Too big an idea for a short story,' said Robert, but he made a note about it. Later he disappeared into his study and wrote eighteen pages, single-spaced, of notes on ideas which the Mowgli suggestion had started rolling in his brain. He worked on those pages the whole night, and came out with a batch of papers titled The Man from Mars.

Three years later, July 1952, Heinlein wrote to his literary agent Lurton Blassingame about the problems he was having with the novel he was trying to write:

The story itself is giving me real trouble. I believe that I have dreamed up a really new SF idea, a hard thing to do these days—but I am having trouble coping with it. The gimmick is "The Man from Mars" in a very literal sense. The first expedition to Mars never comes back. The second expedition, twenty years later, finds that all hands of the first expedition died—except one infant, born on Mars and brought up by Martians. They bring this young man back with them.

This creature is half-human, half-Martian, i.e., his heredity is human, his total environment up to the age of twenty is Martian. He is literally not human, he was raised by Martians, he has never heard of sex nor seen a woman, has never felt full earth-normal gravity. Absolutely *everything* about Earth is strange to him—its orientations, motives, pleasures, evaluations. On the other hand he himself has received the education of a wise and subtle and very advanced—but completely nonhuman—race.

That's the kickoff. From there anything can happen.

And it did. And who it happened to was not only Valentine Michael Smith and his friends and the rest of the Earth, it was also Robert Heinlein. That, I suspect, is why the novel took another eight years to be finished. Robert and Ginny's premise (their child, if you will; they had no fleshly progeny) came alive in Robert's mind and talked him into things he'd never imagined himself believing or anyway admitting publicly. Robert was snagged by his greatest trump card as a storyteller and science fictioneer: his respect for a premise and his commitment to the logical and earnest development of its implications. Like Jubal and Ben and Jill in the novel, he listened while Michael talked, observing humanity from his "man from Mars" perspective. The reference is to the often-mentioned hypothetical outside observer of a situation who is somehow able to look at it without seeing through the distorting lenses of universally accepted local concepts and assumptions and value-biases. "How would this look to a man from Mars?"

October 21, 1960, when the novel was done, Heinlein reca-
pitulated to Blassingame: "This story is supposed to be a completely free-wheeling look at contemporary human culture from
the nonhuman viewpoint of the Man from Mars (in the sense of
the philosophical cliché). Under it, I take nothing for granted
and am free to lambaste anything from the Girl Scouts and
Mother's Apple Pie to the idea of patriotism. No sacred cows of
any sort, no bows and graceful compliments to the royal box—
that is the whole idea of the framework. . . . Using the freedom of
the mythical man from Mars . . . I have undertaken to criticize
and examine disrespectfully the two untouchables: monotheism
and monogamy."

My study of Heinlein's correspondence (in the posthumous
book *Grumbles from the Grave*, put together by Virginia) does not
suggest that his intention from the outset was to write a novel
criticizing these "two untouchables." Rather, his focus, as he
expressed it in July '52, was on "how to manipulate the selected
elements for maximum drama," in order that the story not
become "static and philosophic." Okay, so he built in a conflict
with a despotic planetary government that wants to imprison or
exploit this man from Mars. To make the struggle more even, he
gave Smith more power, in the form of enormous wealth and
then also in the form of certain yogic tricks (telekinesis, and the
ability to slow down or speed up his bodily functions) that he
learned from his Martian tutors.

Another form of story-stimulating conflict arose when Heinlein found himself creating a future USA in which an energetic
evangelic church is gaining power by combining skillful use of
modern media like TV with equally skillful use of good old-
fashioned mob psychology—and of course the principals of this
Fosterite Church of the New Revelation regard the Man from
Mars as either a useful ally or dangerous competition. So this creates conflict, and Valentine Michael Smith of course responds by
asking questions about all the things he doesn't understand
(everything Earthly, but especially sex and religion), and his
friends, notably a cranky old writer of popular fiction named
Jubal Harshaw, try to explain in ways that are true to their feel-

ings but could possibly make sense to a charmingly innocent and curious man from Mars.

Smith then processes all this input and tries to make it jibe with the Martian way of looking at things. Another power Heinlein has given Michael, or that he has seized for himself as characters in novels sometimes will beyond the expectations of their creators, is an extraordinary charm deriving from his extreme and very genuine innocence combined with a tremendous self-confidence that would have to be called arrogance if he weren't so likable. Other characters love him and find his youthful idealism and earnest boyishness irresistible, as do readers. And as does the author, who finds himself arguing with his creation via various surrogates, and inexorably losing the argument, that is, succumbing to the seductive charm of this Mars-born, premise-born, creature.

So Michael evolves into the ultimate small-c communist and the shockingly charismatic leader of a freewheeling religious cult, in the face of his Author's fervent skepticism and staunch anti-communism. And some innocent and arrogant part of most readers learns and evolves along with him. My point is that Heinlein didn't necessarily plan this. It's just that when he finally did find a way to work his premise into an acceptably dramatic plot, his lead character, the personification of that premise, hijacked the story and turned it into a raucous wild party full of criticism and disrespectful examination of the two untouchables. Oops. The creature from the depths of the unconscious. "I am aware of the commercial difficulties in this ms.," Robert wrote Lurton in 1960, "but if it *does* get published, it might sell lots of copies." And so it did. Valentine Michael Smith really did arrive from Mars in 1961 (slightly earlier in Robert Heinlein's study), and he's been encouraging and seducing Earthlings to look at things through his eyes ever since. "Thou art God!" is his primary message. "This is not offered as a creed but as an existential assumption of personal responsibility, devoid of all godding," Robert (or maybe Jubal?) told his agent in 1960. "It says, Don't appeal for mercy to God the Father up in the sky, little man, because he's not at home and never was at home, and couldn't care less. What you do with yourself, whether you are happy or unhappy—live or die—is strictly your business and the universe doesn't care. In fact you may *be* the universe and the only cause of all your troubles. But, at best, the most you can hope for is comradeship with comrades no more divine (or just as divine) as you are. So quit sniveling and face up to it—Thou art God!"

From here anything can happen. That's the beauty of Coltrane's "India" and "Up 'Gainst the Wall" and Heinlein's *Stranger in a Strange Land*. And the last thing I have to say is that although there's no sex in *Old Path White Clouds* (entry #12), this reader finds that the yearning and idealism stirred up in him by reading Nhat Hanh's biography of the Buddha seem almost identical to the feelings still stirred in him by reading *Stranger*. "Remember, kid," he writes to himself now, "what you do with these works of art is strictly your business. Face up to it."

Since I (the person writing these chapters, and the list-maker and -defender) survived a serious head injury at the age of forty-six, a few years before I began this book, you might suppose that my selection of a short story and a very short essay by the Argentinian master of miniatures, Jorge Luis Borges, for my "greatest hits of the 20th century" list was influenced and prejudiced by the fact that Mr. Borges wrote his most successful and famous stories, his first metaphysical fictions, while still recovering from a severe head injury at age thirty-nine that left him "near death, bereft of speech and fearing for his sanity."

Yes, but. I didn't know about Borges's head injury until this week (early August 1999, one hundredth anniversary of JLB's birth) when I did some biographical research in preparation for this chapter. And I didn't know about my own future "brain injury victim" status when I fell in love with this story and this essay and several other Borges pieces when I was seventeen, a few years after the first English-language books of his writings appeared (*Ficciones* and *Labyrinths*, both 1962).

"Like all men in Babylon, I have been proconsul; like all, a slave." This is the first sentence of "The Lottery in Babylon." The statement, while certainly a line of poetry, is meant literally: The narrator tells how, as a citizen of Babylon, he has been a lifelong participant in a lottery that awards its players (every citizen) with prizes both favorable and unfavorable. That last was an innovation that became a permanent feature, because the public, the customers (back when you still had to buy a ticket), *loved* it. The narration continues, with all the impact of a six-page punch in the stomach. A compact *Ulysses*. An outwardly silent "Sister Ray." A brick on the noggin. "Nothing has been the same now that Meatball has struck me at last!" An R. Crumb comix character said that (circa 1970), and it's a fairly good description of how you, dear friend, are quite likely to feel after reading "The Lottery in Babylon" attentively for the first time. Or twelfth time. "Get me outta here, my dear man!" quoth Bob Dylan, circa 1967. Hmm. He had recently bumped his head, too.

The other Borges jewel I include here on my list of "treasures to grab first if the collective human operating system begins to crash" is an essay (nothing fictional in these pages, but "sense of wonder" enough to support a science fiction novel) called "The Wall and the Books." The essence of this durable delight can be found in its *two* opening sentences:

> I read, some days past, that the man who ordered the erection of the almost infinite wall of China was that first emperor, Shih Huang Ti, who also decreed that all books prior to him be burned. That these two vast operations— the five to six hundred leagues of stone opposing the barbarians, the rigorous abolition of history, that is, of the past—should originate in one person and be in some way his attributes inexplicably satisfied and, at the same time, disturbed me.

I could comment for days on the wondrous prose (in any language) and reverberating thoughts in every paragraph of "The Wall and the Books," but I have to cut straight to the information (gleaned partly from looking up Chinese history in my trusty one-volume *Columbia Encyclopedia*) that, like news of JLB's head injury, has just this week reached me: that primary among the books and potent forces of the past the emperor wished to obliterate was the *I Ching* (see entry #4). Okay, the Wall still stands. But so does the book, nyahh nyahh.

Borges in "real" life was a librarian. So it's fitting that "Borges," the protagonist or implied narrator or scribe of all his stories and essays, is the archetypal ideal reader, the nationless, timeless, but not unfeeling intellect who has the confidence and enthusiasm to browse freely and attentively amidst the intelligent and inspiring voices of literary or aesthetic history, those voices and minds any student or energetic book-lover may freely romp with and learn from and with.

JLB does not limit himself or his studies to a particular continent or era. The world is his oyster. And for this reason it is easy and safe to predict that Borges miniatures like the two examples cited here will continue to be read enthusiastically in future centuries and civilizations, by readers still experiencing laughter and fear and awe and awakening in all the right places.

It has been suggested (read "The Lottery in Babylon" just before or after *Gravity's Rainbow* and you'll certainly understand why) by several including TP himself that without Borges there could be no Pynchon. Nor could there be a 20th century, in my opinion, without Pynchon and Borges and Dylan and Picasso and Chaplin and Kafka. And me. And you. Borges certainly represents *my* ideal reader, the reader-participant, the one who makes his own lists in response to this one, the one who enjoys chewing on riddles like "the wall in space and the fire in time." Zen reader. So I'll let him participate in our ongoing discussion by quoting here the last three sentences of "The Wall and the Books:"

> Music, states of happiness, mythology, faces belabored by time, certain twilights and certain places try to tell us something, or have said something we should not have missed, or are about to say something; this imminence of a revelation which does not occur is, perhaps, the aesthetic phenomenon.

This would concord with the last words of entry #1:

Someday, when we're dreaming
Deep in love, not a lot to say
Then we will remember
Things we said today. . . .

HIT 33

The Little Prince
by Antoine de Saint-Exupéry
(written summer and fall 1942)

Mi primer encuentro con El Principito fue en español, cuando lo escuché decir "Por favor, dibújame un cordero." A lo largo de los años mi cariño por la historia y por este pequeño hombrecito fue ceciendo. Fue hasta después que El Principito se habla ganado un lagar indeleble en mi, que comencé a leerlo en inglés y francés.

—Manuel Delgado of Venezuela, quoted from his 1997 Internet website dedicated to *The Little Prince*

What is a greatest hit? Oh, do not expect, grown-up readers, to be able to count and measure the answer with your minds. "It is only with the heart that one can see rightly. What is essential is invisible to the eye."

A great and widely recognized work of art is, among other things, a solid rock to which one can cling (or upon which one can rest) amidst the uncertainties and ambiguities of human life. Of course, that solid rock may be only a small asteroid tumbling through space. "What good is *that*?" you ask. Good enough for a 20th-century aviator/storyteller temporarily exiled in New York now that the war in Europe had engulfed his homeland, France. And good enough for hundreds of millions of 20th-century readers from Venezuela to Vietnam, who have found comfort and encouragement in clinging to the little prince's ball of rock, Asteroid B-612—an inspired science-fictional extended metaphor for homo sap's love of home and his capacity to appreciate the joys of the simple life, including non-sexual love and friendships (including interspecies friendships).

Antoine de Saint-Exupéry was forty-two years old when he wrote *Le Petit Prince* (*The Little Prince*) in the summer of 1942, two years before he and his airplane disappeared over the Mediterranean while returning from a wartime reconnaissance mission.

Saint-Ex, as he was called by acquaintances not intimate enough to call him Tonio, first rode in an aeroplane in 1912. A true man of his century, he began flying in 1921 after he was drafted into the French military, and went on to fly for eleven years (1926–1937) as a civilian test pilot and mail pilot. Drawing on this experience, he wrote two novels, three books of nonfiction (memoirs and other essays), and one fable.

His fable, *The Little Prince*, is certainly his masterpiece, but he is beloved by those in the know around the world for his other writings. I read *Wind, Sand and Stars* (1939) twice as a young man, with great pleasure and a sense of having been generously mentored by an experienced and insightful friend. I earnestly recommend that any reader who has ever treasured *The Little Prince* and has wished for more of the same, find a copy of *Wind, Sand and Stars* and read the little eight-page chapter called "Oasis." The prince is not in it. But you will find more of his spirit in this little essay/memoir/fable than anywhere else in world literature except in his own book and in the hearts of that book's readers. Moreover, in this earlier tale the beings that spirit inhabits are female, two young Argentine girls the author encountered when he was sheltered overnight by their family after "a minor mishap forced me down in a field." A tiny sample (translation by Lewis Galantière; the French title of this book is *Terre des Hommes*):

Space is not the measure of distance. A garden wall at home may enclose more secrets than the Great Wall of China, and the soul of a little girl is better guarded by silence than the Sahara's oases by the surrounding sands. I dropped down to earth once somewhere in the world. It was near Concordia, in the Argentine, but it might have been anywhere at all, for mystery is everywhere.

"Hmm," you might think, "interesting that the French author was in Argentina, and found himself thinking about the Great Wall of China!" Look, these "greatest hits" constantly leak into each other, like all earthly objects and creations and beings. By way of one small example, consider the resemblance between the king in chapter ten of *The Little Prince,* who commands his subjects to do what they might reasonably be expected to do anyway, and Eliot Rosewater of entry #29, who, as a sort of American king with almost limitless money to dispense, loves his subjects for being who they already are and gives them grants to do what they can reasonably and affectionately be expected to do anyway. The satirists' messages in both accounts are similar, as is their tone. The subject in both cases is the feasibility of benevolent monarchy.

By way of another odd connection or echo between hits, note that entry #7, the Universal Declaration of Human Rights, hearkening back as it does to the Magna Carta, is another 20th-century portrait (like chapter ten of *TLP*) of the possible (in this case, from the people's point of view, the ideal) relationship between kings (governments) and subjects (people).

One more example (and then I have to go back to my asteroid to pay some attention to a rose):

"You—you alone—will have the stars as no one else has them. . . . In one of the stars I shall be living. In one of them I shall be laughing. And so it will be as if all the stars were laughing, when you look at the sky at night."

"Ananda, if you but open your eyes and look, you will see Sariputta in yourself, in all the people Sariputta taught, and along every path Sariputta traveled to spread the teaching. Open your eyes, and you will see Sariputta everywhere. Don't think Sariputta is no longer with us. He is here and will always be."

"Jubal our beloved father . . . please stop and grok the fullness. Mike is not dead. How can he be dead when no one can be killed? Nor can he ever be away from us who have already grokked him."

—entries #33, #12, and #31

Gandhi

by **Richard Attenborough** and **Ben Kingsley**

(released December 1982)

I want to be a great storyteller and have people come a long way to hear the stories I have to tell. That's what acting is all about," Ben Kingsley said in an interview in 1983, after winning a "Best Actor" Academy Award for his performance as Mohandas Gandhi in this 1982 film ("Best Picture") produced and directed by Richard Attenborough ("Best Director").

I like the idea that acting is all about storytelling, just as I like the idea that Matisse and Picasso were performers, as passionate and spontaneous and as present in the moment as Billie Holiday or Umm Kulthum or John Coltrane or Jack Kerouac.

So as I watched this film yet again last night, and heard my viewing-partner exclaim about what a great story it is, the thought spontaneously crossed my mind that among the relatively few works of art chosen for discussion in this book-length essay, three are true stories (*Gandhi*, *Kundun*, *Old Path White Clouds*), and in all three a nation is a primary character, a major or indeed dominant player in the story being told. And in two of these three, that nation is India. For some reason.

India, of which Georg Wilhelm Friedrich Hegel said (in *The Philosophy of History*):

> It strikes everyone, in beginning to form an acquaintance with the treasures of Indian literature,

that a land so rich in intellectual products, and those of the profoundest order of thought, has no History; and in this respect contrasts most strongly with China—an empire possessing one so remarkable, one getting back to the most ancient times.

No History—in the view of the historically influential (quick quiz: Write a brief essay on the history of Marxism as an idea, and on the impact of that idea on the history of the 20th century) 19th-century German philosopher Mr. Hegel—yet great stories, Siddhartha, Mahatma, stories that far outlive their own time. Hmm. What is history, but a story? Ask Borges, ask Pynchon.

And what is it about these particular stories that makes it so easy for us readers and watchers to identify with Mr. Gandhi and Mr. Sakyamuni and their family members and friends and followers? Maybe, Georg, just maybe, a truly great story has the ability to transcend History and make it unnecessary. Or maybe a culture that intrinsically sees through or just doesn't "get" the illusion of History just naturally gives rise to finer stories.

What do Buddha and Gandhi have in common? A lot. Both men were stubbornly and actively (not passively) nonviolent. Both of them were extraordinarily successful (enough so to stand out as universally recognized great men of their centuries and eras) at moving the hearts of other men and women primarily because of their ability to see themselves and present themselves as the equals of other humans regardless of race, class, and life-circumstances.

Gandhi-ji wore the clothes of a poor peasant, and rode in the "third class" sections of trains. The Buddha took the same approach, and both of them improved the lot of their countrymen by genuinely caring about them and thereby earning their trust and sincere and energetic attention. And both of them consciously made of their own lives great stories that would inspire and nourish men and women of India and of all other nations for centuries and millennia to come.

Powerful dudes. And yet, in the hands of great storytellers like Kingsley and Attenborough and Nhat Hanh, they become persons that you or I can "identify" with. Despite the innate superiority that such greatness implies, we story-listeners and -watchers can see these guys as imperfect, vulnerable individuals like ourselves and can therefore understand the dramatic (and sometimes undramatic) and difficult choices they made in their lives—we can imagine ourselves behaving similarly in such a situation. Universal heroes. Models to live by. Storytelling is all about positive and negative models. Hey, we gotta learn somehow. And the greatness of the art of storytelling is that it successfully engages our interest and attentiveness and receptivity. Sucks us in. Gives our attentive minds instant gratification. And maybe long-term gratification as well. I mean, that Hegel line is something I read once, thirty-three years ago, an assignment in a college philosophy class. I remember I read it while participating in a week-long student fast at three universities to protest, or at least publicize our doubts about, the war in Vietnam. So Hegel's outrageous comment shook up my smug notion that I know what I mean by "history," and that was good for one foodless afternoon's entertainment—but look! damn thing's still stuck in my brain all these aeons later. That's what hits are for.

And I can quote it to you now more precisely than "India don't got no history," thanks to a librarian friend who located it based on my memory that what I read that day was a booklet called *Reason in History*. So don't let them burn our libraries, friends. Don't let them be replaced by digital media which, it turns out, self-destruct irretrievably five hundred months after you've mulched the books you just digitized. But I digress. Except that the same thing applies to movies. Too bad you readers in 2188 can't see this superb work of film art because 21st-century archivists had a misplaced trust in new storage formats and so most of those old movies are gone like the contents of the Alexandria Library. Well, that's show biz.

Back to *Gandhi*. Like *Old Path White Clouds*, it's an epic, starting with the hero's awakening and following his entire career until just after his death. The whole film rests on the shoulders of one actor, who does indeed give a great, and memorable, performance—thus enabling me to further acknowledge the performing arts in this volume, by nominating a work of acting as an art object worthy of inclusion in a greatest-hits time capsule. As with concerts, dance and drama performances are difficult to include unless there's a recording that can be considered at all comparable to the experience of having been present at the show, the moment of creation. True, I have fond memories of seeing Sam Shepard's *Buried Child* the week it opened, in San Francisco—but I'd have to do some serious research to come up with the names of the actresses and actors and director who did such a terrific job that night. And I know I've seen at least one performance of George Bernard Shaw's *Saint Joan* that touched me as deeply as some of the other selections in this book—probably at the Loeb Theater in Cambridge, Massachusetts in the 1960s, but I can't be more specific than that. And the purpose of this rambling aside is to affirm again that what goes into anyone's time capsule/curriculum is necessarily based not only on quality but also on what can be conveniently pasted in the scrapbook. A truly great example of film acting can be watched in future centuries (unless the digital archiving nightmare comes true), but stage acting cannot (except for films of stage plays, which are seldom comparable to the real thing). This can create distortions in the historical record, whereby we are aware that there was great play-writing being done in England at the time of Shakespeare, but no one talks about the perhaps equally impressive accomplishments of actors and actresses and directors in that glorious era.

Ben Kingsley was born Krishna Bhanji in Yorkshire, England, at the end of 1943, of an Indian father and a Russian-Jewish mother. He is an accomplished stage actor who had performed with the Royal Shakespeare Company for most of a decade but had only appeared in one movie before Attenborough hired him to play Gandhi in the film Sir Richard had been working on (thinking about and doggedly seeking support for) for most of two decades.

So Kingsley was a stage actor turned movie actor; Attenborough was an actor of both sorts turned director/producer, and

Gandhi was an attorney turned Mahatma. A freedom fighter. A man who improvised brilliantly. As we see in almost every moment of this remarkable film.

So zoom the camera in, please, on a young theological student at a lecture in Philadelphia in 1950, a black man from Georgia, twenty-one years old, thoroughly captivated by the lecturer's description of Mahatma Gandhi's long nonviolent campaign against British domination that ultimately brought freedom to India. The young man, Martin Luther King, Jr., immediately went out and bought several books about Gandhi. "As I read," King recalled later, "I became deeply fascinated by his campaigns on nonviolent resistance."

See what a well-told story can do? Imagine the impact Dick and Ben's movie might have on some young woman or man who sees it at the right moment (for her or him) in 2188 or any time. . . .

One more little tale, partly because it backs up my statement about the value of libraries (repositories of greatest hits of past centuries): Autumn 1908. South Africa. Thirty-nine-year-old London-trained Indian-born lawyer Mohandas Gandhi is in jail for the first time. He borrows a book from the prison library, and reads therein a 19th-century "hit" (remembered) essay by Henry David Thoreau called "On the Duty of Civil Disobedience." This occurred when Gandhi had already improvised new techniques of nonviolent resistance to authority over the past two years, in response to circumstances affecting Indian immigrants in South Africa, techniques he called *satyagraha* (firmness in the cause of truth and love). In Thoreau, Gandhi found a kindred spirit, and thus much support and encouragement. He quoted Thoreau's essay in his own writings, and called it "a masterly treatise" which "left a deep impression on me." This scene is not in the movie but I add it here because it reveals Mohandas as one of us—a reader, an art appreciator, a person deeply affected by great hits from other times and places. Like you and me and Martin.

This is an unusual entry because it credits two artists as collaborators on the listed artwork (certainly Coltrane and Holiday and Roosevelt and Wilhelm and Dylan and Leone also had collaborators, but they were not co-billed in the chapter heading). This is because the director is generally considered the author of the film, but certainly the actor or actress is the author of the performance, and in this entry I honor film and performance simultaneously, as they are truly inseparable. And by way of an illustration of great minds thinking alike, here is a quote from Sir Richard Attenborough from an interview with the *New York Times* when *Gandhi* was released:

> I work as an actor works to involve an audience by engaging their emotions. . . . [So Gandhi also worked, not so much in his speeches as in his public actions.] I have no interest in being remembered as a great creative filmmaker. I want to be remembered as a storyteller.

So be it. And (gasp) one more footnote to non-History. While studying law in England, young Mohandas, like his soul brother Henry David, read the *Gita* (the Hindu scriptures) for the first time, under the influence of two British theosophists. They also recommended a relatively recent great hit by poet Sir Edwin Arnold, a biography of the Buddha in the form of a long poem called *The Light of Asia* (1879). Gandhi reports in his *Autobiography:* "I read it with even greater interest than I did the *Bhagavadgita*. Once I had begun it I could not leave off."

The purpose of great art (speaking for myself as listener/observer) is revelation. That's certainly what I get reliably from rock and roll and "Sister Ray" and *The Rolling Stones, Now!* As Henri Matisse told us, back in entry #13, "each century seeks to nourish itself in works of art, and each century needs a particular kind of nourishment."

Am I suggesting that this thrown-together collection of recordings of young British white boys playing and singing American blues and "r&b" songs, plus a few imitative originals, deserves to be regarded as a work of art capable of "communicating divine truth"? Yes, but . . . notice that another definition of *revelation* is "an act of revealing to view or making known." In this respect, I find the young Rolling Stones to be committed artists working in the same tradition as Matisse: the tradition of art as a secret the artist has been told by other artists, and by his senses, which he now intends to shout as loud as he can—for the benefit of the ordinary person who hasn't necessarily heard of or heard Cézanne or Howlin' Wolf but who has certainly had private visions and experiences related to Wolf's and Cézanne's and Matisse's and the Stones'.

This is it. Everybody needs somebody to love, needs a particular kind of nourishment, and these twelve performances are it. For me and for quite a few other men and women of my time and place.

"Reveal" (*Webster's New Collegiate Dictionary*): "to make something secret or hidden publicly or generally known."

"Come on along boys, it's just down the road apiece!" —the Rolling Stones in Chess Studios, Chicago, June 1964, quoting Chuck Berry in 1960 quoting Don Raye circa 1942.

"Everybody here listen to my song tonight, gonna save the whole world. . . ." —Mick Jagger in RCA Studios, Hollywood, October 1964, loosely quoting Solomon Burke (from an obscure single, earlier in '64).

"Tour de force" (*The Random House College Dictionary*): "an exceptional achievement using the full skill, ingenuity, resources, etc., of a person, country, or group." Of the twelve songs on this rock-and-roll album, fully six are, in my opinion, tours de force. Exceptionally ambitious and successful performances. Major statements.

Statements like (I'll augment these songs' title phrases to summarize what they and therefore this album have to say):

"Everybody Needs Somebody to Love."

"I am the Little Red Rooster."

"Ohhh, you're *so* Down Home Girl. . . ."

"There's a place you'll really get your kicks; it's open every night about twelve to six . . . it's just Down the Road Apiece."

"You Can't Catch Me, 'cause if you get too close, I'll be gone like a cool breeze."

"I'll tell you, Mona, what I want to do: build a house next door to you!"

These six statements may not look exceptionally profound on paper—but to hear the Rolling Stones in 1964 singing and playing them live in various recording studios on two continents is to discover hidden depths not only in these direct, vernacular statements, but also in you, their listener. "Yeah! Yeah yeah yeah, Mona!!" At the right moment, this statement or exclamation can have the force of revelation. For me. And I daresay for almost any receptive male or female adolescent or once-adolescent listener in any era. "Turn up the volume!" That's the appropriate response to greatest hits. Or maybe I just say that 'cause I'm a 20th-century guy. "You can never go fast enough. . . ."

Matisse again: "A painter doesn't see everything that he has put in his painting. It is other people who find these treasures in it, one by one, and the richer a painting is in surprises of this sort, in treasures, the greater its author."

"New Jersey Turnpike in the wee wee hours, I was rolling slowly, 'cause of drizzlin' showers." This is a remarkable treasure that has been found in "You Can't Catch Me" (vinyl album side one, track three) by millions of people, as they have simultaneously found other treasures in the form of particular guitar sounds and sonic patterns ("riffs") and rhythm section sounds and vocal phrasings ("cooooool breeze . . .") and in the form of specific feelings generated in them by the song and the ensemble performance. How about that guitar solo (and the jazzlike interaction between soloist and rhythm instruments) after the turnpike verse? Almost inexhaustible treasures . . .

The author of the turnpike lyric quoted above is a great poet-performer from Missouri named Charles Edward Berry. But the author of most of what you and I, the listeners, experience here is: the band, the performers of this recording, five men ranging in ages from twenty to twenty-eight when these songs were recorded. All born in England, and all but one during wartime (all children of *Gravity's Rainbow* characters, in other words). Charlie Watts, drums; Bill Wyman, bass guitar; Brian Jones, guitar and miscellany, Keith Richards, guitar; Mick Jagger, vocals and harmonica and some percussion. These five guys, the Rolling Stones, are joined on a few of the tracks of this album by guests Jack Nitzsche and Ian Stewart, both on piano. A band definitely analogous to the swing band described in loving verbal detail (and extraordinarily evocative musical detail) in "Down the Road Apiece."

The rock-and-roll band, if you like that sort of thing, and I did and do—but what they actually were was a blues band loosely modeled on Chicago blues combos and British skiffle bands, keen young record collectors mostly recording (at this historical moment) American r&b songs they found on 45-rpm records purchased randomly in stores in black neighborhoods in the United States or stores in England that imported such items. Very often the Stones' recording—of "Down Home Girl" or "Oh Baby (We Got a Good Thing Goin')"—was made very soon (sometimes only hours) after first listening to the song in question.

Revelation occurs (in the case of this particular greatest hit, this "rock and roll" or "pop music" album) as a result of the cumulative and collective impact on the engaged listener of the surprises and treasures he finds in these recorded performances. Something secret is made known. Something big enough and vital enough to seem (especially to a sixteen-year-old boy, which I was when I first heard *Now!*) like divine truth. Made known, not to the mind alone, but to the body and the mind and the heart all at once. The heart leaps, the body shakes, and the mind stutters. It doesn't know what to say, but it knows it wants to (and sometimes does) scream with joy. "Turn up the volume!" "Let's dance!" "Come here, baby, I want to introduce you to my spiritual teacher!" "I mean, 'build a house next door to you!'" "I mean, it's a secret and I don't know how to explain it but I somehow feel like it could save the whole world. And somehow it has a lot to do with my emerging sexuality and self-awareness." "Come on along boys, it's just down the road apiece!" Those guitar licks. Divine fucking truth.

Tours de force? What makes "Down Home Girl" (as recorded by the Rolling Stones, October 27, 1964) an exceptional achievement is precisely the way it uses and displays the *full resources* of these five-plus-one musicians. Collectively they create a sound here that is sensual, hypnotic, innovative and unique and visionary.

That visionary quality is what impressed me so much when I was a sixteen-year-old blues fan and very skeptical about "rock and roll." The Rolling Stones converted me by confronting me with musical experiences like this one, rooted in the blues idiom and every bit as convincing and surprising and self-contained as the Howlin' Wolf and Bo Diddley and Sonny Boy Williamson tracks that had recently changed my life by confronting me with what I can only call auditory visions of a world that was immediately profound and familiar and revolutionary and endlessly enticing. "Oh don't you hear me crying?" "Ohhh, you're *so* down home girl. . . ."

As I type these words at age fifty-one and find myself in trouble and my life in upheaval because of the power of sexual feelings, I have to acknowledge that it was Wolf and Bo and the Stones and a few other blues singers and players who seemed to open this door in me originally. And what drew me to the doorway, in every instance, was the unique sound of the music.

And I can argue for this stuff as great art of the era because I know I'm not the only one to whom it felt like a revelation. In fact, what particularly pleases me about the Rolling Stones and this album is that their music is primarily about being in love with and, yes, under the spell of, such works of art. "It's just an old piano and a knockout bass."

Similarly, Chuck Berry sings and covers Don Raye's swing song because Berry's oeuvre (including the songs he selects to "cover") is itself a celebration of the joys of the listening life ("Rock and Roll Music," "Johnny B. Goode"). As Matisse's art is about his experiences of communing with the human species and himself by looking at other people's paintings. Solomon Burke means what he says when he preaches that he believes the world can be changed by listening to a song. As does Mick Jagger when he repeats Burke's rap, in the same spirit in which his mate Keith repeats Berry's guitar licks. One great chain of music. Based, among other things, on the spontaneous creation of remarkable sounds. Auditory visions opening the doors to further visions. And more trouble. Wolf: "Tell me baby, where did you stay last night?" Jerry Leiber and Jerry Butler, via Alvin Robinson and now the Rolling Stones: "Every time you move like that, I've got to go to Sunday mass. . . ."

And I'm here to assert that the rhyming of "Sunday mass" with "fiberglass" is a defining moment in 20th-century art. And that that rhyme cannot be separated from Mick Jagger's singing of it, nor from Brian Jones's and Keith Richards's and Jack Nietzsche's and Charlie Watts's and Bill Wyman's guitar and piano and

drum and bass playing during and before and after it on this extraordinarily textured recording.

As with the five other major works on *Now!*, the exceptional
power of "Down Home Girl" is a product of both ambition and
accident. Regarding ambition, the Rolling Stones when they
recorded "DHG" were in Hollywood for the first time (and in the
United States for the second time)—just as these six lads when
they recorded "Down the Road Apiece" four months earlier were
in Chicago and the USA for the first time. Their ambition, as
any young musician of any era can understand, was to imitate and
emulate and join their musical heroes and, more modestly, to
somehow communicate via their playing and singing and their
choice of songs, their vision of this glamorous and mythical place
(America, the black South) that they'd encountered via these
mysterious records. Not just to go to America and play in the
same studios as those guys (!), but to become that kind of musician and tell stories in that musical language. To share, just by
singing a song or playing a guitar, how it feels to be us, twenty-
year-old urban British males in a world every bit as exciting and
ominous and sexy as what we found in these art objects that first
called us into this work, this spiritual path. Mick Jagger and Brian
Jones and Keith Richards and pals are keenly aspiring to capture
their youthful vision of rural America, and of the flavor of adulthood they would choose for themselves, as they perform this song
together on October 27, 1964. You can hear it and feel it in every
moment of the performance.

Regarding accident, I'll start with an easier example, illustrative of the fact that pop music as an art form is inevitably shaped
by silly arbitrary decisions involving which performance, which
recording session take, ends up being the, um, the "White Christmas" that umpteen million people have heard Bing Crosby sing.
The performance of "Everybody Needs Somebody to Love" you
find at the beginning of your copy of *The Rolling Stones, Now!*
may be the three-minute version that leads off the 1965 album,
or it may more probably be the five-minute version that was
always on *The Rolling Stones No. 2*, the rather different British
equivalent of the *Now!* album. I have here a 1986 American CD

that shows on its sleeve that this track is 2 minutes and 57 seconds long, but when you play it it's the 5:00 take from the British album. (Both recorded the same day and quite different-sounding, distinctly different performances.) To make matters more confusing, you'll find statements in the literature (books about the Rolling Stones, in this case a survey of their recording career by fine U.K. music journalist Roy Carr) like: "The version of 'Everybody Needs Somebody to Love' that appears on the American [release of] *The Rolling Stones, Now!* is in actual fact a studio run-through that was issued by mistake." Nice mistake! Both versions (recorded the same day) are excellent and have their champions, but after recent comparisons I remain certain that the weirder, shorter one is the only one of the two that de-serves to be listened to forever as a masterful example of inspired (and reckless) 20th-century musicianship.

And if one of the two performances done at different times on that same October 27 as "DHG" is so much more distinguished than the other, to what can we attribute this? Same day, same song, same great band at the height of its early creative power . . . Maybe one of the two times the singer or the drummer acciden-tally did something different, and where they went from there and how they felt about it as they played changed completely as a result. And of course, which version you the listener happen to hear and get used to is also a matter of accident and geography and other illogical factors.

This might be a good place to mention that in the opinion of the undersigned, you're not listening to the worthy-of-Greatest-Hit-status *Rolling Stones, Now!* album unless you're listening to it on vinyl or on an analog tape recording made from a clean copy of the vinyl record. The CD's okay and you would certainly fall in love with it if it were the only version on your desert island, but the sound is not the same, and the vinyl version is twice as won-derful. *Caveat auditor.*

And for me what points to the accidental nature of the mag-nificent *RS Now!* version of "Down Home Girl" is listening to the rare Alvin Robinson version that the Stones copied as closely as they could. The original doesn't hold a candle to the counterfeit. The vocal has less humor, less conviction, less soul, and the band sound is far less interesting. So where did this magnificent white European version come from? Inspired accidental blues-flavored ensemble arrangement by Jones Jagger Richards Watts Wyman Nietzsche? Evidently. You can't plan these things. They just happen.

And lest I seem to be ignoring the other tours de force (as I am glossing over the six other album tracks, all of which contribute in meaningful and pleasurable ways to the excellence of the album experience as a whole), let me say quickly that "Little Red Rooster" is a treasure-filled three minutes even apart from its distinction as the only pure blues performance ever to be a #1 record in England (and one of the few out-and-out trance performances ever to be a pop #1). In this case, if you compare it with Howlin' Wolf's original recording of this Willie Dixon song, you notice that Mick Jagger is certainly no Howlin' Wolf, but you may also notice that the Stones' version is the more distinguished and memorable recording. (And remember, Wolf didn't feel ripped off, he and Dixon were grinning all the way to the bank.) (For Wolf the payoff wasn't songwriting royalties but record sales and tour bookings.) And I've already alluded a few times here to what sublime live band performances "You Can't Catch Me" (written by Chuck Berry, but mostly unheard till *Now!* even by Berry fans) and "Down the Road Apiece" are.

And then there's "Mona," the earliest recording on the album (February 1964). In this case these white punks are copying one of my personal choices of top five all-time greatest rock-and-roll or r&b singles, and the Stones' version is totally lacking the remarkable African moans that dominate Bo Diddley's 1957 recording. And yet, the amazing thing is that there's room in this world and in my consciousness for two quite different versions of "Mona (I Need You Baby)"—both sublimely redolent with the kind of conviction and musical presence and visionary freshness that I require of any work of art worthy to be called a "great hit" of its century. Revelation guaranteed. Yeah! Yeah yeah yeah . . .

And if somebody out there is bothered that the Rolling Stones didn't write any of these songs I've singled out for praise, let me point out to you that the great modern composer John Coltrane didn't "write" "My Favorite Things." That doesn't make Coltrane's recording of Rodgers and Hammerstein's song any less of a masterpiece. Great creative work almost always includes some kind of collaboration.

HIT 36

Dune by **Frank Herbert** (published 1965)

I remember with what excitement I walked, at age seven, to a corner drugstore two miles away whenever I had ten cents to buy a new comic book. What was I excited about? I was anticipating reading a new Superman or Batman or Wuff-the-Prairie-Dog story. I could already feel myself going into that other world I enjoyed so much, that place between the pages of those comics that always managed to hold my attention and stimulate my imagination. It was an almost addictive experience. Soon, of course, I was reading science fiction paperbacks from my parents' bookshelves, and that adventure lasted a lot longer than the comic book phase, and took me much further.

I read a huge amount of science fiction between age ten and age fifteen and was distracted after that by other passions. So *Dune* reached me as it reached most of its millions of readers, by friends' recommendations, at a point where I'd slowed down to only two or three science fiction books a year. Somebody got across to me in early 1968, three years after my romance with *The Rolling Stones, Now!*, that it was quite important that I read this book as soon as possible. They were right. Little did I know in January that I would be out of the city and living in "the country" by October. Huge numbers of my contemporaries seemed to get the same idea that year or in the next year or two. The first Earth Day was celebrated in April 1970 (not coincidentally, nine months after the first moon landing), and all the media coverage of this gave Frank Herbert the opportunity to put together a nonfiction paperback on environmental topics to be published in conjunction with Earth Day. In his introduction to that book, *New World or No World*, Herbert wrote:

> I am a human living on the planet Earth, a condition shared by about three and a half billion of my fellows in this year 1970.
>
> Only about one-third of us are sufficiently well fed that we can take the time to write such words as these. Food is energy is time. Pollution is lost energy.
>
> This is insanity.
>
> I feel constrained to say these things in just this way because of a pledge I have made. I refuse to be put in the position of telling my grandchildren: "Sorry there's no more world for you. We used it all up."
>
> It was for this reason that I wrote in the mid-sixties what I hoped would be an environmental awareness handbook. The book is called *Dune*, a title chosen with the deliberate intent that it echo the sound of "doom." In the pages of *Dune* there is a man named Pardot Kynes, a planetologist, which is a kind of super-environmentalist. I put these words into his mouth:

> Beyond a critical point within a finite space, freedom diminishes as numbers increase. This is as true of humans in the finite space of a planetary ecosystem as it is of gas molecules in a sealed flask. The human question is not how many can possibly survive within the system, but what kind of existence is possible for those who do survive.

The Beatles and the Rolling Stones and Bob Dylan are rightly remembered for the impact their sincere and energetic pop culture creations had on millions of individuals and, therefore, on the collective human consciousness at what seemed to be a moment of unusual receptivity in the species ("Yeah, bring it on!" we shouted. "We're ready!"). But humankind's urgent need to communicate with itself at that moment didn't only manifest through pop music. "The two most popular science fiction novels of the last twenty years," scholar David Hartwell wrote in his 1984 book *Age of Wonders*, "are *Dune* by Frank Herbert and Robert A. Heinlein's *Stranger in a Strange Land.*"

Stranger in a Strange Land, you'll remember, had its origins in an intriguing premise suggested to the novelist by his wife in 1949, which led to twelve years of rumination and writing-process before the book was completed and published. Oddly enough, something very similar can be said about *Dune*. "Back in 1953," Herbert told an interviewer in 1985, "I was going to do an article (which I never finished) [he was a newspaper journalist] about a pilot project of the U.S. Forest Service in Florence, Oregon, studying how to control the flow of sand dunes. The whole idea fascinated me, so I started researching sand dunes, and of course from sand dunes it's a logical idea to go into a desert. Before long I saw I had too much data for an article, and far too much for a short story . . . I finally saw I had something enormously interesting going for me about the ecology of deserts, and it was, for a science fiction writer anyway, an easy step from that to think: what if I had an entire planet that was a desert?"

As far as I know, the idea of writing about the relationship between humans (i.e., U.S. Forest Service scientists) and the ecology of sand dunes was not specifically a suggestion made by Frank Herbert's wife Beverly. It could have been, but that doesn't matter, because I know from personal observation for many hours over the course of years of friendship with Frank and Beverly that the writing of the great and beloved creative work known as *Dune* (and the *Dune* series) can be properly described as an act of collaboration between author and spouse just as significant as and perhaps even more tangible than the collaboration between Robert and Virginia Heinlein that gave us *Stranger in a Strange Land*.

Joseph Conrad's turn-of-the-century great hit *Heart of Darkness* (1902) artfully calls attention to the collaborative nature of all storytelling by including the tale's listeners (Marlow's ship-mates) as visible characters in the narrative. Bev Herbert is not a visible character in *Dune* unless the reader is able to look deeply enough to recognize in Lady Jessica and Chani the author's powerful love and appreciation and respect for and sometimes genuine awe toward the primary female presence in his life, his constant companion and the mother of his children. The relationship between the reader and the characters and the narrator is important in any novel, and it is unmistakable that *Dune*— which opens like T. H. White's *The Once and Future King*, with scenes of the young hero's hands-on education in the care of remarkable and very likable instructors—flatters and seduces its readers (and brings out the best in them) by its evident confidence in their intelligence and attentiveness and their willingness to work and their ability to appreciate and grasp subtle distinctions and insights while simultaneously glimpsing and holding in their minds the big picture (humankind against a backdrop of centuries, continents, planets). So we identify with Paul Atreides from the outset and thus are all the more ready to be the author/narrator's students as he teaches us about this grand imaginary universe of Arrakis and sandworm and Space Guild and Padishah Emperor (and, by implication, about our own Earth as well), because after all this may be just what we need to learn in order to fulfill our own, ahem, grand and destined roles.

Where Bev comes in, as Frank told me and as I saw for myself in the Herberts' living rooms in Seattle and, later, Port Townsend, and in restaurant meals during science fiction conventions and book trade shows, is that her remarkable intelligence and genuine interest and stimulating contributions to the conversational exchange all gave him permission and opportunity and inspiration to use his own mental skills and articulate his (and, often, their) insights into the subtleties of everyday human communication and into the "big picture" of life in this era and historical moment and in this particular natural and human environment in which we find ourselves. Bev gave the storyteller a story to tell and the essayist-instructor a set of insights to pass on, by being such an active and immediate and collaborative audience for his monologues and excited observations, and via her own inventive contributions to their ongoing dialogue.

One imagines Robert and Virginia Heinlein's collaborative process was similar, though I never had dinner with them.

Science fiction's hold on the youthful attentions of (and ability to stimulate the imaginations of) a century of readers is primarily a function of the quality of the relationship that this unique form of discourse creates with its readers, its audience, its students—the respect in which they feel themselves being held and the satisfaction they get from successfully participating in its mental exercises and how much fun it is to learn about life and the world in this manner (like Wart, young King Arthur, in the "Sword in the Stone" section of *The Once and Future King*, getting to learn about life by actually sharing the mind of a wild animal for an hour thanks to Merlin's sorcery).

The listener creates the storyteller, and vice versa; and together they collaboratively create, and indeed live, the story. The novelist thinks and writes and researches and rewrites for twelve years, and the reader for his part or her part walks miles to obtain a copy of the novel and, in Coleridge's splendid phrase, actively participates in the creative process via the "willing suspension of disbelief for the moment, which constitutes poetic faith."

Why did they call it the 20th century? Well, not all of them did. Some of the beings that lived on that planet didn't talk, and those that did talk had many different languages and calendars and names for themselves and for their era. In the large sector of the human-populated landmass called "the West" (funny name, on a sphere—west of what? Wasn't the western sector also east of something?), the most widely used calendar measured "time" in reference to the birth or arrival date of a local deity named Jesus Christ, also called Lord, or Dominus. So "20th century" meant almost twenty hundreds of "years" since the birth of Christ. Individual year-dates like 1969 were properly written "A.D. 1969," the letters a reference to a long-unused language called Latin, the language that first employed the letter-shapes they still used: A for Anno, year, *D* for Domini, Lord, the "i" suffix indicating possession. And so it came to pass that on the one thousand, nine-hundred, sixty-ninth "year of our Lord" a small group of unsuspecting worshipers found themselves the acclaimed authors of a big hit record (#4 in the United States, #2 in England) called "Oh Happy Day."

"Oh happy day, oh happy day, when Jesus walked [i.e. when He was among us, when He walked on Earth], oh when He walked, He washed my sins away. . . ."

It was an accidental hit, and certainly no examination of the greatest hits of the 20th century could be complete without discussion of an accidental hit, and, by extension, the apparently accidental nature of all hits. But we have to be careful. Some of those beings believed passionately that there are no "accidents," or rather that what humans perceive as accidents are actually events consciously and purposefully arranged by unseen forces, or deities. Your humble scribe does not presume to take a position on such lofty matters, but here are the "facts" as they were passed down to me:

Edwin Hawkins (the credits above are as they appear on the original 45-rpm record, and if they're a bit unwieldy, that does serve to remind us again that it isn't always obvious who deserves credit for a great work of art, and under what name he or she or they should be acknowledged) in A.D. 1967 was the director of the choir at the Ephesians Church of God in Berkeley, California, and for the purpose of a performance at an annual Christian youth convention back east at which there would also be a Southern California State Youth Choir, Hawkins (then age thirty-four) and a woman named Betty Watson organized the Northern California State Youth Choir, which included Dorothy Combs Morrison (then age thirty-two) from Longview, Texas, who began singing gospel as a child with a family ensemble called The Combs Family. Also present was nineteen-year-old Walter Hawkins, Edwin's younger brother, later a minister and (like Morrison) a successful professional singer. In order to raise money to attend the convention, Edwin and the choir recorded an album on two-track recording equipment called *Let Us Go into the House of the Lord*.

They did manage to sell five hundred copies of the album to friends and neighbors, and a year and a half later a San Francisco rock music promoter found a copy of it in a stack of records in a warehouse, bought it and gave it to a local disc jockey, who listened to it and started playing one track, "Oh Happy Day," on his popular radio program on KSAN. His listeners loved it and insisted on hearing it again and again, and so Buddah Records in

New York City bought the rights and put out a 45-rpm single, re-naming the choir The Edwin Hawkins Singers. Soon millions of copies were sold worldwide, and thus "Oh Happy Day" became what has been called "the only crossover gospel hit in chart his-tory." And, um, we use the word "accidental" because obviously Edwin Hawkins didn't plan or anticipate this outcome when he rearranged a tune he'd found in an old Baptist hymnal belonging to his mother, and taught it to his choir and included it on their homemade album.

And the four-minute-and-fifty-nine-second performance and recording that resulted (available free on the Internet, our spe-cies' bulletin board, right now if you look for it) is indeed a great work of art, as universal and compact and delicious as *The Little Prince* or *Dance* or "Good Vibrations." This is a superb expression of the human spirit, speaking of and beyond the moment when these singers and this choir director were alive and creating it. Or re-creating it—maybe "art" is actually a series of stories passed along like a juicy rumor from mouth to ears to mind to mouth to ears, for centuries and maybe longer. "He taught me how . . . to walk . . . right, and pray! Good God! Oh yeah. . . ." No two minds hear it quite the same way, so it is transformed in a living and creative fashion as it's passed along.

And "Oh Happy Day" is here on this list because I'll stand it up against *Ulysses* or the Charlie Chaplin or Marx Brothers film of your choice. Listen to what this young woman and her scream-ing companions are doing to these words! This is a truly Ameri-can art form and truly universal and, on this perfect and funky recording, truly 20th-centurian. Do you feel that change (chord change, miraculous mood change) when "He taught me how" comes in?? What we have here is five minutes of ecstasy, compa-rable to the similarly intentionally ecstatic devotional music of Nusrat Fateh Ali Khan. Of course. The love of God is a common starting point for many of the world's great art forms and creative traditions.

And because this five-minute "accidental" recording really is so aesthetically perfect and brilliant, I can use it as evidence that you don't need to be an acknowledged "genius," a Matisse or a

Joyce or a Brian Wilson, to produce exceptional work that will nourish humans forever if the word is passed along. Search those warehouses, friends. Who knows what great works of art may be waiting to be discovered! And please remember, as the Buddha said, that *you* are already qualified to discern which things to accept and which things to discard. And, if you get a chance, listen to "Oh Happy Day." Great joy awaits you.

HIT

38

Kundun

by **Martin Scorsese**

(released December 25, 1997)

"A thing of beauty is a joy forever," John Keats told us 181 years ago, and he hasn't been proven wrong yet. I put *Kundun* on my best-of-the-century list in late January 1998 because I'd experienced this movie as a thing of great beauty when I saw it for the first time two weeks before that, and had been equally impressed when I saw it again a week later. And I didn't want my list to deny, for its readers or its author, the possibility that we are not always wrong to believe we're experiencing "greatness" in the present moment (when else?)—even though another part of our minds insists we wait an appropriate number of months or years before declaring that the novel we just turned the last page of, or the new record we just listened to repeatedly, or the concert we just walked out of, is undoubtedly "one of the greatest books or records or shows I've ever read or heard or seen!"

Okay, so I put it on my list partly to defy that part of me (and of all of us) that insists that greatness can only exist in the past, i.e., at a safe critical distance. But mostly because I was *sure*—absolutely confident that the great beauty I was seeing and hearing in the cinematography and music and directing and performing and writing and audiovisual composition of this film was the real thing, universal and enduring, not just a joy for me alone or for this week only. A greatest-hits candidate, in other words.

This was reaffirmed, quite emphatically, last night (twenty months later) when I saw *Kundun* a third time, this time on home video instead of in a theater. My viewing companion (same person I saw the film with the first two times, and the same one who was impressed with what a "great story" the film *Gandhi* tells) said afterward, through tears, "I love stories that are about the greatness of the human spirit." Me too, Cindy. And Bill Faulkner agrees with us (see entry #16):

> It is the writer's privilege to help man endure by reminding him of the courage and honor and hope and pride and compassion and pity and sacrifice which have been the glory of his past. The poet's voice need not merely be the record of man; it can be one of the props, the pillars, to help him endure and prevail.

The movie *Kundun*, in my opinion, is (and will continue to be, as long as men and women watch "movies") exactly such a prop or pillar, as the Buddha's teachings (his sutras, his spoken poems) are for His Holiness the 14th Dalai Lama of Tibet, the hero of this biographical film—who is, remarkably, still alive and still living his extraordinary life story today as I write these words.

Still alive in the body of the 14th, I should say, because the premise of the film is that it is the story of an immortal being named Kundun, focusing in on the late-20th-century segment of his long and winding (but unbending!) tale.

In his autobiography (on which this film is based), Tenzin Gyatso writes,

> I am held to be the reincarnation of each of the previous thirteen Dalai Lamas of Tibet (the first having been born in 1351 A.D.), who are in turn considered to be manifestations of Avalokiteshvara, Bodhisattva of Compassion. I am often asked whether I truly believe this. The answer is not simple to give. But as a fifty-six-year-old, when I consider my experiences during this present life, and given my Buddhist beliefs, I have no difficulty accepting that I am spiritually connected both to the thirteen previous Dalai Lamas, and to Avalokiteshvara and to the Buddha himself.

That's a good answer, but the triumph of Martin Scorsese's film is that, particularly because of the irresistible "discovery" sequence early in the movie, it manages to sell its premise even to a confirmed skeptic like me. The colors in almost every frame of this movie are so beautiful, and the various actors who play Gyatso at different ages so convincing and likeable (even and especially the marvelous brat of a two-year-old, played by Tenzin Yeshi Paichang), that before I know it I am lulled into a keen desire to identify with this hero and his glorious and painful circumstances, just as I naturally identified with Paul Atreides while reading *Dune*—and to my surprise I find that this act of identification automatically includes (as in *Stranger in a Strange Land*) surrender to and acceptance of the story's premise. And anyway, in the unlikely event you can watch this movie and still find it impossible to believe in a six-hundred-year-old, regularly reincarnated entity, the story still works its magic, because if you decide Gyatso *isn't* Kundun, then immediately he becomes that classic fictional character, the poor boy unexpectedly elevated to royal status, like a winner or loser in Borges's Babylon Lottery. Either way, we the viewers are with him every step of the way as he tries to be a good person in the face of intolerable circumstances and absurdly difficult choices (cooperate with the Chinese or fight futilely? stay in Tibet or flee to India?).

Like *Gandhi*, *Kundun* is a movie about an individual who wakes up and finds himself in the 20th century and then has to improvise furiously to cope with things as they really are, here and now. Just like you and me, even if they are supermen. How's *that* for a movie premise: Superhero of Compassion?? Yeah, but will anybody believe it? Um, I know this movie wasn't a big hit, in spite of all the publicity it got when China threatened to boycott the Disney Corp. forever if they didn't back off, but I find it hard to imagine *anyone* watching this film and not believing in and rooting for this superhero. One widely remembered scene: The Dalai Lama is crossing the India/Tibet border on his way to exile, and a guard asks him, "Are you the Lord Buddha?" His Holiness (played as an adult by Tenzin Thuthob Tsarong) replies,

"I think I am a reflection, like the moon on water. When you see me, and I try to be a good man, you see yourself."

As with *For a Few Dollars More*, I love the music (composed by Philip Glass) and the faces of the characters, the landscapes, the vignettes (brief interactions between characters), and, as I said, the colors, like a two-hour walk through a Matisse exhibition. And then within all that and beyond it, I love the story, of this man and this nation. I so identify with the Paul Atreides character, I mean the Dalai Lama, as he stumbles under the burden of his role and of his love for his people and for all people, even for his enemies. "Why am I here?" you see him thinking. And you even see him struggling with the premise himself ("I guess I'm here, as my advisers say, because I chose it; when I was the thirteenth Dalai Lama I chose to be reborn close to the Tibet/China border as a way of sticking my tongue out at the Chinese"). Great story. And can you believe that this great hero and his people and the amazing place they live in are not the inventions of a science fiction writer? They're real. So real that when I turned on my computer to write this chapter after watching the movie the night before, I found the Dalai Lama broadcasting live on the Internet on behalf of helping all human beings. How do you turn off this VCR? The movie won't stop, the character just keeps talking, and I've become a player in the drama myself. Here's what he just said to me (I didn't search for this; when I turned on my Internet provider there was a new button on the home page saying, "The Dalai Lama, Live from India"! and also offering a sample chapter from his brand-new book):

On a recent trip to Europe, I had the opportunity to visit the site of the Nazi death camp at Auschwitz. Even though I had heard and read a great deal about this place, I found myself completely unprepared for the experience. My initial reaction to the sight of the ovens in which hundreds of thousands of human beings were burned was one of total revulsion. I was dumbfounded at the sheer calculation and detachment from feeling to which they bore horrifying testimony. Then, in the museum which forms part of the visitor center, I saw a collection of shoes. A lot of them were patched or small, having obviously belonged to children and poor people. This saddened me particularly. What wrong could they possibly have done, what harm? I stopped and prayed—moved profoundly both for the victims and for the perpetrators of this iniquity—that such a thing would never happen again. And, in the knowledge that just as we all have the capacity to act selflessly out of concern for others' well-being, so do we all have the potential to be murderers and torturers, I vowed never in any way to contribute to such a calamity.

Events such as those which occurred at Auschwitz are violent reminders of what can happen when individuals—and by extension, whole societies—lose touch with basic human feeling. But although it is necessary to have legislation and international conventions in place as safeguards against future disasters of this kind, we have all seen that atrocities continue in spite of them. Much more effective and important than such legislation is our regard for one another's feelings at a simple human level.

Okay, he got my attention, since I had the same experience visiting Auschwitz when I was sixteen, and then I appreciate that he acknowledges the Universal Declaration of Human Rights and goes on to talk about how effective you and I as individuals can be in improving the world by making the effort to be kind in our daily interactions with others (it's all becoming blurred to me now—was that Eliot Rosewater talking, or the Little Prince?).

And as my 20th-century book comes to its melodramatic close (it's September 17, 1999, as I write this), this hero who just stepped off my VCR screen seems to want to talk to me and us about, per Dr. Doi (see entry #20), the importance of the universal need to *amaeru*:

Almost without exception [the Dalai Lama says in his new book], a mother's first act is to offer her baby her nourishing milk—an act which to me symbolizes unconditional love. Her affection here is totally genuine and uncalculating: she expects nothing in return. As for the baby, it is drawn naturally to its mother's breast. . . . What we see is a relationship based on love and mutual tenderness, which is totally spontaneous. It is not learned from others, no religion requires it, no laws impose it, no schools have taught it. It arises quite naturally. This instinctual care of mother for child is crucial because it suggests that alongside the baby's fundamental need of love in order to survive, there exists an innate capacity on the part of the mother to give love.

I find that whenever I meet people and have a positive disposition toward them, there is no barrier between us. No matter who or what they are, I feel that I am encountering a fellow human being with the same desire to be happy and to avoid suffering as myself. By keeping in mind that ultimately we are all brothers and sisters, that there is no substantial difference between us, that all others share my desire to be happy and to avoid suffering, I can express my feelings as readily as to someone I have known intimately for years. And not just with a few nice words or gestures but really heart to heart, no matter what the language barrier.

Relinquish your envy, let go your desire to triumph over others. Instead, try to benefit them [let them *amaeru*]. Welcome others with a smile. Be straightforward. And try to be impartial. Treat everyone as if they were a close friend. I say this neither as Dalai Lama nor as someone who has special powers or ability. Of these I have none. I speak as a human being: one who, like yourself, wishes to be happy and not to suffer.

So in 1999 the guy from the movie is using the Internet and the mass medium of modern book publishing to do his best to live up to the vow we see him take early in the movie: "To be a protector for those without protection. A ship for those with oceans to cross. A place of refuge for those who lack shelter. And a servant to all in need." And the primary plot line, the chess game between the ancient comrades known as Tibet and China, continues—from the film, we know that the 14th Dalai Lama, as sincere as he is about his wish to help all of "the earth's nearly six billion human beings," also believes that the best thing he can do for his land and people is to be visible like this as a Tibetan lama, to use his star quality to rally support for a tiny nation in the shadow of its neighbor's power. Turn off your VCR, Paul, turn on your computer, the hits just keep on happening!

And a very good movie keeps playing before your eyes and ears and in your heart and mind long after you've rewound the cassette. A joy forever, for all of us with oceans to cross before we sleep . . .

HIT 39

A Private Correspondence

by Lawrence Durrell and Henry Miller

(published 1963)

I t's more than ever clear that Tibet is winning the war—this war and the next half dozen," Lawrence Durrell wrote (from Alexandria, Egypt) in a letter to his good friend Henry Miller (in Big Sur, California) on August 22, 1944.

This is another sort of accidental art, in which two novelists become characters in an unplanned narrative, a collection of letters they wrote back and forth between 1935 and 1959, the story of their lives in those years and thus the story of the world and the era they lived in, as seen through the minds and experiences and conversations-on-paper of these two correspondents. "This book has a superb plot," the editor of *A Private Correspondence*, George Wickes, boasts in his introduction. It does indeed. Good plot, good characters, first-rate writing, stimulating insights, and the opportunity to get inside the minds and lives and motives of remarkable men. What more could we ask from a novel? Should the book be left off the list, omitted from the curriculum, because this masterpiece is an accidental rather than a conscious creation, because we the readers are actually eavesdroppers?

The story begins, oddly enough, with a fan letter. A young man (twenty-three) wants to acknowledge his new hero (forty-three) for having written one of the greatest hits of the era: "Dear Mr. Miller: I have just read

Tropic of Cancer again and feel I'd like to write you a line about it. It strikes me as being the only really man-sized piece of work which this century can really boast of . . . it really gets down on paper the blood and bowels of our time. I have never read anything like it. I did not imagine anything like it could be written; and yet, curiously, reading it I seemed to recognise it as something which I knew we were all ready for."

Right, Larry, that's how I felt when I was sixteen and read Kurt Vonnegut's *Cat's Cradle* (and, the same year, heard Bob Dylan's "It's Alright, Ma"). Durrell at this moment is the archetypal reader, listener, noble partner in the artist-audience relationship. Great works of art come to life when someone reads or sees or hears them and experiences a private and personal epiphany: "This is it! This is for me. This is what I and everyone like me has been waiting for! I have a stronger and happier sense of who I am because of this painting, this book, this song, and the first thing I want to do is tell the author, tell the world, sing with joy!"

Miller returned the favor, switched roles from artist to appreciator, from beloved to suitor, two years later after reading an unpublished manuscript his friend mailed him. "Dear Durrell, *The Black Book* has come and I have opened it and I read goggle-eyed, with terror, admiration and amazement. I am still reading it—slowing up because I want to savor each morsel, each line, each word. . . . This is way beyond Lawrence and the whole tribe. You are out among the asteroids. . . . The whole thing is a poem, a colossal poem. It's like the Black Death, by Jesus. I'm stunned."

Other times, of course, the protagonists of this book are very critical of each other's new writing, misunderstand each other and feel misunderstood. As though the accidental author of this story were being careful to maintain balance and drama in the narrative. He certainly holds our interest via many plot-twists (success, failure, poverty, celebrity, elation, depression, peacetime, wartime, wives found and lost, babies born) and changes of venue (Paris to Hollywood to Big Sur, Greece to Argentina to Yugoslavia).

But why does Durrell say Tibet is winning the Second World War? Well, you can't jump into a novel in the middle and expect it to make sense. In the Durrell-Miller correspondence, "Tibet" had become a code word, shorthand for the wisdom of the East and the possibility (much desired by Miller) of personal escape from a world ruled by materialism. Henry in Paris to Larry in Corfu, May 10, 1937:

> I must write you a whole special letter about things Tibetan: the film *Lost Horizon*, your magic book on Tibet, the book *I Ching* [see entry #4], which I am still burrowing for, "the most extraordinary book in the history of world literature," says Keyserling. And more, please, about the first twelve years of your life there in the passes [Durrell was born in India near the Tibetan border]. If I go any-where from here it will be there. Maybe I shall be the next Dalai Lama—from America sent! This is one of my quiet megalomaniac days. I believe anything is possible.

Reading *A Private Correspondence* in 1969, I found myself overwhelmed by a powerful longing to write and publish books, and to have a friend with a similar life-purpose with whom I could exchange sympathetic and stimulating letters about our difficulties and aspirations. I wanted to enter the universe of the story I was reading, in other words. And so I did. Now, reading Wickes's and Durrell's and Miller's book again thirty years later, I feel a not-quite-overwhelming longing to close my email account and sell my fax machine and even my telephone and go back to writing "snail mail" letters as a primary way of communicating with friends I don't live with and see every day. Because I miss the slowness and steadiness and commitment and all-encompassing nature of this form of friendship. Faster communication has its advantages, but like all change it carries with it that painful dis-advantage called loss. ("Things change, Kundun," the monk teaches the boy in the movie. "Today you lose, tomorrow you may win." Or both at once.)

And so, an excellent reason to include this eccentric and accidental work of art, this well-edited scrapbook of private cor-respondence, in my 20th-century hits list and time capsule, is that it preserves and exemplifies the way we used to communicate with each other back then. Not that all of us were as articulate and visionary and hardworking (or separated by as many miles) as Miller and Durrell; but still there is a startling universality in the portraits these letters paint of places and people and situations and mind-states. Expressed with love for life and love for language. Paintings of the essentially "Tibetan" character of an American bohemian in Paris and an India-born English civil servant on an island in Greece. Writers both—and like all artists essentially megalomaniac because of their addiction to creating universes, using their most private experiences and thoughts and perceptions as building blocks. Creating universes in collaboration with their readers, I should say. The unique thing about writing letters is that you know (and sometimes meet in person) the reader you're talking to and co-creating with. You can indeed express your feelings as readily as to someone you've known intimately for years. Like a true Tibetan should. This book, *A Private Correspondence*, can be read as a textbook on friendship and intimacy. An opportunity to study a curriculum that, as the Dalai Lama suggests, could make the values expressed in the Universal Declaration of Human Rights (see entry #7) more present in our lives as individuals and nations ("Treat everyone as if they were a close friend"). APC is a fine example of two humans using their poet voices to help each other endure and prevail. And, incidentally, a "record of man" in the mid-20th century at the same time. And lots of fun to read.

"Lost Highway"
by Hank Williams
(recorded March 1, 1949)

Sam Shepard, playwright and actor, and Bob Dylan, songwriter and performer, got together on an August afternoon in 1986 and, as friends will, as Durrell and Miller did, found themselves talking about great works of art and memorable artists of their era. Dylan: "Sometimes I wonder why James Dean was great. Because—was he great or was everybody around him great?" Shepard: "He was great. Remember the scene in *Rebel Without a Cause* [1955] where he's holding Plato [Sal Mineo] in his arms, and in the other hand he's got the bullets? That's spectacular acting. Where do you see that kind of acting these days?"

Dylan [we can eavesdrop on this conversation because Shepard recorded it and published it as a "play" in a magazine]: "What was it that he did that was so different? What made that scene so incredible?" Shepard: "It was this pure kind of expression. Most actors in that scene would express nothing but self-pity, but he put across a true remorse . . . for this dumb death of an innocent kid."

Dylan: "So he actually did have a cause, then?" Shepard: "I don't know." Dylan: "'Rebel with a cause.' See, that's the devil's work." Sam: "What?" Bob: "Words have lost their meaning. Like 'rebel.' Like 'cause.' Like 'love.' They mean a million different things."

Sam: "Like Hank Williams?" Bob: "Naw, you can never change the meaning of Hank Williams. That's here to stay. Nobody'll ever change that."

Hiram Hank Williams was twenty-five when he recorded "Lost Highway." The son of an Alabama tenant farmer who'd abandoned his family, Williams had just recently released his second hit record, "Lovesick Blues," the one that made him a "star," that sold a mass audience (and a generation of future music stars) on Williams's particular "pure kind of expression." For the next few years the young man with a guitar ("The 1949 Folk Music Recording Sensation!" according to MGM Records' ad for "Lost Highway" in a radio trade magazine) would have many more hits by singing about and for the "common folk," in spite of continuing difficulties with severe alcoholism and drug dependence that led to his death at age twenty-nine in the back of a car while being driven to a performance at a theater in Ohio.

Shepard: "Did you used to listen to him a lot?" Dylan: "Overload. Who can you listen to if you can't listen to Hank?" Sam: "Did he mean the same thing to you as James Dean?" Bob: "Yeah, but in different ways. They both told the truth." Sam: "They both died in cars." Bob: "Yeah." Sam: "A Cadillac and a Porsche."

> I'm a rolling stone, all alone and lost,
> For a life of sin, I have paid the cost.
> When I pass by, all the people say,
> "Just another guy on the lost highway."

This book begins with a rather upbeat ("visionary," I called it) song written by the artists who performed and recorded it. But it ends with a downbeat (bleak yet somehow jolly) song not written by its performer, even though the performer/singer/guitarist/bandleader is rightly praised by Dylan and others as a great songwriter. But that's okay. The important thing is not who wrote James Dean's scene; it's the truth that artist tells his audience (you and me, Sam and Bob) at that moment.

Leon Payne, author of the words and music of "Lost Highway" and the lines quoted above, was a blind musician (white and poor, like Hank) who'd released the original version of "Lost

Highway" on the Nashville-based Bullet label in October 1948. His widow later told an interviewer:

> In the early days of Leon's career, he hitchhiked from one place to another, finding jobs wherever he could. Once he was in California hitchhiking to Alba, Texas, to visit his sick mother. He was unable to get a ride and finally got help from the Salvation Army. It was while he was waiting for help that he wrote this song.

"Lost Highway" (MGM 10506, backed with "You're Gonna Change (or I'm Gonna Leave)," released September 9, 1949) was not as big a hit as "Lovesick Blues" or "Wedding Bells," or "Move It On Over" or "Long Gone Lonesome Blues," or the posthumously released "Your Cheatin' Heart." But even if it wasn't one of the best-selling records of Hank Williams's brief but meteoric career, I confidently include it in my selection of the twentieth century's greatest hits because both Leon Payne's title and Hank's recording have that quality that is universal to all great hits of any era: resonance.

No one with any feel for the aesthetics and essential character of the 1901–2000 era in human history could fail to recognize the resonant and evocative quality of the two words "lost highway." As a direct result of (and tribute to) the Payne song and Williams recording, "Lost Highway" has also been used as the title of a dramatic film (by David Lynch, 1996), and of a book (by Peter Guralnick, 1979, subtitled "Journeys and Arrivals of American Musicians"), and of a popular radio program (KUSP, Santa Cruz, California, late 1990s), and of course of various websites. Two irresistible words, especially once they've reached your ears and consciousness by way of Hank Williams's voice. The first words of the song, "I'm a rolling stone, all alone and lost," quite likely helped inspire Muddy Waters to write and record his 1950 tune "Rollin' Stone," which in turn gave the Rolling Stones (see entry #35) their name. The popular late-20th-century weekly magazine *Rolling Stone* draws its name equally from Muddy and the British rockers and from Bob Dylan's 1965 hit "Like a Rolling Stone,"

which unquestionably reflects the impact of hearing "Lost Highway" on the radio as a young man ("nobody'll ever change that").

But resonance is not just a matter of a choice of words. It's a
sound, a matter of pure musical expression, often musical expression through a human voice—the instrument that delivers those
striking words. So I suggest that if you want to study what it is in
works of art that gives them their power to endure and to influence men and women and move hearts far beyond their place and
time of origin, start by listening to the first thirty-four seconds of
"Lost Highway" (the first verse, the lines quoted above) and
observing closely how the sounds of these instruments and of this
singer's voice resonate in you as a listener. Reel your mind in from
the grand perspective of a hundred years of paintings and novels
and songs and movies and let it focus on just a few seconds of one
performance—and observe, if you can, what happens to your feelings and your consciousness in those seconds, just you alone with
this twenty-five-year-old man and his voice and these stringed
instruments that seem to resonate with that voice like piano
strings setting each other vibrating.

What do you feel? Why? Notice, for example, the four simple
guitar notes in the first two seconds that seem so full of emotional
meaning and that reach such a satisfying dramatic climax on that
fourth note as the other instruments join in. And notice the individual words that seem to be emphasized by the melody and by
the singer, as though our attention is meant to linger on each one
as its implications resound, ring like a bell, in our minds and
hearts: "stone," "sin," "by," "guy," with the most fulfilling emphasis on that vague adverb "by," which seems to carry a mysterious
profundity, as though the heart of the singer's and the song's message is in that phrase "when I pass by," with the implication being
that as he sings "by . . ." we are actually seeing him, and all the
pain of his awareness of how he appears in others' eyes is lightly
and convincingly (almost telepathically) conveyed in that musical moment, in the stretching of the vowel in "by" so that it's the
longest and most dramatic moment in the whole short and
momentous verse. Have you observed what parts of yourself are
awakened by these sounds, this story? And what is this feeling of

affection you find in yourself for this singer, this work of art, this friend? Is it that when you hear his voice, you know you're not alone? Of course, you aren't alone if you feel this way. You are as one with millions of others people who love and have loved Hank Williams and what they hear in his voice and his recordings. It's a kind of gold standard. "You can never change the meaning of Hank Williams." And you don't want to.

"He was all right," Kitty Wells, another country singer of the time, recalls. "Hank always enjoyed getting out and singing for the people. People loved him. He stood tall and lanky. You could always tell he meant the songs he was singing." "Hank was not for any certain time, but for all time and all people," Mrs. Jeanette Davis wrote to the Montgomery, Alabama, daily newspaper shortly after his death. "No one will ever take Hank's place in the hearts of millions, as well as my own."

In the first chapter of his new book, His Holiness the Dalai Lama writes of the thousands of seekers, Tibetan and otherwise, who come to see him at his home in India: "Many have unrealistic expectations, supposing that I have healing powers or that I can give some sort of blessing. But I am only an ordinary human being. The best I can do is try to help them by sharing in their suffering." It strikes me that Hank Williams and Elvis Presley are regarded as almost holy figures by millions of people precisely because they are or were only ordinary human beings, with healing powers that derive from their ability to speak in the voice of the ordinary man and woman and thus to share in each listener's suffering.

The lost highway leads somewhere, in other words. That's the riddle. And the music, the moment of connection between artist and audience, is the answer. "Just another guy on the lost highway . . ." Like me. Like us. So, paradoxically, we find ourselves wanting to follow this lost soul. "There must be some way out of here," Bob Dylan sang in 1967. Maybe the greatest hits of any era are a trail of clues leading us out of the labyrinth.

Citations

Entry #1

13 Lyrics quoted are copyright © 1964 Northern Songs Ltd.

Entry #2

22–23 Lyrics quoted are copyright © 1968 Oakfield Avenue Music.

23 Reed quote as cited in *Lou Reed: The Biography* by Victor Bockris (London: Hutchinson, 1994).

Entry #3

26 "Ars Poetica," Archibald MacLeish, 1926; copyright © 1985 by The Estate of Archibald MacLeish.

26 The book/catalog referred to is *Pablo Picasso: A Retrospective*, edited by William Rubin (New York: Museum of Modern Art, 1980).

27 *Familiar Quotations* by John Bartlett, 14th Edition (Boston: Little, Brown, 1968).

27 Picasso quote ("Academic training . . .") as cited in *Picasso on Art: A Selection of Views*, edited by Dore Ashton (New York: Viking Press, 1972), p. 11 of Da Capo reprint.

27 Arnason quote from *History of Modern Art*, by H. H. Arnason (New York: Abrams, 1977).

28 Berger quote from *The Success and Failure of Picasso*, by John Berger (London: Penguin Books, 1965).

Entry #4

34 "Revolution" quotes from Hexagram 49, *The I Ching or Book of Changes*, translated by Richard Wilhelm, rendered into English by Cary F. Baynes (New York: Bollingen Foundation, 1950).

36 Jung quotes from Foreword to the 1950 Bollingen Foundation edition as above.

37–38 Information about Wilhelm and Lao and extended quote are from *Understanding the I Ching: The Wilhelm Lectures on the Book of Changes* by Hellmut Wilhelm and Richard Wilhelm (Princeton, N.J.: Princeton University Press, 1995), p. 145.

Entry #5

41 The Campbell biography cited is *A Fire in the Mind: The Life of Joseph Campbell* by Stephen and Robin Larsen (New York: Doubleday, 1991).

Entry #6

44 Information about the 1933 film is from *Leonard Maltin's TV Movies and Video Guide*, 1991 edition.

47 Herzog quote as cited in chapter 10 of *Wishing on the Moon: The Life and Times of Billie Holiday* by Donald Clarke (New York: Viking, 1994).

49 Frank Sinatra quote as cited in chapter 6 of *Wishing on the Moon*. Miles Davis quote and Billie's response from *Talking Jazz* by Max Jones (New York: Norton, 1987).

50–51 The 1994 MCA CD mentioned is MCAD 20254. The 1996 CD *American Legends: Billie Holiday* is LaserLight/Stanyan Records 12 736.

51 The *Billie Holiday Songbook* CD is PolyGram/Verve P2-23246. *The Complete Billie Holiday Mastertakes Collection*, Vol. 7 CD was issued in 1993 in Italy by Camarillo Music Ltd on the King Jazz label. *The Golden Years* vinyl anthology was released by Columbia Records in New York in 1962.

Entry #7

54 Lash quote from *Eleanor: The Years Alone* by Joseph P. Lash (New York: Norton, 1972).

56 "The International Bill: A Brief History" by Peter Meyer is in *The International Bill of Human Rights*, edited by Paul Williams (Glen Ellen, California: Entwhistle, 1981).

Entry #8

58 *Ubik* by Philip K. Dick (Garden City, N.Y.: Doubleday, 1969). *Been Down So Long It Looks Like up to Me* by Richard Fariña (New York: Random House, 1966).

Entry #9

64 "What matters to me is . . ." Philip K. Dick in "Notes Made Late at Night by a Weary SF Writer," written in 1968 and included in Lawrence Sutin, ed., *The Shifting Realities of Philip K. Dick* (New York, Pantheon, 1995).

64 "In *Martian Time-Slip* we see the world . . ." Patricia Warrick, *Mind in Motion: The Fiction of Philip K. Dick* (Carbondale: Southern Illinois University Press, 1987), p. 76.

66 "I remember I was in my teens . . ." Philip K. Dick in D. Scott Apel, *Philip K. Dick: The Dream Connection* (San Jose: The Permanent Press, 1987), p. 63.

Throughout: *Martian Time-Slip* by Philip K. Dick (New York, Ballantine, 1964).

Entry #10

71, 72, 73, 74 Lines quoted from "Howl" are copyright © 1956 by Allen Ginsberg.

71 "Schumacher suggests . . ." in Michael Schumacher, *Dharma Lion* (New York: St. Martin's Press, 1992), p. 203.

72 "superb footnote," ibid., p. 203.

73 "Saw Moloch smoking building . . ." quoted in Barry Miles, *Ginsberg: A Biography* (New York: Simon and Schuster, 1989), p. 192.

73 "Part I deals sympathetically," Allen Ginsberg, quoted in Schumacher, p. 206.

Entry #11

78–79 Lyrics quoted are copyright © 1966 Irving Music, Inc.

79 "layered vocals and sound textures," David Leaf, *The Beach Boys and the California Myth*, New York: Grosset and Dunlap, 1978, p. 82.

79 "We prayed for guidance . . ." Carl Wilson, in *The Making of* Pet Sounds by David Leaf, p. 22, published by Capitol Records, Hollywood, 1997.

80 "I was watching Diane . . ." Brian Wilson (with Todd Gold), *Wouldn't It Be Nice: My Own Story* (New York: HarperCollins, 1991), p. 135.

81 "It's about a guy who was crying . . ." quoted in Leaf, *California Myth*, p. 80.

82 "As a twelve-year-old . . ." Carl Wilson, in Leaf, *The Making of* Pet Sounds, p. 22.

82 "He used to go in and record . . ." Tony Asher, quoted in Leaf, *California Myth*, p. 78.

83 "I find it possible . . ." Brian Wilson, in Leaf, *California Myth*, p. 89.

Entry #12

85 "Pierre Menard, Author of the *Quixote*" is included in *Labyrinths* by Jorge Luis Borges (New York: New Directions, 1962).

88 "TNH's own story," told in *Cultivating the Mind of Love* by Thich Nhat Hanh (Berkeley: Parallax, 1996), p. 8.

Throughout: *Old Path White Clouds* by Thich Nhat Hanh, translated from the Vietnamese by Mobi Ho (Berkeley: Parallax, 1991).

Entry #13

93 "Notes of a Painter," text from Jack Flam, *Matisse on Art* (Berkeley: University of California Press, 1995).

94 The newspaper critic interview is with Charles Estienne, and can be found in Flam, *Matisse on Art*.

95 The quotes from Barr are from *Matisse: His Art and His Public* by Alfred H. Barr, Jr. (New York: Museum of Modern Art, 1951), pp. 134 and 136.

95 The quotes from Gilot are from *Matisse and Picasso: A Friendship in Art* by Françoise Gilot (New York: Doubleday, 1990), p. 46 and pp. 90–91.

96 1950 interview is with Georges Charbonnier, from Flam, *Matisse on Art*. Definition of *farandole* is from *Webster's New World Dictionary*.

96 1941 interview is with Francis Carco, from Flam, *Matisse on Art*. 1935 essay is "On Modernism and Tradition," included in Flam. 1936 quote is from a statement recorded by E. Tériade, "On the Purity of the Means," included in Flam.

98 The 1929 comment is credited in Barr—and in *Modern Art* by Sam Hunter and John Jacobus (New York: Abrams, 1976)—as a statement to Christian Zervos. A very similar comment can be found in Flam, where it is part of a 1929 statement to E. Tériade, "On Fauvism and Color."

99 Growing quote is from *Matisse* by Lawrence Growing (London: Thames and Hudson, 1979), p. 107.

99 1931 quotes are from an interview with Pierre Courthion, included in Flam, *Matisse on Art*. Van Dyke Parks quote can be found in David Leaf's liner notes to a 1990 reissue of the Beach Boys albums *Smiley Smile* and *Wild Honey*.

100 Matisse's 1907 comment to Apollinaire is in Flam, *Matisse on Art*. The text as I cite it is from Barr, *Matisse*, p. 101.

Entry #14

105 Information and quotes from *The Lost Worlds of 2001* by Arthur C. Clarke (New York: New American Library, 1972), pp. 18, 29, 31–32, 35, 38.

112 Kubrick quote is as cited in *Arthur C. Clarke: The Authorized Biography* by Neil McAleer (Chicago: Contemporary, 1992), p. 204.

Entry #15

114 Virginia Danielson, *The Voice of Egypt: Umm Kulthum, Arabic Song, and Egyptian Society in the Twentieth Century* (Chicago: University of Chicago Press, 1997) p. 138.

114 Naguib Mahfouz, *Miramar*, original Arabic edition published 1967, English translation by Fatma Moussa Mahmoud published 1978 by The American University in Cairo Press.

115 The discography in the back of Ysabel Saïah's biography *Oum Kalsoum* (Paris: Denoël, 1985) on p. 245 gives the date of enregistration of "al-Atlal" as 07/04/66 and notes "premier concert après la mort de Kasabgi."

116 The 1978 interview in which Bob Dylan called Om Kalsoum his "favorite singer" appeared in *Rolling Stone* in early 1978; Dylan also talked about her in a 1978 interview published in *Playboy*. The 1984 quote is from a radio interview syndicated by Westwood One.

117 "The song depends . . ." as cited in Danielson, *The Voice of Egypt*, p. 139.

118 Racy's essay "Creativity and Ambience," quoted in Danielson, p. 138, appeared in *World of Music* in 1991. "Umm Kulthum's performance . . ." quote is from Danielson, p. 155.

118 The documentary film is *Umm Kulthum: A Voice Like Egypt*, produced and directed by Michal Goldman, 1997.

119 Quote is from *A Woman of Egypt* by Jehan Sadat (New York: Simon & Schuster, 1987), p. 56.

Entry #16

122 Ellison quote, as cited on Faulkner website at www.mcsr.olemiss.edu.

123 Faulkner quote from *Faulkner in the University: Class Conferences at the University of Virginia, 1957–1958*, Gwynn and Blotner, eds. (New York: Vintage, 1959).

125 Quotes from *Three Famous Short Novels* by William Faulkner (New York: Vintage, 1961): Lion quote from p. 229; "They will endure" quote from p. 282; "His creation" quote from p. 273.

Entry #17

127–128 Dylan to Ginsberg, quoted in *Wanted Man: In Search of Bob Dylan*, John Bauldie, ed. (London: Black Spring, 1990), p. 108.

128 "Questions to Sam Shepard" from *Rolling Thunder Logbook* by Sam Shepard (New York: Viking, 1977), p. 13.

128 Dylan quote from interview conducted by Jonathan Cott, published in *Rolling Stone* early in 1978.

129 Dylan to Ginsberg, from Bauldie, ed., *Wanted Man*.

Entry #18

134 Quote from *Slow Learner* by Thomas Pynchon (Boston: Little, Brown, 1984).

135 Quote from *Old Path White Clouds* by Thich Nhat Hanh (Berkeley: Parallax, 1991).

136 Quote from *Gravity's Rainbow* by Thomas Pynchon (New York: Viking, 1973).

Entry #19

142 Excerpted material first appeared in an essay titled "From Patti to Nusrat in a week and a half, with Lobos, Maceo, Marcia, Maldita, Johnny, Jonathan, Les Etoiles, Terrance, Mike and more (!) in between," by Paul Williams, *Crawdaddy!* new #10, early autumn 1995.

Throughout: *The Anatomy of Dependence* by Takeo Doi, M.D., translated by John Bester (New York: Kodansha International, 1973).

Entry #20

152 Vonnegut quote from *God Bless You, Mr. Rosewater* by Kurt Vonnegut, Jr. (New York: Holt, 1965), p. 29.

Entry #21

157 Ginsberg essay "The Great Rememberer" published as afterword to Penguin paperback edition of *Visions of Cody* by Jack Kerouac.

157 "Ananda has the finest memory among us," from *Old Path White Clouds*, p. 346. Mahakassapa challenges Ananda, ibid., p. 570.

158 Mark Twain fooling with journalism/fiction boundaries: e.g., the piece he wrote in the *New York Times* interviewing a young black man whose speech seems to have been a basis, later, for Huck Finn's.

158 Details of the writing of *On the Road:* from Ann Charters's introduction to the 1991 Penguin edition of *On the Road.*

159 "godsend" from *Desolate Angel* by Dennis McNally (New York: Random House, 1979), p. 133.

160 "Gerard was St. Francis": Ibid., p. 5. Jack thought of Gerard as a saint: *Selected Letters of Jack Kerouac*, Ann Charters, ed. (New York: Viking, 1995), p. 540.

161 "How Early": G. K. Chesterton, *St. Francis of Assisi*, 1990 Doubleday Image edition (originally published 1924), p. 59. "He swore": Ibid., pp. 41–42.

162 "In this there are": Ibid., pp. 42–43. "popular with everybody": Ibid., p. 39. "great liking": Ibid., p. 40. *On the Road* quote: p. 160 of Signet paperback.

163 "It was a solid": Chesterton, *St. Francis*, pp. 72, 74.

163 Quote from *Desolation Angels* by Jack Kerouac (New York: Coward-McCann, 1965).

164 Ananda's reluctance to act when asked to be Buddha's attendant: *Old Path White Clouds*, p. 346.

164 Quotes from *On the Road* by Jack Kerouac (New York: Viking, 1957).

Entry #22

167 "$15,000 fee" per *Clint Eastwood* by Stuart M. Kaminsky (New York: New American Library, 1974).

168 Kiral interview with Frayling from http://film.terranet.com/director/s.leone/articles/prof.

169 Nudge quote from www.imagesjournal.com/issue06/infocus/spaghetti.

Entry #23

171 Delany quote from an interview with Paul Williams, cited in "Theodore Sturgeon" by Paul Williams in *The Berkley Showcase, Vol. 3*, edited by Victoria Schochet and John Silbersack (New York: Berkley, 1981).

173 Heinlein quotes from "Letter to Theodore Sturgeon, February 11, 1955," by Robert Heinlein, published in *The New York Review of Science Fiction*, August 1995.

173 Sturgeon quotes from *The Proceedings; CHICON III*, edited by Earl Kemp (Chicago: Advent, 1963).

174 Quote from "An Interview with Theodore Sturgeon" by Darrell Schweitzer in *Science Fiction Review*, February 1977; also can be found in *Science Fiction Voices #1* by Darrell Schweitzer (San Bernardino, Calif.: Borgo, 1979).

176–177 Quote from "And Now the News . . ." which is included in *The Golden Helix* by Theodore Sturgeon (New York: Dell, 1979).

177 Quote from "Mr. Costello, Hero," which is included in *A Touch of Strange* by Theodore Sturgeon (Garden City, N.Y.: Doubleday, 1958).

Entry #24

178 "The Fruit of Awareness Is Ripe" from Thich Nhat Hanh, *Call Me by My True Names* (Berkeley: Parallax, 1993).

178 Lyrics quoted are copyright © 1975 Linda Music Corp.

179 Patti Smith quote from *Patti Smith Complete* (New York: Double-day, 1998), p. 7.

180 "We went through all kinds of . . ." quoted in Clinton Heylin, *From the Velvets to the Voidoids* (London: Penguin, 1993), p. 192.

Entry #25

188 Maltin quote from *Leonard Maltin's TV Movies and Video Guide, 1991 Edition* (New York: Penguin, 1990).

188 Reference is to *Rock and Roll: The 100 Best Singles* by Paul Williams (New York: Carroll & Graf, 1993).

188 Hellman quote is from an interview with Monte Hellman conducted by Beverly Walker for the British Film Institute in 1971, which is reprinted as the introduction to a paperback book of the screenplay, *Two-Lane Blacktop* by Rudolph Wurlitzer and Will Corry (New York: Award, 1971). Walker's pages of descriptive text that precede the conversation with Hellman provide background information about the making of the film, including why Will Corry's name is on Wurlitzer's screenplay.

Entry #26

191–192 As this book goes to press, *Live/Dead* is available on Warner Bros. Records CD #1830-2, and *Fillmore East 2-11-69* is available on a Grateful Dead Records double-CD, #GDCD 4054, distributed by Arista Records/BMG.

192 Quotes from Paul Williams interview with Timothy Leary, Feb. 21, 1969, are from *Pushing Upward* by Paul Williams (New York: Links, 1973).

Entry #27

Throughout: the June 13, 1920, Sunday page discussed in this chapter is reproduced in *Krazy & Ignatz: The Komplete Kat Komics, Volume Five, 1920, Pilgrims on the Road to Nowhere* by George Herriman (Forestville: Eclipse, 1990), p. 29.

198 Spiegelman quote from "Comix 101: Forms Stretched to Their Limits" by Art Spiegelman in *The New Yorker*, April 19, 1999.

198 Seldes quote as cited on the back cover of *Komplete Kat, Vol. 5*.

199 Blackbeard quotes from "Kat in Nine Bags: A Twenty Year Quest for a Phantom," by Bill Blackbeard, in *The Komplete Kat Komics, Volume Two, 1917, The Other-Side to the Shore of Here* by George Herriman (Forestville: Eclipse, 1989).

202 Kerouac quote as cited in "About the Krazy Kat Cartoon Strip" at www.krazy.com/coconino.htm.

Entry #28

Throughout: lyrics quoted copyright © 1956 Arc Music Corp.

203 Sam Phillips quotes from *Deep Blues* by Robert Palmer (New York: Viking, 1981).

206 Gordon McGregor quote from his essay "Howlin' Wolf (aka Chester Arthur Burnett)" at www.hub.org/bluesnet/artists.

Entry #29

210 The Mead book is *Culture and Commitment* by Margaret Mead (Garden City, N.Y.: Natural History Press, 1970).

212 Klinkowitz insight from *The Practice of Fiction in America* by Jerome Klinkowitz (Ames: Iowa State, 1980), p. 98.

Entry #30

215 LSD trip quote, cited in J. C. Thomas, *Chasin' the Trane* (New York: Doubleday, 1975), p. 215.

216 Dolphy left group because of discomfort at criticism, per John Fraim, *Spirit Catcher: The Life and Art of John Coltrane* (W. Liberty, Michigan: GreatHouse, 1996), p. 115. Also liner notes to *The Complete Village Vanguard Recordings*, by David Wild, p. 12.

216 Fraim quote from Fraim, *Spirit Catcher*, p. 116.

217 Kirk quote from Thomas, *Chasin' the Trane*, p. 151.

217 "In the same year," from *John Coltrane* by Bill Cole (New York: Schirmer, 1976), p. 146.

218 Amram quote from Thomas, *Chasin' the Trane*, p. 77.

219–220 Fraim quotes from Fraim, *Spirit Catcher*, pp. 34–35.

220 "At clubs during this period": Ibid., p. 108.

Entry #31

221 First paragraph: 1955 letter in Robert A. Heinlein, *Grumbles from the Grave* (New York: Del Rey, 1989), p. 225. Other book titles from *Grumbles*, p. 233.

221 Mars crater information from front matter page in *The Moon Is a Harsh Mistress* (New York: Tor, 1996).

222 Kurt Vonnegut, "Heinlein Gets the Last Word," *The New York Times Book Review*, Dec. 9, 1990 (the "original uncut" version was officially published a few weeks later, in 1991, so in this chapter I say the Vonnegut piece is from '91 to avoid confusing the reader).

225 "Robert was looking": Heinlein, *Grumbles*, p. 52.

226 "The story itself": Ibid., pp. 223–224.

227 October 21, 1960: Ibid., p. 228.

228 "If it *does*": Ibid., p. 226.

228 "This is not offered": Ibid., p. 229.

Entry #32

230 "Near death, bereft of speech . . ." from *Merriam Webster's Encyclopedia of Literature* (Springfield, Mass.: Merriam-Webster, 1995).

230 Quote from "The Lottery in Babylon," which is included in *Labyrinths* by Jorge Luis Borges (New York: New Directions, 1962) (story translated by John M. Fein).

231 Quotes from "The Wall and the Books," which is also included in *Labyrinths* (translated by James E. Irby).

Entry #33

234 Opening quote: The address for the quoted page of Manuel Delgado's site is www.inteligente.com/b612/books.htm.

235 The information that *TLP* was written in summer and fall 1942 is from *Antoine de Saint-Exupéry: His Life and Times* by Curtis Cate (New York: G. P. Putnam's Sons, 1970), p. 471.

236 Quote from *Wind, Sand and Stars* (New York: Harcourt, Brace & World, 1967) (translated by Lewis Galantière), chapter 6, first two pages.

236 The quotes are from *Stranger in a Strange Land*, chapter 38; *Old Path White Clouds*, chapter 79; and *The Little Prince*, chapter 26.

Entry #34

238 Quote from Ben Kingsley 1983 interview is from *Current Biography*, November 1983. Hegel quote is from the Introduction section of *The Philosophy of History*.

242 The story of young MLK finding out about Gandhi at a lecture and the King quote are as cited in *Martin Luther King, Jr., and the Freedom Movement* by Lillie Patterson (New York: Facts on File, 1989), p. 27.

242 The story of Gandhi reading Thoreau in prison and the quotes from him about Thoreau's essay are from *The Life of Mahatma Gandhi* by Louis Fischer (New York: Harper, 1950), pp. 87–89.

243 The Attenborough quote is from an interview conducted by Barbara Crossette in *The New York Times*, Nov. 28, 1982.

243 Gandhi quote about Arnold's *The Light of Asia* is from *Autobiography: The Story of My Experiments with Truth* by Mohandas K. Gandhi (Boston: Beacon Press, 1957), pp. 67–68.

Entry #35

244 See Entry #13 notes for sources of Matisse quotes.

248 Stones' recordings made very soon after first listening to the song in question, per Keith Richards, quoted in *The Rolling Stones:*

An Illustrated Record by Roy Carr (New York: Harmony, 1976), p. 24.

Throughout: recording dates and locations for specific tracks from *The Rolling Stones Complete Recording Sessions* by Martin Elliott (London: Cassell, 1990).

250 "studio run-through": From Carr, *Illustrated Record*.

250 The Alvin Robinson "Down Home Girl" is included on a 1989 Charly Records (UK) CD called *Stoned Alchemy*.

Entry #36

254 Herbert quote from the introduction to *New World or No World*, edited by Frank Herbert (New York: Ace Books, 1970). This citation can also be found in *The Maker of Dune*, edited by Tim O'Reilly (New York: Berkley Books, 1987).

255 Hartwell quote from *Age of Wonders: Exploring the World of Science Fiction* by David Hartwell (New York: Walker & Co., 1984), chapter 2, p. 31 (of the McGraw-Hill paperback).

255 "Back in 1953 . . .": From *The Maker of Dune*, ed. O'Reilly, p. 102.

257 Coleridge quote from *Biographia Literaria* (1817) by Samuel Taylor Coleridge, chapter 14, as cited in *Familiar Quotations* by John Bartlett.

Entry #37

259–260 Sources for details of the story of the recording of the song and of its discovery and success are: *Behind the Hits* by Bob Shannon and John Javna (New York: Warner Books, 1986), p. 27; *The Faber Companion to 20th-Century Popular Music* by Phil Hardy and Dave Laing (London: Faber and Faber, 1990), p. 348; and www.gospelweb.com/profiles/edwin_hawkins,www.lovecenter.org/WHawkinsBio, and http:// alexmgmt.com/dorothys_bio.

Entry #38

263 Gyatso (the 14th Dalai Lama's birth name) quote is from *Freedom in Exile: The Autobiography of the Dalai Lama* (London: Hodder and Stoughton, 1990), p. 11.

265 Quote is from *Ethics for the New Millennium* by His Holiness the Dalai Lama (New York: Riverhead, 1999), chapter 5.

267 Second quote from Dalai Lama: Ibid.

268 The "vow" as I quote it varies slightly from the version in the film; I have chosen to use the wording of the same prayer or vow as printed on the last page of *Ethics for the New Millennium* and included in the excerpt I downloaded from the Internet.

Entry #39

269 *A Private Correspondence* by Lawrence Durrell and Henry Miller, edited by George Wickes, was published in New York in 1963 by E. P. Dutton & Co. It is now out of print, but a new and different collection of their correspondence has since been published.

269–270 The fan letter from LD to HM is dated August 1935.

270 The HM to LD letter about *The Black Book* is dated March 8, 1937.

Entry #40

273–274 The Shepard/Dylan conversation in play form appears in *Esquire*, July 1987.

274 Lyrics to "Lost Highway" by Leon Payne are copyright © 1949 Fred Rose Music, Inc.

274 The "Lost Highway" ad from a "special disk jockey supplement" to *Billboard* magazine is reproduced in the booklet that accompanies a 1990 PolyGram Records CD box set called *Hank Williams: The Original Singles Collection*.

275 "In the early days" quote from Myrtle (Mrs. Leon) Payne is from a 1972 telephone interview, as cited on Manfred Helfert's website at www.yi.com/home/HelfertManfred/lost.htm.

277 Kitty Wells quote as cited in *In the Country of Country* by Nicholas Davidoff (New York: Pantheon, 1997), p. 69.

277 Jeanette Davis quote as cited in Colin Escott's liner notes in the booklet in *The Original Singles Collection*.

Throughout: I am indebted to *Hank Williams: The Biography* by Colin Escott (Boston: Little Brown, 1994) for background information helpful to the writing of this chapter.

Index